HONORING THE LEGACY OF BP CHAN

HONORING THE LEGACY OF BP CHAN

Celebrating a Life of Martial Arts and Qigong

RON LAMBERT

無名

In Their Own Words:

Memories of
Qigong Master and Martial Arts Teacher
BP Chan, 1975-2002

CONTENTS

This book is dedicated to the memory of
Guillermo Bun Piac Chan

May 30, 1922 - March 7, 2002

"When we learn the martial arts, practice together, everybody is right & everybody is wrong. Who is right, who is wrong - nobody knows. How do we solve this riddle?"
—BP Chan

INTRODUCTION

Not "Master Chan."

Not "Sifu" or "Shifu", the Chinese words of respect for teacher or Master.

Mister Chan. Mr. Chan. Always Mr. Chan. Simply Mr. Chan.

I had never heard of BP Chan until I joined a martial arts school in Westchester County, NY in 2002. My teacher, a direct student of Mr. Chan, and the school's students, always spoke about him with respect and admiration. There was almost a reverence in their words when they used his name.

"Mr. Chan did it this way."

"Mr. Chan always said…."

"I learned so much from Mr. Chan."

I never met Mr. Chan, but after having spent 18 years at that school surrounded by a teacher and his students that did know him, I almost feel as if I do now.

I decided to write this book because I believe that BP Chan has flown - a better word is soared - under the internal martial arts radar in this country. BP Chan taught martial arts for four decades in the United States and Europe. Yet, he did not do interviews. He wrote no books or magazine articles. In addition, he did not particularly like to be filmed or photographed. He preferred to remain "nameless" to the greater martial arts com-

1

munity... and to his students. Mr. Chan passed away 22 years ago, so even just talking to him now is not possible.

Probably the longest written composition he wrote was an essay titled "How to Prepare to do One Move," and that was only meant for his students to see. Bob Schefsky, a direct student of BP Chan, said that BP Chan told him that he didn't want anything written about him while he was alive, but didn't care if people wrote about him after he had passed away.

There have been no books written about him – until now.

In his lifetime, Mr. Chan taught hundreds of students (One student, Ken Cohen, puts the number over one thousand). He taught at the schools of William CC Chen, CK Chu, Richard Chin's Asian Martial Arts Studio, and others. He did workshops (he called them "shopworks") in Connecticut, New York State, and New Jersey. He created space for, and offered, martial arts workshops and study at the Tai Chi Farm in Warwick, NY. How is it that this man's encyclopedic body of knowledge and training, which included Tai Chi (Push Hands, Tai Chi Staff, Tai Chi Knife, Tai Chi Ruler), Xing-Yi (Five Elements, Linking Form, Dui Da Paired Form, Twelve Animals, Eight Posture Form and Applications, Bagua Zhang (Eight Outer Palms, Inner Palms, Standing Set, Eight Two-Person Sets, Bagua Push Hands, Applications), Qigong, Five Animal Frolics, Daoist Meditation, Northern Shaolin Kung Fu, I-Chuan, An Mo, Eight Immortals Staff, Eight Immortals Sword, and much, much more, has hardly been noticed by those outside his classes or workshops?

To this day, 22 years after his passing, some of his students are still reluctant to share their personal memories of him with "outsiders." They feel that what he transmitted to them was so very special, so unique, and touched them so personally that they simply want to keep those cherished memories to themselves.

I hope this book opens that door of guarded silence around Mr. Chan just a crack so you can understand what a treasure of a human being and martial arts teacher he really was - to those who knew him.

There are bits and pieces of information about BP Chan in various corners of the well-known search engines. I know, because I've spent countless hours looking, but found nothing comprehensive. You are holding the first book ever written about this unique man, and even with all my hours of effort, this volume of his legacy is still far from exhaustive.

But it's a start.

CONFESSION TIME AND ACKNOWLEDGEMENTS

I'm neither an author, journalist, professional writer, nor biographer.

I have a confession to make. I really didn't write this book.

The content comes from the memories, recollections, anecdotes, and experiences of those who were fortunate enough to be students of BP Chan from 1975 until 2002. I was merely a facilitator; a collector and compiler of information; a cheerleader; simply someone who pulled all their wonderful content together and consolidated it into this book. Nothing more.

A big "Thank You" to those 1st generation students of BP Chan who graciously shared their memories, contributions of content, and encouragement with me. I enjoyed speaking to all of them, listening to their stories, and learning about BP Chan. It was a wonderful opportunity for me to meet folks I never would have met otherwise; folks who share a common interest with me about BP Chan. This book truly would not have seen the light of day without these folks:

Ray Hayward, Frank Allen, Mark Jones, Linda Lehrhaupt, Alan Stolowitz, Bob Schefsky, Jim Fogarty, Tim Regan, Tim Folger, Andy Lee Zalcman, Marsha Nolan, Dr. Richard Chin, Richard Raab, Fran Buckelew, Alvin Fayman, Ron Gee, Gar Wang, Becky Herdt (for Paul Gallagher), Kenneth Cohen, Rudy Curry, Andy Diaz, Mike Trombetta, Peter Chema, Martin Wessels, Patti

Walsh, Jeffrey Pascal, and Cooper.

In addition, two 1st generation students of BP Chan who contributed to this book chose to remain anonymous. You know who you are.

Thanks also to Loretta Wollering, Sal Canzonieri, Matt Parsons, Lynn Teale, Ron Statler, Jess O'Brien, Debbie Shayne, and Bruce Marcus for their support.

If I omitted anyone, please understand that it is entirely unintentional and accept my sincere apologies.

Ron Lambert
Rye Brook, NY
March 2024

"IN THEIR OWN WORDS"

My working title for this book was "In Their Own Words: Memories of Qigong Master and Martial Arts Teacher BP Chan, 1975-2002." Going forward, you will find that I have interspersed Mr. Chan's student's memories of him with other material.

Aside from the few brief verbal snippets of personal information about himself that BP Chan selectively gave to his students and others, not much information is known about him. Up to now, there have been no books written about him, or by him. Most written material about him that can be found on-line are tributes and articles in martial arts magazines or journals written after his passing by his students. There is no oral history. He was never interviewed. He didn't want that. You can see that this presents a formidable obstacle to anyone wanting to write a book about the life of this martial arts teacher and Qigong Master. My work-around for this challenge was to ask Mr. Chan's students themselves to tell me about their experiences with him. They are the last remaining sources of information about their teacher. Who could be a better source of information about BP Chan than his students?

Embedded in our consciousness are our life experiences. We are all unique, different people, and no two of us can have the exact same life experience. When we die, what is lost is the totality of those personal life experiences. The genesis for this book was a quest on my part to seek out and to preserve those life experiences of the direct students of BP Chan, especially their memories and recollections of him. By "direct students" I mean those who were taught specifically by him; not second or third generation students who would have been one or two teachers removed from him. Was he unique as a human being? Was he unique as a teacher of the martial arts, or was he, as characterized by one of his students, "simply a diminutive man who walked this earth"?

The memories and recollections in this book were obtained via essays written by the students themselves, by written communication, telephone communication, Zoom meetings and face to face meetings with the direct students of BP Chan themselves. Electronic transcriptions of the original interviews were edited by me for grammar, punctuation, clarity, and continuity. In almost every instance, they were also edited by Mr. Chan's students themselves. The views, comments, and opinions expressed in this book are solely those of BP Chan's first-generation students. They are all we have left to give us insight into the character and persona of Mr. Chan.

Some of Mr. Chan's students reading these recollections might think, "Well, that wasn't my experience." Well, maybe not, but we each see, feel, and experience things according to our own senses. It's not that any one person's experience is correct- or true- and another's not; it's simply that we are all different and we have our own unique set of experiences. It's hard to "fact check" someone's memories. You had to be there to do that, and even then, no two people see or feel the same thing. Time erodes details.

My goal was not to seek consensus of memory or experience

from Mr. Chan's students; I was seeking the totality of their community experience to better understand his relationship with his students.

You will see that indeed, there are common threads that run through the recollections of Mr. Chan's students. Maybe, in a way, that's all the fact checking we need to establish the truths about Mr. Chan.

1. BAGUA COMES TO NEW YORK CITY

Frank Allen

It began for us in our Lower East Side group in December of 1974. I was studying with a couple local luminaries, Jan the Iron Man Lang and Irish Jimmy O'Meara. I was working in Jan's store.

Jan the Iron Man Lang had a little curio shop on 6th Street, just off 2nd Avenue in the East Village, which doubled as his Kung Fu studio. It was a very unique store with all the display cases either on pulleys or wheels, allowing the space to be emptied out and turned into the workout space in a few minutes. Jan got his Iron Man moniker by his ability to withstand any blow and seemingly come away unscathed. A few of us did hardcore training with him based on arduous standing practice and contact sparring. The store/studio was aptly named The Silver Lining.

It was a cold and gray winter day, and the Iron Man was about to cross the avenue in pursuit of yet another rot-gut coffee from the Greek diner when he heard a familiar voice yell, "Hey Man, it's Bagua!" He turned to see Slick Tyrone skidding his bicycle to a stop. Tyrone was "Slick" to some and "Oily" to others. It sort of depended which side of the deal you were on. "Bagua?" replied the Iron Man, "What? Where?" "At William's," said Tyrone. "He's got a new instructor who's going to begin teaching Bagua in January." Tyrone was one of the senior students at one of the best-known Tai Chi schools in the city,

William C.C. Chen's school of Tai Chi up on 23rd and 7th Avenue. William had the distinction of being the only fighting Tai Chi school in New York. "Damn! Bagua, finally!" exclaimed the Iron Man. And Jan said, "So when it starts, I'll go up, I'll check him out, I'll let you guys know what's up." And he did, he went up there and took the first class. He came back and said, "This guy's great, we're all going to study with him. Get your money together, we're going up to Williams'."

It was noted that a bunch of the Tai Chi people in town were interested in Bagua, although we knew very little about it. The only sources of Bagua at that point were two books, the Robert Smith book and the Li Ying Arn book. And of course, we all owned them, looked at them. Smith's book is mostly the straight-line drills of the Gao Yisheng school. A little bit of circling in the back of the book. Li Ying Arn wrote a little introduction, had some nice pictures, a nice picture of Cheng-Yu Lung and some of the other people, Sun Lutang. But most of it he had reprinted, probably without getting permission because you didn't have to, you know, Chinese and copyrights.

Li Ying Arn's Bagua's self-defense book is all the little drawings of the chubby little guys in black and white. And we looked at those, and looked at those, and they were like hieroglyphics to us. We were fascinated, but without doing Bagua, we couldn't figure them out at all. But we looked at them all the time. We were really excited about Bagua, but there's no one teaching it to non-Chinese, at least in New York, and maybe I think the East Coast. About the only people in the country that were teaching it was Johnny Lee, who was in Louisiana at the time, later moved to Florida. And I think John Painter may have been starting to teach his variation. Maybe Jerry Allen Johnson. I don't know if Jerry started then or not. But that was it. That was like Louisiana, Texas, and Colorado. And there's no way for us to get anywhere near it. So we're all really excited that William had this guy.

So, in January of 1975, Jan Lang went up to 23rd Street and 7th Avenue to the William Chen Tai Chi School and began to learn the esoteric art of Bagua Zhang. After eight weeks of practicing the basics of the art, the second cycle began, and the Iron Man graciously decided to bring his entire student body to the classes. At my first class in March of 1975, we met Mr. BP Chan. I pretty quickly figured out this guy's a walking martial arts encyclopedia and had more knowledge than anybody we'd ever met, but he was really into his humble thing. He made the point he wasn't a teacher, he wasn't a Sifu, he certainly wasn't a Master, he was Mister. One of his favorite phrases was," I don't teach, we just practice together."

It was BP Chan, we had no idea what the BP stood for, but when you asked him, he'd say something like "Bureau of Police." And later we found out that it was originally from Fujian province. It's some Fujian dialect name I've never heard of before or since.

I have no idea how it's pronounced, really. If you were to look at it in English, it looks like bun piak or something like B-U-N-P-I-A-C or something like that. And I'm sure that's not the real pronunciation. And of course, like anybody that's been around Westerners, he had a Western name. We also later found out he was from the Philippines, and his Spanish name was Guillermo, which is Spanish for William. They quickly figured out William Chen and William Chan in the same school was gonna be way too confusing for the students. So he became BP Chan.

Later, we found out the story of what was going on, that Mr. Chan had left the Philippines rather quickly. I mean, there's speculation about that later, it was pure speculation. He had two daughters here and left behind his wife and his other kids. He had eight kids, so the other six- maybe he had six- the other four, had a bunch of kids. He came and stayed with a daughter upstate who was a nurse. Through 1974 he lived with her and he taught a small class of nurses in her basement. Five, six, seven nurses. His other daughter lived in New York City, so he moved down and was living with her and her family and she lived on 7th Avenue between 22nd and 23rd. And one of the first things he asked her is, did you ever see any Tai Chi schools around here? She says, yeah, there's one right around the corner. I walk past it every day. So he walked around the corner to 23rd Street and walked into William's. They got talking, and William realized all the stuff he knew, and that the guy was up for teaching, and hired him on the spot. They decided that he would begin with Bagua.

Jan took us up there to William's. Jan was like, any student's got the money, let's go, we're all going up. Jan and Mr. Chan developed a relationship; Jan was there from the minute Mr. Chan started teaching at William's, and he studied with Mr. Chan until Mr. Chan's death in 2002, over 25 years, although I think a lot of that last 20 years was once or twice a week. Mr. Chan went to Jan's storefront where he had that martial arts space where he taught, and it was all private lessons. But Jan and Chan were together for the rest of Chan's life. And Jan was always bringing everybody that he could. Anybody that studied with Jan for a while ended up studying with Mr. Chan, also.

What he taught was simply called Bagua, and even spelled in the old way of Pa-Kua. Those of us students in the know snidely looked down on those who pronounced the P and the K while Mr. Chan humbly treated everyone the same.

So, we started studying Bagua, and when we had finished 24 weeks of learning a 10 exercise Chi Kung set along with our eight palm changes, all of a sudden Chan said, "Well, that's it, come back, learn something else." Like, what?? Most of the students just left. But the Jan Lang students - Tinker the Locksmith, Cooper the Hustler, Michael 919 the Businessman, Alan the Mover, and I with the Iron Man, sort of surrounded Mr. Chan outside the office and told him "We know this isn't it, Mr. Chan, we know this is a lifetime study." He started to smile. We said, "We want to learn more. We know there's lots more of this." He said, "What do you want to learn?" We said, "We want to learn to stand." His grin covered his whole face.

BP Chan loved standing. His basic thing was standing. He thought you could learn pretty much everything from standing.

When he showed up and said that to William, William said, "No, no, you can't teach Westerners standing. You start to teach them standing, they get bored, they quit, we don't make any money, they all leave, you cannot teach them standing no matter what."

"What else?" he asked. "We want to learn to breathe properly, Mr. Chan." And the smile returned. "Anything else?" At which point the Iron Man blurted out, "We want you to hit us." Jan had done Iron Body training with previous teachers. "What?" said Chan. As we already knew about Chan's power in his iron palm, which belied his diminutive size of about five foot three inches, the rest of us chorused "No Mr. Chan, we don't want that. Don't listen to him." and he smiled again. Then came the big question "When do you want to do this?" We all knew the answer that would get us our training, but as late-night hippies we dreaded the prospect. Until then, we had all been jubilant, heads up and smiling. To a man we looked down, shuffled our feet and quietly said, "Early morning, Mr. Chan," and a Tuesday morning, 6AM to 8 AM Bagua class was born. And so that began our Tuesday mornings. Went on for a couple of years in the studio, I think. A year and a half or whatever. Every Tuesday morning from 6 o'clock to 8 o'clock we trained Bagua with Mr. Chan. And the first half hour of every session was standing 20 minutes in universal post, then you went into a Bagua stance on one leg and stood there for five minutes, and then you changed direction and stood five minutes on the other leg. That was the opening half hour. Then we'd do an hour and a half of forms in two person and whatever else we were doing. And we had some relatively well-known martial arts instructors come down for that class, and usually after a couple of classes with the standing, they were gone. But Jan kept bringing people in, and other people filtered in that actually got into it. And we had a good steady group that we trained with in William's studio.

And then I'm not sure what happened, but suddenly, we weren't using the studio anymore. By this time Mr. Chan's daughter had moved, I think, to Stuyvesant Town, the housing thing on 14th street that goes up a few blocks and then over and so we started training there. Yeah, we were there for a year or so and outside every morning. Then we moved to Tompkins Square Park where he was there for years. When we got to Tompkins Square Park, he started training us in iron palm and iron wrist. We started hitting the trees, mostly wrists, wrists, wrists, and then the palms. And he had his own liniment that he gave us.

One of the standard things he'd say was, "Liniment, strong, no liniment, crippled." So we had to apply his liniment before we did the iron palm or iron wrist. He was constantly yelling at me because I was getting carried away and I'd get these cuts on my wrist. It was fun putting the alcohol-based liniment on (Ouch! Frank laughs), but I didn't care. When I was hitting the trees, Mr. Chan would yell at me, "No BREED! No BREED!" – "Bleed" with his accent.

We were completely satisfied with what we were learning, as it included the 8-palms solo set and 8-palms two-person set that matched the solo set, our 10-exercise Chi Kung set, and an 8-palm meditation set which made a complete little system. We did leg stretching, his hanging leg exercises. We would do the hanging leg exercises on the fence, the wrought iron fences that were there. Put your leg up on the fence and touch the toes and touch the toes of the standing leg as well as the up leg and see if you can touch your forehead to your knee. We did a lot of hanging leg and hitting trees as well as doing the forms.

At one point he got invited to teach up at Cecil Chu's school on I think it's 46th and 6th. And Cecil was a good friend of William's and was actually a student of William's who opened his own school. There's a whole story there too, but it doesn't have anything to do with Mr. Chan. But Mr. Chan started teaching them and he started inviting them down to the Park. And of course, being the Lower East Side Park, the Lower East Side people had gathered with a few other people; at first, we were not real happy with what we used to call the "Chus" coming down to our morning classes.

But later we got to know them, in fact later I became pretty good friends with Domingo Colon, who was one of the main students there. Eventually he opened his own school in Westchester. But we did a lot of Park training as well as the classes. By the end of 1975, William got Mr. Chan teaching other things. He started teaching Qigong. By 1976, Mr. Chan was also teaching Hsing I Chuan, the 24 Posture Yang Style Tai Chi and Chin-Na, locking and grasping, which we also studied with him.

The Qigong set, when we got it, was known as the Ten Bagua Exercises. And when he started teaching Qigong, it suddenly became known as the Tao Ten, which these days it's still pretty much known as. And at that point, Bagua was just Bagua. No explanation, no talk about lineage, it was just Bagua. And it was years later before I found out what it was. We were assuming - we knew that he knew the Jiang Rong Chao original form, but he wouldn't teach it to us because his etiquette said if anyone else in town was teaching a form, he wasn't going to teach the same form. And there was some old guy in Chinatown with five or six students teaching the Jiang Rong Chao original form, so he wouldn't teach it. So he taught us this one, and we used to assume it was something from the Jiang Rong Chao school. Many years later, Novell Bell, known as the Black Taoist, studied with BP Chan, and was brought there by his teacher, Rudy Curry, who was with Chan early on. Twenty years down the line, Chan started opening up and telling people stuff. And that's how we discovered that it was the Dragon Claw Palm set of Cheng-Yu Lung. It was made for him by his father, Cheng-Ting Hwa, and I got that information from Novell. And along with Qigong, in fact I think the first thing he started teaching about halfway through 1975 was adding Xing-Yi. We didn't discover what that was like until they published in English the Sun Lu Tang Xing-Yi book, and we looked at it and went, well this is exactly what Mr. Chan is teaching us. Now whether it came down the direct Sun Lu Tang line or not, I don't know because we knew that he was really, really enamored of Wang Xiangzhai, who was the last student of the great Guo Yun Shen of the Divine Crushing Fist. Wang Xiangzhai founded Da Cheng Quan, Great Achievement Boxing, and later in life, Universal Post Therapy, where you stood in universal post and did a variety of things with your mind and of course Chan loved standing. His hero was Wang Xiangzhai. His favorite story was Wang being old and some friend of his putting on a big demo and wanting Wang to demonstrate and Wang said, "I don't do anything anymore." The friend said, "I know you do something, just come and do what you do." And Wang again said, "I don't do anything anymore." And finally, he said, "Okay," and walked out on the stage, went to Universal Post, stood there for 10 minutes and walked off the stage. Chan thought that was the best thing he'd ever heard. It was wonderful.

We later started getting stories filtering back through here and there. And we heard that Chan started studying martial arts at 10 years old. Because his father sent him to his friend, the martial arts teacher, because he felt he needed some training and discipline. At 10 years old, for his first six months of training, he stood in a deep horse stance facing a wall from a few inches away. And every time he turned around and looked at the class behind him, the teacher hit him with a stick. That was his original six months of training.

He had some really tough training in the early days, but he was really vague about it. We didn't know how much of it was in Fujian and how much of it was in the Philippines, because he trained in both places. He was apparently in the Second World War, but he used to say that he had never been in a fight in his life. The time the two guys tried to mug him didn't count (see below.) And we kind of speculated, again pure speculation, that he may have been in the famous broadsword brigade because he had all the details and he fit all the criteria. He talked about how the broadsword brigade picked out short-statured trained martial artists who could roll in a tight ball with a broadsword. They figured out that the Japanese machine guns were fixed and that they couldn't point them down. So they'd get people as small as they could to roll under the machine gun fire and then jump in the trenches with their broadswords. And he had all these details, and he was certainly a small-statured martial artist who was highly trained. He did say he had no part in the Second World War but he did have all these details on the broadsword brigade. And pure speculation, it may have nothing to do with anything, but we used to speculate on why he did come to America very quickly and left his family behind. Took him like eight years to get the paperwork to bring the rest of the family over.

And he used to tell the story of the two guys that tried to mug him. How these two Filipinos came up at 45-degree angles and pointed knives at his side, and how he grabbed the knives, turned them around, and stepped into the thrust - the thrust looking throat level. At which point he would stop the story and go, "Oh, but I made a mistake, cut my hands bad. Look." He started showing us the scars on his hands but never continued the story. So we always wondered if maybe he seriously injured or killed these guys which is why he came to the United States very quickly. But that was just our speculation. May have had nothing to do with nothing.

He was totally into the humility thing, refusing to say he was a teacher. When we went and did anything public, he would not go with us. First time that happened was on January 25th of 1976, when we piled into Slick Tyrone's car, after training just a year, and headed to the Chinese Businessmen's Association of Fairfield County, Connecticut. Cooper and I were doing Bagua, Jan and a couple of people were doing Tai Chi. His main people doing Xing Yi at the beginning were some of the women. And Prudence did Tan Tui, Erin and Emily did Xing-Yi. And we all went up there, we're all terrified, we're only doing this for a year. We're not good at this, we really suck. They're gonna know because Chinese people know Kung Fu; they're gonna know we're no good. It was a big realization when after we did our thing and we knew we were "eh," they all started coming up and talking about how good we were and how wonderful we were, and we thought "those people don't know Kung Fu." If those people knew anything they wouldn't think we were this good.

We now understood from that demonstration that the general Chinese public did not necessarily know Kung Fu. We tended to do demonstrations, Cooper and I, those first few years; we were playing Bagua demonstrations and we demonstrated at some of William Chen's Chinese New Year's parties. It was 1978, I think, huge East Coast Chinese demonstration, people from Boston to Baltimore, in Columbus Park in Chinatown. The BP Chan demonstration team did that, also. That was the biggest. I got a few pictures from that one. On September 9th of 1978, the team was sent down to Columbus Park in Chinatown to participate in the huge Universal Tai Chi Association demonstrations that not only included every Tai Chi school in New York, but schools from as far away as Baltimore, the famous Lady Master Bow Sim Mark and her school from Boston, including her teenage son, Donnie Yen, and a couple Masters from Taiwan. Amid this illustrious company, Cooper and I yet again were picked to show Mr. Chan's Bagua Zhang. As part of his humbleness thing, Mr. Chan himself refused to attend any of these demonstrations.

We also demonstrated at the William Chen Tai Chi School Annual Chinese New Year parties, like the 1979 Year of the Sheep party. Mr. Chan attended those parties.

He had these adages, which I always put as the wisdom of BP Chan. He was always working, working, working on his English. When he got here, he spoke Mandarin, Fujianese dialect, and Spanish, totally fluent Spanish, but he was working on his English. Of course, everybody asks "How many years do you study?" Mr. Chan would say "How many years you study doesn't matter. The question should be how many hours do you practice?" That was one of his. And one of the ones that I have always tried to keep to, that most teachers don't want anything to do with, is, "If the students don't become better than the teacher, there is no progress in the art." I have definitely trained students who got better than me, and I figured I'm supposed to, from what he said. That was really an important one: "If the students don't become better than the teacher, there is no progress in the art." And of course, his whole thing on dying, "Everyone gets the invitation, but we do exercises, ours comes a little later."

And my favorite of all Chan stuff was "Who has the best Tai Chi?" "Who is old and happy? He has the best Tai Chi." As for his Spanish, when we were training in Tompkins Square Park for a year or so, we had this group of Spanish kids, you know, like probably 15 to 19, that lived down in Alphabet City. And what we're quite sure they were doing was they would go to the West Village at night, and then at 6, 6:30 in the morning, they'd be heading back home to Alphabet City, and then walking through Tompkins Square Park.

The first time they stopped to watch us train, they're sitting there, and all of a sudden Mr. Chan walks over to them and starts talking to them in Spanish. They're totally blown away. The little Chinese guy walked up and started talking to them in Spanish. And they loved him. And for a year or so, they came and visited class over and over again.

They didn't necessarily train. They came and they wanted to talk to the little Chinese guy who spoke perfect Spanish. It was an incredible thing, this gang. But they came to watch him because he always told them how, when they first moved to the Philippines, they moved to a neighborhood that wasn't so good.

His father had always told him, "You make friends with people they call the good people. Trouble comes to the door, they say good-bye, you go outside. So, you make friends with people they call the bad people. Trouble comes to the door and they say, you stay here, I'll take care of it." And with that in mind, when they first got to their neighborhood, his father liked to go for long walks in the evening. He immediately saw and checked out who the muggers were. And he walked up to each and every one of them and said "I'm old Chan. I like to walk for entertainment. I like to walk every night."

So every night he'd give each a couple bucks. And it turned out that the muggers of his neighborhood ended up being his security guards, because they knew if there was no one that got mugged that night, that at least they'd get a couple of bucks from old Chan. And if anybody else came and gave him trouble, hey, you can't get in the way of our couple of bucks from old Chan. So, he turned the muggers of his neighborhood into his security guards. His father didn't do martial arts, but he was like a 33rd degree Mason. That's as high as it gets.

And we remember when he went home for his father's 100th birthday. Apparently, he had some longevity genes going for him. And yeah, his father lived to be a hundred.

Studying with Mr. Chan was always informative and fun. All our guys assumed Chan must be perfect. There was the school picnic the first year when Tinker, caught up in his ideas of what a Kung Fu Master should behave like, came upon Chan drinking a cream soda and exclaimed, "Mr. Chan, you are drinking soda." Chan promptly dropped his middle finger over the word soda and retorted, "Oh no, is Sparkling Cream." Or the time that he was trying to explain to us how parts of the body can fill with blood and energy to become harder, and he said, "It's all the same banana" and then wagging his index finger towards Jan's crotch continued, "There's no bones here." "It's all the same banana" became one of our favorite sayings for years. In the early years Chan's adaptation of the English language offered a few problems and a bit of amusement. For the first couple of years, we were constantly Posting and Toasting. Now, we knew what to do when he said these words, but we had no idea what he actually meant. It went on so long that Jan, who was a true village artist, painter, musician, sculptor, sketch artist, and filmmaker, was about to make a sculpture of a piece of toast on a post to commemorate the phrase when Chan's English improved, and we discovered that we were actually Pausing and Thrusting.

RAL: Sounds like he really was a character.

Yes, he was a character. I mean, he didn't like to put up with bullshit either.

And Cooper, who was Jan's partner, had moved to New Mexico and lived there for a few years. And Jan got on the phone and said, you got to come back and study with this guy. And he moved back to New York City to study with Mr. Chan, been back in New York City ever since. But Cooper was married to this woman. They got to be heavy-duty vegetarians and all this and that.

So they decided that they were going to take Mr. Chan to dinner. They're going to bring Cooper's relatives from this really straight, totally New Jersey middle-class family that knew nothing from nothing. And I think his wife's mom came and her little Chinese friend from Taiwan. And they went to dinner. Mr. Chan wasn't really into it. They kind of browbeat him into going to dinner with them. They arrive and the first thing is Chan orders a meal and everything has meat in it. EVERYTHING. So then Cooper and his wife go, "But Mr. Chan, you know, you know we're vegetarians." So, okay, he orders this dish called Monks and Nuns Vegetable, which doesn't have a recognizable vegetable in it. That's what he ordered for a vegetable dish.

And then their cute young lady friend from Taiwan shows up a little bit late, and you see Chan bristle when the straight lady goes, "Oh, she's cute, like a little China doll." And Chan's like... (Frank laughs.) But then she turns to Chan and says, "My brother has asthma. Can you tell us something that's good for asthma?" And they're sitting there, they've got all this weird food all over the place and looking at it. Chan tells them this story, and goes, "Oh yes, Philippines, we have special thing. Cure asthma every time. First, you get a monkey. Take monkey, we have thing, puts metal around his forehead, holds him dangling. Then you start fire on the monkey. Monkey goes really, really crazy. Make completely crazy. Take big knife, cut off top of head. Give kid spoon, have eat the brains. No more asthma." It could work because if you go to the hospital with a heavy, heavy asthma attack, what do they do? They shoot you up with adrenaline. What's that monkey's brain become when you light the fire under him? Full of adrenaline. And he proceeds to tell these straight people at this dinner that's the cure for asthma.

RAL: Did you hear this from Cooper?

I think I heard it from Jan. Cooper didn't talk about it so much. But he told Jan.

When Cooper first came back, Jan and Cooper, they had studied with Bruce (Frantzis) in '72 and then four years later Bruce came back in '76. Well, at the time they met Mr. Chan, Jan and Cooper were like, "If we could get Bruce and Chan together, go to dinner with them, can you imagine what we would learn just listening to them? Could you imagine?" Bruce comes back and sure enough they set up the dinner and they go to dinner. Bruce and Chan speak Mandarin all night long and they have no idea what they said. Later we found out one thing though, which was Bruce bragging about his lineage. And Mr. Chan said, "Oh, your lineage is much better than mine, you should teach these boys." Bruce replied that he was not going to be in town long enough. And then, like a week later, he started his classes that he ran for a year. So we studied with both of them for a year, then Bruce disappeared for another decade before he came back. But yeah, studying with Chan was amazing. Amazing. And I was there for about the first five years. and then my daughter was born. After that I just saw him on and off. You know we did Chinese New Year's demonstrations at my place, and he'd come by and hang out, watch and every now and then give some advice. I was demonstrating his Bagua at one point and apparently, I wasn't getting this stuff right. Afterwards I went over it with Mr. Chan. He just said our Xing-Yi looked good. He said to me, "Mr. Flan, Mr. Flan, one palm up, one palm down. Like yin, like yang. We used to do these things......"

RAL: All these stories and recollections, amazing. When was the last time you saw him?

The last time I saw him was probably at the Tai Chi Farm in the 90s. I just went up there when it first started, but he loved the Tai Chi Farm. He became friends with Jou Tsung Hwa who started the Tai Chi Farm. And people don't realize that all the improvements, the garden building, the little house building, all the improvements that happened was because Chan used to round up all the students that he could get during the good weather, and then go up there every weekend and work, cleaning and building the Tai Chi Farm. The Tai Chi Farm and all those improvements were made by Mr. Chan and his students. Not me, I'm not real handy, I'm not real fun about doing stuff, but he got the people, and they were up there every weekend working on the Tai Chi Farm. He loved that place. And I think he was kind of heartbroken when Jou Tsung Hwa died. Chan put so much effort into that, so much. Yeah. He loved that; he loved that place. So I'm not really sure, it was either up there or at one of our parties that he came by, and last saw him.

In 1982, when I decided my guys and I were going to compete, we ended up competing in one of the last of the Fu Jow Pai (Tiger Claw) tournaments. When Novell ran his Man-Up Stand-Up a few years ago, it was almost as tough, but because he had to abide by the rules, Novell had to tell them light contact, blah blah blah, and then when the people started fighting, he'd stand on the edge and start screaming, kill them, and they'd go full blast. Back in the old Fu Jow Pai tournaments, it was cups, mouth guards, 10-ounce gloves, try to knock each other out. And when Chan heard that we were doing that, he told Jan to bring me up. At that point Jan and Chan were doing their private lessons still at William's Studio, and he had Jan bring me up to his private lessons, and they started training me for fighting because Chan was into "These guys don't look like they're doing their martial arts. You should look like you're doing your martial arts. The best one would be Xing Yi. You need to work on your Xing Yi and look like you're doing Xing Yi." And then Chan said, "OK, Mr. Flan." The first time the guys introduced me to him, they said, "This is Frank." Chan said "Nah, nah, we have flan, this noodle pudding." And then the guys called me Noodle Pudding for the next two years; my nickname was "Noodle Pudding."

"Okay, Mr. Flan, you do Xing Yi, nothing but Xing Yi. Mr. Jan, you do whatever you want. So, needless to say, Jan's kicking my ass all over the studio. I'm trying to do just Xing Yi and he's doing freeform and Bagua and all kinds of stuff. I did get my moment. At one point the phone rang, and Mr. Chan walked into the office and the minute he did, Jan kind of looked at him, and I was supposed to be doing just Xing-Yi anyway, and I front kicked him in the solar plexus as hard as I could, knocking him down. He's been beating the hell out of me, with me stuck doing just Xing-Yi for like 45 minutes already.

Like I said, Mr. Chan went into the office; yeah, he used to do that. He'd set up people doing stuff and then he'd end up going in the office. A big one was he'd stop us in stance. He'd be doing a form, he'd hit a stance and he would say, "Hold it." And then he would go in the office. And by the time he came out, there'd be three or four students still holding the stance: Jan and me and a couple of Jan's other students. Everybody else had totally quit and was walking around and whatnot. We're the only ones that would hold the stance until he came out, no matter what.

We did it one day when we were in the Xing-Yi Dragon posture. He said "Hold it" and went into the office. Jan and I were next to each other and we're both feeling shaky. I look at Jan, he's looking kind of gray, I don't know what's going on. Jan said he's looking at me and going, "Frank, getting kind of green." We went home from class; we both came down with this wicked flu. And you know, all this stuff will run a disease through you quicker which means if you're at the middle of disease when you're training it'll go to the end. But if you're at the beginning of the disease you can train in a couple hours, go to the middle and the height of it. And that's what had happened to the two of us. When we're standing in Dragon stance, we're both coming down with the flu and it revved it up and we went like from the beginning of the flu to the height of the flu with that one stance, which is why he was looking gray and I was looking green. He was sick for a week and a half, I was sick for a month. Yeah, we came down with the flu while standing in stance.

Chan, amazing, amazing guy. I didn't do too much of his Qi-gong. I really didn't. I did a few classes, but I did his Bagua and his Xing-Yi and his Yang Style Tai Chi. And his Yang Style Tai Chi was rather interesting because William said, "You know, you don't do the same Yang style as I do, and why don't you, why don't you do the 24?" Everybody does the 24 now. Chan had left China for the Philippines before they made the 24. He said, "Ooh, I never did that." William said, "Here's the postures" and he gave Mr. Chan a list of the 24 postures. So he took his long form and put togeth-er the 24 posture straight out of his long form. Years later when I learned the PRC 24, they were almost exactly the same. It like shot hell through this whole thing that Communist Tai Chi isn't the real thing, yada yada.

Later in China, I discovered that all these amalgamated forms were where the government got the masters together and said make an amalgamated unified form that we can teach in colleges and use for tournaments. And you could see that though Chan had never even seen the PRC-24, his 24 was almost exactly the same. A sub-division of that that I like is there is no unified form of Bagua. Well, apparently, whenever they got all the Bagua Masters together, no one would agree on anything, and they never got to see an amal-gamated form. What they did is eventually take the forms from the general Jiang Rong Chao school and use them for the standard.

RAL: Frank, what life lessons would you say that you learned from BP Chan?

Well, a lot of them are the stuff in those adages. It's mostly important to be happy, and it's all about being healthy and hap-py, and that you've got to try to make the best of any situation.

RAL: Did you stop being a student of Mr. Chan's because you started your own martial arts school, or you decided to study with some other people?

Well, no. At that moment I wasn't studying with anyone, and I was occasionally seeing Jan, every now and then. I'd see Mr. Chan a little bit.

In 1979, I founded my own martial arts organization, the Wu-Tang Physical Culture Association, then in 1980, my daughter was born. These events began to take up both my time and funds, and I drifted away from Mr. Chan.

I still saw Mr. Chan occasionally, such as when he would attend our Chinese New Year demonstrations at my place, and he'd come by and hang out, watch and every now and then give some advice. I remember at one of these, he gave me a thumbs up after watching our demonstration of his 24 posture, Yang Style Tai Chi Form.

RAL: Did Mr. Chan know that you had formed your own school? And did he say anything to you about that?

Nothing directly, but like I said, he came to some of our Chinese New Year's demonstrations at school, at my school. And that's where I got the like-yin and like-yang thing. Yeah, he never said anything directly about it, but he was fine with it. Sorta. There were certain people that told him that I just had a fighting place where we beat each other up all the time, but then he came down and saw the demonstrations and knew that wasn't true. We were doing stuff including his stuff. My first 14 years doing Bagua was Mr. Chan's Bagua. That was it. No other Bagua.

And Xingyi even longer. Although I picked up a few bits and pieces of Xingyi from Bruce, I didn't really teach the Xing-Yi from Bruce. Mr. Chan's Xingyi was my Xingyi until I was studying with Liu Jing Ru in China. That's why now I'm bringing it back. You know, we're doing the Dragon Claw Bagua in class. And Xing-Yi, we've started doing his Xing-Yi, and trying to make sure that my people have both Mr. Chan's and Liu Jing Ru's Xing-Yi.

RAL: You had mentioned that you never did any of BP Chan's Qigong.

Well, I did the Tao Ten, because they were the Ten Bagua exercises. And I did a lot of standing, because we did standing in classes. and I did little bits of stuff. Like I said, I took his Qigong for a few months. Yeah. About six, seven months I took his Qigong. There was a Williams boxing class just before Mr. Chan's class and Jan and I would go up an hour early, go to the corner, drop in the Universal Post and not move for an hour and watch William's boxing class and get everything we could absorb by watching. A lot of my Fighting for Health internal boxing class comes from just standing and watching William's boxing class.

Everybody was like, the Westerners are standing for an hour. They're not moving for an hour. We got to watch that class for free for a year, by standing in Universal Post while we watched. And then others started showing up, just wandering around and watching for free. That's when William's wife came up with the famous "half price to watch." I understand it is still half price to watch. But for a year, Jan and I got away with watching that class, because we stood in Universal Post while we watched.

RAL: Do you have any mementos from your time with Mr. Chan that perhaps no one else might have? Like a letter from him or an object that he gave you or anything like that. Anything physical?

No, nothing. We used to go up to his house occasionally and a lot of times he'd give us tea. Jan hated tea. But when Mr. Chan gave tea, Jan would drink it. But then we'd go up there and he'd have this mung bean and garlic drink. And you may have heard I detest garlic. I can't stand garlic. But when he made the mung bean and garlic tea, I drank it because it came from Mr. Chan. And when first going up there with the cold weather, I thought it was the worst thing in the world. It wasn't. In the summer he had an iced mung bean and garlic drink, which was much worse than the hot tea.

RAL: At that time, Mr. Chan was living in Queens?

No. Oh, he was in Manhattan. Yeah, at that point, I think that was really early on, we used to go up to his place on 7th Avenue. And then, like I said, he lived at Stuyvesant Town. Then he worked stuff out and was back at his daughter's place in Stuyvesant Town.

And, you know, by the time he was in Queens, I wasn't seeing him at all. But that's when I imagine Rudy Curry hooked up with him. Rudy Curry studied with him quite a bit, and Rudy Curry was Novell Bell's teacher, and he turned Novell on to BP Chan. Novell has always been really nice to me and gives me the respect of being a senior brother in the BP Chan thing because I was with Chan ahead of him. He's actually a really good guy. Everybody is a product of their own environment. But yeah, he's one of the champions. He and Rudy Curry are two of the Chan people that are around that are still serious, serious martial artists and still alive. It's like an awful lot of people from when I started out aren't. I think Rudy did some of the other Yin Fu stuff that Novell got into. But he was primarily a teacher of BP Chan's material. He's a really nice guy.

Jan continued to study with Mr. Chan until Chan's death at 80 in 2002. It was a shock as Chan always seemed like one of those guys who would never die. It was equally shocking when Jan passed away at 70 in 2010. I miss both of these remarkable men and try to carry on the many lessons that I learned from them.

2. THE YIN AND YANG OF LINEAGE

It's hard to find books about Chinese Martial Arts teachers that don't contain references to that teacher's lineage. My sense is that books about martial arts teachers are not considered "complete" without a discussion of lineage. I debated whether to even include lineage in this book, since BP Chan himself downplayed his own lineage, preferring only to share that information sparingly. But those interested in the martial arts want it regardless, so I'm happy to offer two summaries of the lineage of BP Chan here.

The importance of lineage in the Chinese (or Japanese, or Southeast Asian, for that matter) martial arts rests in the eye of the beholder. Many who study the martial arts directly from a lineage holder believe it lends authenticity and credibility to the teacher and ultimately, to his/her students. Many believe that it is a purer form of that teaching; the knowledge and teaching has not been diluted and has not taken detours through other non-lineage teachers. Let's face it, there is prestige associated with being a lineage holder.

On the other hand, others will tell you that lineage really doesn't matter. Just because you study with a lineage holder is no guarantee that you will reach a high level of skill in that style. It's the results that count.

But what did Mr. Chan think about the importance of lineage? Although Mr. Chan would sometimes be forthcoming and provide a minimum of detail around his teachers, asking Mr. Chan about his lineage seemed to irritate him. To paraphrase, Mr. Chan would say, "Why are you asking about my lineage? It's me you're studying with, right?"

Researching lineage has always been a slippery slope. Identifying past teachers has always been difficult due to lack of written records, certain levels of secrecy surrounding teaching of the internal martial arts, verbal histories passed down which may have lost detail over time, etc., etc. In this book, you will find several students who have offered up details of Mr. Chan's lineage. I will leave it to the readers of this book to decide for themselves which lineage paths - or none - they choose to follow.

Sal Canzonieri*, although not a direct student of BP Chan, invested years of research to document lineage of the martial artists his teachers have studied with. One of his martial arts teachers, Warner Ollie, was a direct student of BP Chan. Here is Sal's research on the lineage of BP Chan that he provided for this book. I have not edited, changed, or verified the content.

WARNER OLLIE
- Chief Systems: Chen Tai Ji, Xing Yi, Tai Ji Ruler
- Chief Teachers: **BP Chan** – Chen Tai Ji, Yang Tai Ji, Xing Yi, Bagua.
- Warner Ollie studied Taiji Ruler, Chen TJQ, and Xingyi Quan with **BP Chan** in NYC.

BP CHAN (1922-2002)
- Internal Arts teacher of Warner Ollie, Frank Allen, Ken Cohen, and Others
- Chief Systems: Old Chen style and Old Yang style Tai Ji, Xing Yi, Bagua, Qigong, Taiji Ruler, and more.
- Chief Teachers: Chan Jingming, Lian Dak Fung, Lui Chow

Munk, Chow Changhoon, Liu Hingchow, Zheng Huai Xian, Leung Kaychi, Tung Ying Chieh.

BACKGROUND

BP Chan was born in 1922 in Fujian province. His birth name is Chan Bun Piac. At the age of 10, he began Taoist meditation and Qigong with the monks of An De Guan monastery (安德觀 - Monastery of Peaceful Virtue), not far from his home in Fujian province. At 11, he began training with the famed Southern China Master of Wu Zu Quan (Five Ancestors Boxing - 五祖拳) Chan Jingming 陳景銘, from whom he learned Fujian White Crane Boxing, Standing Meditation (Zhan Zhuang), and various qigong techniques. Later he learned Shaolin boxing with Lian Dak Fung.

Shortly thereafter, he studied Taiji Ruler Qigong from Master Lui Chow-Munk, student of Zhao Zhongdao.

During World War II, Chan was inducted into the Chinese military. Chan probably had other teachers as well, including combat instructors in the military. He knew and taught Yunnan Consecutive Step Boxing – Lian Bu Quan 雲南連步拳, which was part of standard training for Nationalist troops during the Second World War.

After he moved to the Philippines, when World War II was over, he continued cultivating the Tao and learning Bagua Zhang and Xingyi Quan with Liang Ji Ci 梁紀慈 (Leung Kay-Chi in Cantonese), with whom he taught for many years. He later studied Yin Bagua and Chen Tai Ji Quan with Liang Ji Ci (Liu's first disciple, teaching in Boston. His wife is the daughter of Han Qing Tang.)

He also mastered Xingyiquan with Chow Chang Hoon and developed his Baguazhang with Liu Hing Chow, teaching the Cheng style Dragon Bagua Zhang set. BP Chan also learned Jiang Rong Qiao "Original" style Bagua Zhang.

Chan was deeply connected with the tradition of Sun Lutang 孫祿堂 through his training in various arts (most likely Xingyi

Quan 形意拳) with Sun's famed disciple Zheng Huai Xian (1897-1981) 鄭懷賢..

He studied Old Yang Tai Ji Quan with Tung Ying Chieh, also learning and becoming proficient in the Tai Chi Staff, Tai Chi Knife, and the various methods of Push-Hands.

In 1974, Chan moved to NYC and taught martial arts and Qigong at the school of friend and colleague William C. C. Chen. He taught classes in Yang and Chen Style Taiji Quan; Bagua Zhang; Xingyi Quan; Yunan Boxing; Taoist Meditation; Taiji Ruler Qigong; Lying Down Qigong (Wo Gong); Standing Meditation, and more. Chan was friends with Jou, Tsung Hwa and taught regularly Jou's Tai Chi Farm in Warwick, New York State.

In NYC, Chan taught Qigong to Ken Cohen. Ken Cohen learned Taiji Ruler from BP Chan and taught it as well. According to Cohen, Chan was an avid reader and deep thinker. He especially admired the book "A Study of Xingyi Quan" 形意拳學 by Sun Lutang 孫祿堂 and often, during private classes, quoted passages from it. He also loved the inner martial arts writings of Jiang Rongqiao 姜容樵. Chan was constantly refining his practice and teaching style.

CHAN JING MING AND LIAN DAK FUNG-SHAOLIN QUAN TEACHERS TO BP CHAN

BACKGROUND

In Fujian, Shaolin Quan Masters Chan Jing Ming and Lian Dak Fung were BP Chan's teachers.

ZHAO ZHONG DAO (CHAO CHUNG TAO) (1891-1959.) -TAI JI RULER TEACHER TO LIU CHOW MUNK AND FENG ZHI QIANG

BACKGROUND

Zhao Zhongdao's name is Zongfan; byname is Zhongdao, also named Xianzhang. His family lived in Xinmin county

Northeast Reagion of China. He died without illness in No. 5 yard Tudimiao Xicheng District in Beijing and buried in Beijing Babaoshan Cemetery. Some say that that he was born in 1843 and died in 1962 at the age of 119 years old. Zhao Zhongdao's family is a martial art family. Zhao safeguarded local security in 1901. He moved to Beijing about 1912. He learned Taiji practice from Wang Yongfu in Beijing Xicheng District.

Taiji Chih or Ruler (no relationship with Taijiquan) is a sacred and secret qigong first made public in 1954 by Zhao Zhongdao. Actually, the original name of the system is "Xian Tian Qi Gong Tai Ji Chi" (Pre-Heaven Qi Training Tai Ji Ruler.) It is called the Ruler (Chi, sometimes spelled Chih) because during the basic exercise the hands are held about a foot apart. You may practice this qigong while holding a foot-long "Ruler" between the palms. The Ruler (also called the 'Stabilizing the Heart Needle') is made of a light porous wood such as willow and rounded at both ends so it fits comfortably in the hands. The physical ruler encourages the flow of ch'i. The Taiji Chih system consists of gentle rocking and swaying movements that build ch'i in the feet, the dantian, and the hands. It can be used for self-healing or as a preparation for any form of massage therapy or therapeutic touch. Your hands will feel warm, vibrating, and full of healing power after a few minutes' practice.

The purpose of the training is to stimulate the 'Pre-Heaven' qi circulation by setting up gentle, circular rhythms in the body. The practitioners believe that holding the ruler between the palms aids in coordinating the movements of the hands and body and helps to connect the energy flow. The training is said to cultivate the Three Internal Treasures (essence, qi and spirit), while externally training the connective tissue/bones, muscles and skin. The hands, eyes, body and steps are also trained. All the movements are slow and gentle, with conservation of energy as an underlying principle of training. Among the sets are a set of 8 exercises with the ruler held between his palms, a second set of 8 exercises done empty handed: Tai Ji Shen Gong; a third set is done with a two-person ruler 42 inches long.

Legend has it that was developed by the famous tenth-century Daoist recluse Chen Xi-Yi. Chen lived on Mount Hua, the Daoist sacred mountain in Shenxi Province. The Jade Spring Temple at the foot of the mountain was designed by Chen and contains a statue of him. Eventually he taught it to Zhao Kuan Yin, before he became the Song Dynasty Emperor. Supposedly, the Zhao family has passed it down through the generations.

He published a book on The Gentle Art of the Taiji in 1928. Zhao Zhongdao introduced in the preamble thereof that: 'After the founding of the Republic of China, when I traveled to Peking, I got the position of survey by the recommended of a good friend, and I met Mr. Wang Yongfu living in the west of the city through my friend, and he taught me about the inner method of Taiji'". He published the Simple introduction of the Gentle Art of the Taiji in 1942 and formed a systemic teaching of Taiji Ruler.

In 1954, he founded in Beijing "The Gentle Art of Taiji Health Society," the first school to publicly teach the Taiji Chih. The Society was like a university teaching hospital. Scientists and qigong practitioners from all over China came to learn the art. Patients with debilitating and chronic diseases arrived for treatment. The Society was very successful treating digestive and nervous system disorders, insomnia, high blood pressure, and numerous other problems that had failed to respond to medical treatment. Zhao taught Lui Chow-Munk, who taught the Taiji Ruler to BP Chan. He also taught Feng Zhi Qiang, who taught Bruce Frantzis and Ken Cohen.

CHEN JI MING (陈京铭, (FK. TAN KIONG BENG)-TEACHER OF WUZU QUAN TO BP CHAN

BACKGROUND

Another notable master was Cai Yuming's disciple who took Wuzuquan to the Philippines and started the Beng Kiam club.

He was one of the top ten disciples of Cai Yuming. Chen was a wealthy merchant who moved to the Philippines in 1900 and made a living as a bone setter.

Soon after, the overseas Chinese in Manila became aware of his credentials and sought him out for teaching martial arts. However, in his retirement Chen sought to return home to Fujian and as a result sent his son, Tan Kahong who with some his father's disciples jointly established the Beng Kiam school in 1935.

CAI YU MING (1857-1910) 蔡玉鸣 (FK. CHUA GIOK BENG) – WUZU QUAN TEACHER TO CHEN JI MING

BACKGROUND

Cai Yuming was from Fangwei county, Fujian province. From a wealthy background which then allowed him to focus on his real interests in the martial arts. It is mentioned that he became a student of many boxing teachers and later a disciple of Taizuquan Master He Yang (何阳) in Zhangzhou and later through travels absorbed the techniques of many martial arts formulating Wuzuquan (五祖拳, 5 Ancestors Boxing) which he passed on to disciples after returning to Quanzhou where he opened martial arts schools. He started two schools Longhui (龙会) and ShengGong (圣公.)

Cai Yuming became the most renowned master in Quanzhou and the influence so strong that many Taizuquan masters took tutelage and adopted their teachings. It is for this reason that the Taizuquan and Wuzuquan traditions in Quanzhou later became so interrelated as they shared the same core origin as well as developments.

HE YANG (何阳, 1795-1880) – WUZU QUAN TEACHER OF CAI YUMING

BACKGROUND

He Yang was originally from Yongding, Fujian province who later opened a small Inn within the Yingzhou district of Zhangzhou. He was said to be a 3rd generation practitioner of the

Taizuquan. In the later Qianlong period he later taught martial arts in Zhangzhou (where the martial hall is known as 'Heyang Tang, 何陽堂'.) His martial arts were renowned for hard power often described as 'jing gang jing' (Diamond hard power.) The Taizu Quan style was also known as Wuzuquan or sometimes as Heyang Quan by latter practitioners. His teacher is not known.

Wu Xin (悟心, 1691-1758) is one of 8the earliest recorded practitioners of Taizuquan in Quanzhou records. Wu Xin was said to be a monk residing at Dongchan Temple (东禅寺, Eastern Zen Temple) in Quanzhou and taught the style to lay disciples. Wu Xin was said to have studied from another monk who was an ex-Ming empire loyalist and had converted to avoid persecution.

CHOW CHANG-HOON (ZHŌU CHĀNG XŪN) – XINGYI TEACHER TO BP CHAN

BACKGROUND

As a youngster in the Philippines, BP Chan's Xingyi teacher was Zhou Chang Xun.

LIU HING CHOW (LIÚ XÌNG ZHŌU) – BAGUA ZHANG TEACHER TO BP CHAN

BACKGROUND

In the Phillipines, Liu was BP Chan's Bagua Zhang teacher, along with Liang Ji Ci. BP Chan learned the Jiang Rong Qiao Bagua forms.

ZHENG HUAI XIAN 鄭懷賢 (1897-1981) –SUN STYLE BAGUA ZHANG TEACHER TO BP CHAN

BACKGROUND

Zheng was the disciple of Sun Lu Tang and BP Chan's Sun style Xingyi teacher. See previous pages for information. Zheng also taught Ho Shen-ting.

LIANG JI CI 梁紀慈 (LEUNG KAY-CHI IN CANTONESE) – CHEN TJQ, BAGUA ZHANG AND XING Y QUAN TEACHER TO BP CHAN

BACKGROUND

Dr. Kay-Chi Leung was born in Canton and has spent most of his life studying in Taiwan. He is the son-in-law and favorite student of the late Han Ch'in T'ang, from whom he learned Northern Shaolin, Ch'in-Na, and Yang style T'ai Chi. Dr. Leung is also the Head Disciple of Liu Yun Chiao, who taught him Mi-Tsung, Yin Fu Bagua, Baji-Pi-Kua, and Praying Mantis. Dr. Leung is also a doctor of Chinese Acupuncture, Orthopedics, and western dentistry.

Dr. Leung has had over 15 different teachers who have taught him over 10 systems. Here is a short list: Han Chin-Tang, Liu Yun-Chiao, Du Yu Ze (Tu Yi Che), Chang Xiang San, Wei Xiao Tang, Chao Lien-Feng, Wang SongTing, and Shang Tung-Sheng. Liang Ji Ci learned Tang Lang from the following:

- Zhang Xiang San (Liu He Tang Lang Quan)
- Liu Yun Qiao (Liu He Tang Lang Quan and other Wu Tang association styles, i.e. Ba Ji Quan.)
- Wei Xiao Tang (Ba Bu Tang Lang Quan)
- Liu Zu Yuan (Tai Ji Tang Lang Quan)
- Wang Song Ting (Chang Quan Tang Lang Quan)
- Zhao Zhu Xi (Taiji Tang Lang Quan

While he was learning under Zhang Xiang San, he asked Liu Yun Qiao (Zhang Xiang San gong fu brother) to teach him. That is how he became Liu's first disciple in Taiwan. Liang Ji Ci was one of the few students who got to "touch hands" (spar) with Liu Yun Qiao.

After many years in Taiwan, in 1972 Liang Ji Ci moved to the Philippines where he taught till the mid 80's. There he became BP Chan's Bagua and Taiji Quan teacher. While Liang Ji Ci was in the Philippines, he taught Tang Lang Quan to Xu Wei Peng (a.k.a. Shakespeare Chan, a famous disciple of Zhao Zhi Min.) It is said that Liang Ji Ci learned very in-depth Seven Stars Praying Mantis form Zhao Zhi Min lineage when he lived in Malaysia, but unable to confirm this version.

In the mid 80's, Liang Ji Ci moved to Boston, MA (USA), where he still lives.** He has a school where he teaches Liu He Tang Lang, Ba Ji Quan, Pi Gua Quan, Bagua Zhang, Northern Shaolin, Tai Ji Quan, and some Chang Quan and Xing Yi. He was the personal bodyguard of the president of the Philippines, Ferdinand Marcos.

---

* Sal Canzonieri is the author of The Hidden History of the Chinese Internal Martial Arts, 2014.
**Liang Ji Ci (Leung Kai Chi) passed away in 2022.

3. THE MYSTERY OF B.P. CHAN'S EDUCATION

Mark Jones

One thing that all B.P. Chan's students can agree upon is that he did not wish to disclose much information regarding who he learned his martial arts from. His primary reason for this was that he didn't want the student to be fixated on names and lineages, but rather with the principles of proper body and mind mechanics so they could work and develop their skills based on the premise that focusing on names and biographies of the past would only interfere with his student's practicing. Names cannot teach you a martial art, only hard work can. He didn't even want them to acknowledge himself as their teacher! He presented himself more as a vehicle through which the principles are transmitted. He considered himself to just be a "fellow practitioner" who'd just been practicing for a little longer than his students.

Despite this, Mr. Chan did acknowledge the names of a few of his teachers. There are various ones mentioned on various websites of his students and his photo is readily available in a book showing a Tai Chi class that he was a member of in the early 1950's. He even spoke to me about one of his teachers. But most remain a mystery, and the main ones listed in his various bios come from a source unknown to me – possibly William Chen, Cecil Chu, Ken Cohen? I'm sure there is some basis of fact in those names, however, not only were most written in Wade-

Giles transliteration which is rarely used anymore in favor of the Pinyin system, but many of the old martial artists had several variations on their names and even several names!

The standard bio as reported on Mr. Cohen's website reads as: "He learned Taoist meditation and qigong from monks and masters at the An De Guan (安德觀 Monastery of Peaceful Virtue), not far from his home. At age 11, Chan began training in Northern Shaolin Boxing with Master Lian Dak Fung, and not long thereafter learned Taiji Ruler Qigong 先天氣功太極尺 from Lui Chow-Munk, a direct student of the system's greatest proponent, Zhao Zhongdao. He also studied with the famed Master of Wu Zu Quan (Five Ancestors Boxing 五祖拳) Chen Jingming 陳景銘, from whom he learned Fujian White Crane Boxing, Standing Meditation (Zhan Zhuang), and various qigong techniques. Chan was deeply connected with the tradition of Sun Lutang 孫祿堂 through his training in various arts (most likely Xingyi Quan 形意拳) with Sun's famed disciple Zheng Huaixian (1897-1981) 鄭懷賢. In the Philippines, he continued cultivating the Tao and learning Bagua Zhang and Xingyi Quan with Liang Jici 梁紀慈 (Leung Kay-Chi in Cantonese), who taught him for many years. I have also heard from some of Chan's other students that Chan may have learned Xingyi Quan from Chow Chang-Hoon, though I was unable to corroborate this during his lifetime."

It is pretty certain that he studied Bagua Zhang and old frame Chen Taijiquan with Liu Yunqiao a.k.a. Liu Yun Chiao because other students of Liu's are the only ones I've seen performing the old frame Chen in a similar manner as Chan, with the exception of the older Du Yu Ze a.k.a. Du Yu Tse or Tu Yi Che. The question remains, did Chan ever study directly with Du, who learned from Chen Fake's father Chen Yen Shi or Chen Yen Xi? All I know is that watching Du Yu Ze perform the Chen form is the closest thing to what Chan and his senior students taught me. Adam Hsu can also be seen doing a similar version and he also studied with Liu Yunqiao. There are short videos available of Liu

Yunqiao performing Bagua. His circle walking is indeed exactly how Chan taught it; however his palm changes are completely different. The word I received through the grapevine of various students claim that there are two different sets of palm changes that he learned and there was another Master in New York City who was already teaching the first set; Chan didn't want to show disrespect and teach the same set, so he only taught the second set called "the combined form." I have no idea whether this is true or not.

And the style of Bagua Zhang he taught he called "Dragon Claw." Yet I had read one source claiming that his style was from Jiang Rong Qiao a.k.a. Chiang Jung Chi'ao. Another purports it to be from Cheng Ting Hua. Yet another source claims it was from Yin Fu. The only thing I know for certain is that I've watched videos of all these styles being performed and the one thing they have in common is that none of them resemble what Chan taught.

We are certain that Mr. Chan studied with Tung Ying-chieh (Dong Yingjie.) Yet film of Dong and photos in his "red book," while similar, are not exactly the same as the way Chan taught it.

Herein lies the big mystery. Nearly everything Chan taught from Qigong exercises like the Eight Pieces of Brocade to his Hsing-yi and Bagua and weapons look completely different than that of anybody else. Many of his senior students I've spoken with say the same thing – that "nothing we do looks like anyone else." The things we do are top shelf in effectiveness for sure, but they are unique in the appearance and in the sequence of their forms. The "why they don't look like any other styles" is something nobody will ever know unless an early student or family member comes forth to fill in the blanks.

Yet another mystery can be found in his Yang Tai Chi. There is a book entitled "Tai-Chi Ch'uan: Its Effects & Practical Applications" by one Y.K. Chen of whom very little is known. Even any facts regarding the individual who wrote the preface, C.C.

Chiu is a mystery. What is known is that the line drawings of the Tai Chi postures are nearly identical to those of Chan's, including the order of moves. Did Chan learn what he practiced and taught from this book? Did he and Y.K. Chen study with the same teacher? Is it a total coincidence?

Other questions I've heard raised include whether Mr. Chan learned his Yiquan standing system directly from the founder Wang Xiāngzhāi or possibly from a student of his. Standing meditation was paramount to Chan's teaching and although various standing systems which Chan also taught go back to ancient times, Wang's system was certainly a major component of Chan's teaching. Where he learned it remains an unresolved issue.

Miscellaneous other blanks need to be filled in regarding disciplines he had a mastery of, including the Tai Chi Ruler, cancer healing (did he learn directly from the founder Madam Guo Lin?), and other arts he knew but rarely, if ever taught such as Shaolin Kung Fu and Five Ancestor Fist, which he apparently learned or continued to study in Manila.

In sum, martial arts are not, nor should they be, a fixed set of movements that are immutable. They are a living work-in-progress that are certainly subject to variation and refinement over the years. The only constant immutable feature is the adherence to the principles because they pertain to the laws of physics. It is likely that what Chan taught was, in the final analysis, his own style; one that assimilated the teachings he'd learned from his many teachers and distilled into the essences that he felt were most effective. His Yang style was still basically the Yang style only altered to Chan's liking. Same with all his arts. I imagine it was an evolution over a lifetime – one that spoke most profoundly to Chan's creative and sincere devotion to his art and to disseminating it to anyone who was receptive to learning it.

Yet, for the sake of history, now that Chan is no longer among the living, it would be fascinating to obtain a comprehensive understanding of the exact sources/precedents of his education. In any event, for those of us who were privileged enough to have studied with him and put in the hard work to put his ideas into our bodies and not just our heads, Mr. Chan's many teachers, whomever they may have been, live on in the art we lovingly and diligently practice every day.

4. NEW YORK CITY IN THE 1970'S

I think it's important to look back at New York City in the 1970's to put BP Chan into the context of what life was like at that time in his newly adopted city.

I know what it was like. I was living in Manhattan in 1974, and after getting married in the fall of 1975, my wife and I moved to the Bronx, another New York Borough just above Manhattan Island. At that time, New York City was a dirty, gritty, place to live. Garbage on the streets. Graffiti on abandoned buildings......and on occupied buildings. The subway cars were covered with graffiti; not all cars were air conditioned, and in many cars the air conditioning just didn't work. Some cars still had old-style ceiling fans and wicker seats. Mechanical breakdowns were common. The subway platforms were crowded, hot, smelly, and unbearable in summer. Subways ran erratically. Crime was a frequent traveler on the NYC Subway System.

In February of 1975, the year that BP Chan started teaching at William Chen's School, New York City was in a financial crisis, unable to pay its bills. Although President Gerald Ford never did actually tell Mayor Abe Beame and the City to "Drop Dead," he initially declined to "bail out" the city.

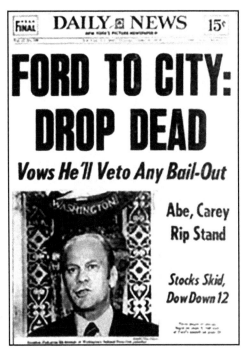

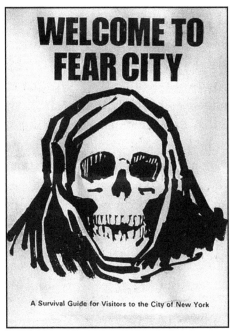

In 1975, a consortium of NYC unions representing 60,000 policemen, firemen and other public-safety officers began distributing pamphlets at NYC airports, bus terminals, and mid-town hotels. The pamphlets offered the following nine guidelines for visitors: 1) Stay off the streets after 6 PM 2) Do not walk 3) Avoid public transportation 4) Remain in Manhattan 5) Protect your property 6) Safeguard your handbag 7) Conceal property in automobiles 8) Do not leave valuables in your hotel room, and do not deposit them in the hotel vault (criminals were regularly breaking into hotel vaults) 9) Be aware of fire hazards.

"Travellers arriving at New York City's airports in June 1975 were greeted with possibly the strangest object ever handed out at the portal to a great city: pamphlets with a hooded death's head on the cover, warning them, "Until things change, stay away from New York City if you possibly can."

"Welcome to Fear City" read the stark headline on these pamphlets, which were subtitled "A Survival Guide for Visitors to the City of New York". Inside was a list of nine "guidelines" that might allow you to get out of the city alive, and with your personal property intact.

The guidelines painted a nightmarish vision of New York; one that made it sound barely a cut above Beirut, which then had just been engulfed in Lebanon's civil war. Visitors were advised not to venture outside of midtown Manhattan, not to take the subways under any circumstances, and not to walk outside anywhere after six in the evening." *

Also weighing heavily on the city was the very active Vietnam anti-war movement and widespread city drug use. It is estimated

* Excerpted from 'Welcome to Fear City' – the inside story of New York's civil war, 40 years on, The Guardian, May 18, 2015.

that over 800,000 New Yorkers fled to the suburbs. Landlords forced viable businesses out of hundreds and hundreds of NYC loft buildings due to J-51 Tax Abatement legislation. Again, I was witness: My business on 24th Street was forced out of Manhattan in 1981 when my lease would not be renewed. The landlord was converting the entre loft building into cooperative apartments because of this legislation. Thousands of other small businesses, the bedrock of NYC, were forced to close or move out of Manhattan.

The "Son of Sam" killings began in July of 1976 and terrorized the City's population. A massive City blackout/power failure provided opportunity for looting and vandalism in July of 1977. There's a whole lot more, but I think you get the picture.

Such was the New York City environment that a 5'2"/ 5'3" small Chinese man from the Philippines chose to call home at the age of 53.

WELCOME TO NEW YORK CITY, MR. CHAN.

"You know…. someday you will be a teacher. Do you know what that means?"

"I think so," I answered.

"No, I don't think you really understand. A teacher does more than just give out information. He is a guide and someone for you to try to copy. He brings about change in the heart of his students. Students imitate their teachers, so the teacher must act as he would have his students act. If you want to know the worth of a teacher, look at his students. They demonstrate what he is really like on the inside."

-Excerpted with permission from
The Making of a Butterfly by Phillip Starr,
Copyright © 2006.

5. IN THEIR OWN WORDS

"Don't Dumb Down"
—Linda Lehrhaupt

This is Linda Lehrhaupt and I'd like to welcome you to the Mindfulness-Based Teacher Project. Podcast number nine: Don't Dumb Down.

One day in the Tai Chi school where I was studying back in 1978, I saw a sign on the board announcing a class in Qigong. And underneath those words it said meditation. And I was immediately pulled into it. Because for some time I had been questioning, what is meditation? I had read that Tai Chi was meditation in motion, and I had been studying it for about nine months, but we never really talked about it in our class, and I thought, oh, okay, Qigong. Maybe here I can learn something about what meditation is about. And so I arrived at the time that was announced on the paper, and I was a bit late, and when I walked into the room, I saw a group of about eight students standing in the middle of the room.

Their arms were chest high, their palms were facing inward, the fingers were almost touching, and that's all they did was stand there. Nobody looked at me. I think most of their eyes were closed. And then suddenly a very small Chinese man appeared in front of me and smiled and waved with his hand, said I should come in and sit down on a bench. And he just kind of gestured to me with a signal as if, you know, sit here and wait. And I did. I wasn't aware. I assumed that the students were performing a Qigong exercise. And I just thought, okay, I'll sit here and watch.

And watch I did. For a long time. And there was such a stillness in the room, and I kept wondering after 5 minutes, 10 minutes, those people were standing there with their arms still up. Try it. It's not easy. And I watched the teacher, who at that point I understood his name was Mr. Chan, I watched him just standing in front of the group. He took the same position that they did and as he settled down into the posture, I had such a sense of stability and quiet strength, not brute force, but a very deep sense of calmness and rootedness. And every once in a while I would see him open his eyes, observing the students slowly from left to right. And it was also not the sense of observing to see if they were doing something wrong, but rather through his gazing at them, he helped to support them in their standing.

After about 25 minutes, he came out of the posture and slowly walked to each student and made slight corrections in their posture.

And if he saw that someone was drooping or wilting a bit, he would just tap them very lightly and give them a big smile and kind of nod his head and slowly the hands would come up to the level that they should be. I was amazed as I continued to watch because I felt in myself that as I watched, a sense of stillness grew within me. And I was also deeply touched by the way Mr. Chan would motivate and encourage the students to keep going. And there was nothing harsh or sharp about it or corrective, but more as if he would come near a student and lend them his strength, his internal strength, to just keep going. After about 45 minutes, the exercise ended. The students did a kind of qigong massage in which they slowly rubbed their arms and legs, leading the energy downward, and then ending with a kind of a tapping on all parts of their body, which I later found out was an equalizing massage where one would regulate the chi so that it was evenly distributed throughout the body.

At the end of the evening I signed up for Mr. Chan's Qigong course and remained his student for the next five years until I moved to Europe. Being a student of Mr. Chan meant entering into a way of learning that I had never really experienced before. For example, we never knew how many classes would be devoted to learning a particular exercise. We would simply continue studying a form until Mr. Chan felt that we had reached a certain level of mastery. It could be one month, it could be four months. And then when we would finish a particular exercise, the next week we might start again from the beginning with an exercise that we might have learned two years before.

And Mr. Chan would begin teaching that exercise that we had learned as if we were beginners, we would start right again with the basics, paying a lot of attention to the posture, to how we would hold our hands, to how we would stand. And I remember that I would be amazed at the level of specificity. I might be holding my hands at a level that I thought was fine and then Mr. Chan would come and adjust them maybe half an inch and in that adjustment, I would feel as if everything was falling into place and then I knew that little things mattered. That it was not just a useless correction, but that there was a very deep precision to what we were doing. At the same time as the years went on, I understood that sometimes if that had been done earlier, I wouldn't have yet been ready to absorb the subtlety of what the difference of a half an inch might mean.

And what became clear over the years was that there was a rhythm in what we were doing. That we would return again and again to a Qigong form that we thought we knew and in that learning again there would be a deepening and a ripening of what had been slowly nurtured before but was not yet ready to blossom to its full fruit.

Mr. Chan also had a very special way of teaching an exercise. Whether it was an exercise that we already knew or one that he was showing us for the first time, he would always ask us to stand and watch him and then he would do the exercise five different times. And then he would ask us to look at different parts of his body each time. One time we would look at the head area, another time at the torso, another at the pelvis area, and then the legs and feet, and then the whole body. And it was like when we would watch the whole body, it was like all of a sudden all the different separate parts that we would be observing would come together in one Gestalt. It was an amazing way to learn, because it not only taught me the intricacies of each part of the form as it related to different parts of my body, but it also trained a way of observation that I find even today, 30 years later, that I can apply to things in my life where I really get a sense of the inner workings of things rather than just the outward Gestalt. So, being a student of Mr. Chan meant not only being a student of Qigong but really being a student of learning how to learn. After I had been a student for almost five years, I remember one night watching him teaching old Qigong movement that we had learned many years before. And we were doing our usual way of observing five times. And I had seen this move so many times, but somehow on that night, my body and my mind and my eyes were unified in a way that I really hadn't experienced before. And then something clicked into place. Something that had been puzzling me about the move for a long time just seemed to appear and be perfect. And at that point I said, Oh! And I'll never forget the way Mr. Chan looked at me, his eyes bright and shiny, a smile coming to his lips, and him saying, nodding, "Finally"!

In that moment, something very special happened. I recall there was a kind of a transmission of a very old knowledge passing between teacher and student. In no way was he teasing me or making me feel as if I was a bit slow. That "Finally" was said with such heart and in a way deep satisfaction that he must have felt as a teacher feeling the harvest of all the teaching and effort that we had both exerted over the years, to come to that moment where my body finally grasped what was happening in that movement. Beyond intellectual knowledge, simply settling in deep into my muscles and deep into my bones. I learned many things about being a teacher from Mr. Chan. One of them was about what happens when we really have faith in the capacity of a student.

There's a tendency to worry about whether or not students can do a meditation to a certain length. There's been a lot of discussion in the mindfulness world about how long the meditations should be. And there's been research that supposedly shows that one gets as much out of a 15- or 20-minute meditation as one does out of a meditation that's 45 minutes. And so, if you ask me now, 35 years later, what was the most important thing that I learned from Mr. Chan? It would not be the Qigong exercises that I learned, although they are very dear to me and play an important part in my life.

What he taught me was that if I just stick with it, I can do it. He taught me to have faith in myself because he had faith in us. He didn't dumb things down so that it would be lighter or easier for us. We may have in that way got it quicker, but the sense of it really being a deep part of ourselves would not have been the same. I was able to stretch because he believed in me; he believed in my capacity to stay with it and to continue to go on. The five years that it took me to get to the point where I could say, Ah! were in no way a waste. And there's always the search now to try to find ways of teaching something quicker or learning something quicker. But the truth is that if it's going to go to any kind of depth, if it's really going to do something in one's life and set a new path, it takes time.

And we must, when we're teachers, be able to support our students through that time of staying with it and letting it go deeper. I hope this story encourages you to not take the shortcut when it seems that a student is becoming disappointed or maybe you yourself are becoming disappointed in the progress of the class. Well, that's a whole other story. Things that go deep take time. Trust in your capacity as a teacher that you can support students because the most important thing that you can really give to them is not the fact that you have something incredible to teach, some wizard exercise. The fact is you've gone the course, you've done the training, and you continue to commit to that because there you are standing in front of a class.

Honor that sense of staying with it and the depth that you have achieved in your own practice and let that be what can be your greatest support and greatest teaching to your students on this path of mindfulness.

"Hsing-Yi goes through the center, Pa-Kua goes around the center, Tai-Chi maintains the center." —*Ray Hayward*

When I was learning Tai-Chi from Master T.T. Liang in Boston, many times he told me I should learn Hsing-Yi and Pa-Kua. I had seen him do some palm changes and a few elements and I asked him to teach me. Liang had three Hsing-Yi teachers, Masters Chang Chun-feng, Yuan Tao, and Wang Shu-chin. He learned Pa-Kua from two of those teachers, Chang Chun-feng and Wang Shu-chin.

Master Liang said he had forgotten those styles, but that he would find a teacher for me. A few weeks later Master Liang said he arranged some private lessons with a teacher, Master B.P. Chan, who was teaching at Master Liang's classmate, Master William C.C. Chen's school. I went down and took four hours of private classes and received my first introduction into these two internal martial arts.

When I first met Master Chan, he told me I was fortunate to study with such a high-level master as T.T. Liang. Chan said

Liang was so strong, even at an advanced age. He also asked me if I knew Paul Gallagher, who he said was one of his best Pa-Kua students.

Master Chan started my lesson with the theory and principles of all the internal styles. He showed how they were similar, and their differences. He then launched into the three centers. There is a training phrase in internal martial arts which states, "Hsing-Yi goes through the center, Pa-Kua goes around the center, Tai-Chi maintains the center." It was the first time I heard about this. When I returned to Boston, Master T.T. Liang gave me further explanation and details. The three centers have become a cornerstone of my practice, understanding, and teaching of the three internal styles.

Master Chan then taught me Pi'/splitting, and Tsuan/drilling, the first two fists or elements of Hsing-Yi. I drilled those two techniques and received many corrections and refinements as well as applications.

After a couple of hours, Master William Chen came in to check on me and to send greetings to Master Liang. While William was there visiting, Chan went out and came back with a carton of milk and some muffins. I told him I wasn't hungry, but he insisted I eat and drink, for him!

I then learned the circle walk with mud stepping. Chan at one point put my hand on top of his head and made me follow him as he walked the circle. Later he put his hand on my sacrum and gently pushed my lower spine as I walked the circle to give me the feeling. I learned two palm changes, Change the Circle, and the Single Palm. My four hours ended all too soon and I went back to Boston to practice.

A few weeks later I received a letter from Master Chan. He was following up with me and seeing how my practice was going. I received three different letters from Chan, and they are some of my prized possessions to this day.

When I was planning to go for more lessons, Master Liang said he had a surprise for me. Not only was I to study with Master Chan's teacher, but my lessons would be right in Boston! Master Liang told me that his Shao-Lin teacher, Master Han Chin-tang's son-in-law, who was B.P. Chan's teacher, was coming to visit Liang in Boston to pay respects. Liang had arranged for me to study Hsing-Yi and Pa-Kua from his friend, Dr. Leung Kay-chi! Dr. Leung learned Pa-Kua from Liu Yun-ch'iao and Han Chin-tang, and Hsing-Yi from Chao Lien-feng.

I called Master Chan and talked about Master Liang's arrangements and Leung Kay-chi coming to America. When I told Master Chan I was to study with his teacher, he was delighted for me! He called me his "classmate" and said I can learn a lot from Dr. Leung. There was no anger, disappointment, or jealousy, only a teacher wanting the best for his student. Leung later told me that Chan not only took all his classes, but he also never missed a single one! And Leung told me that Chan had studied Sun style Hsing-Yi and Pa-Kua with Cheng Huai-hsien/ Zhen Huai Xian.

Although I was studying with Dr. Leung, I attended a seminar in Greenfield MA sponsored by Paul Gallagher and Deer Mountain Taoist Academy. Master Chan greeted me warmly and with no reservation. During a break, I was sitting with Chan and Paul, and Chan said I could ask him any question. I had recently been introduced to the Tao of Love and I asked Master Chan about semen retention. Chan told me the body needed to have all its functions working at the highest level. He said I need to retain to be strong, but sometimes to emit to keep my body able to reproduce.

When I moved from Boston to Minnesota to continue my studies with Master Liang, I stopped in New York to see Master Chan and Master Chen. Chan showed me a finger and thumb massage, which I use to this very day. Greetings were sent to Master Liang and goodbyes exchanged. That was the last time I ever saw Master B.P. Chan. Although I went back to New York to take private classes with William Chen during the 1980's, I never saw Chan again. I continued to benefit from Chan's teachings through Master Paul Gallagher and Master Ken Cohen. I will never forget my first Hsing-Yi and Pa-Kua teacher, Master B.P. Chan.

How to Be a Real Taiji Student
—Paul B. Gallagher

"Taiji teachers are easy to find;
real students are harder to find…"
~~B.P. Chan

Many years ago when I began learning Bagua from Master B.P. Chan in New York City, I had a rather startling experience.

After nine years of Taijiquan study and practice, I prevailed upon a dear friend and colleague of mine, Kenneth Cohen to show me some of the Bagua movements he had learned from Chan. He graciously agreed, and for several days we practiced informally in a local park. Although Ken taught in a very precise manner, our study sessions were very casual, since I merely wanted to learn the rudiments of some Bagua moves so I would have a bit of variation in my practice routine.

After our initial study session, whenever Ken visited my town once or twice a year, we would spend an hour or two in Bagua practice, so I could learn a little more each time. Our practice was never intended by either of us to be an in-depth study, but simply some informal sharing, which I very greatly appreciated.

However, one day I became sufficiently intrigued with Bagua that I wanted to get closer to the source of the teaching. I asked Ken to introduce me to B.P. Chan. Again, he very graciously accommodated my request. So I traveled from western Massachusetts down to New York City to meet Chan for the first time. Of course, I had previously called the Master, seeking his permission to visit a class.

Chan kindly allowed me to observe several classes, and even

spent time with me after his class day was finished to answer some of my specific questions. It was quite evident to me, observing his movements as he demonstrated them in class, that he was a very highly accomplished master (even though, as I later found out he never liked to be called "master," and wanted only to be called a "guide" on the path of study).

I was sufficiently captivated and impressed by what I had witnessed during my visit, that I decided I would like to take a few private classes from him just to "polish up" my very rudimentary Bagua movements. We made an appointment for the following Sunday, when he said he could see me before his regular classes started at 10 AM. So I arose around 4:15, I left my house just before 5, and arrived at Chan's studio right at 9 AM.

He asked to see what I had learned so far, so I showed him what I had learned from Ken who was one of his best students. I told him I had learned the movements very casually, and wanted to refine my movements just a bit, but was not intending a long-term exhaustive study. I hoped he would not be insulted by my request.

He observed my movements silently for a few minutes, then told me he had seen enough. In the most polite terms, he informed me that what I was doing was total crap (not his language), and that I would have to start over from the very beginning. This was NOT a reflection on what Ken had taught me, but rather on the very casual way I had approached both learning and practicing the basics of Bagua that I had learned.

When I had first started learning Taiji, some nine years earlier, I was unable to find a teacher in Boston where I then lived, and so drove for four hours each way to New York and back for a period of 4 1/2 years every weekend to spend Friday afternoons and Saturday mornings in private classes. I had absolutely NO desire to commute to the City again for any long-term study commitment—and yet this seemed to be exactly what Chan was proposing. I didn't quite know how to respond, so I stood silent for a few moments.

Chan scrutinized me attentively, then said, "'Mr. Paul', many of my students want to 'go to the movies'...they want to learn many forms and many arts, but none of them very well. Do YOU want to go to the movies, "Mr. Paul?'"

I was stunned—the master had just thrown down the gauntlet and then waited wordlessly to gauge my reaction. I didn't know what to think—I couldn't even imagine another multi-year period of long weekly commutes to study, yet something about Chan's abilities, and his very presence and demeanor, told me that studying with him would be a completely life-changing experience.

I asked if he could recommend a teacher in Massachusetts, hoping the question would not offend him. He quietly answered, "Teachers are easy to find; real students are hard to find," and then fell silent once more. Somehow, from my very depths, before I could monitor or censor what I was about to say, I simply blurted out, "Mr. Chan—you are the master, and I would be honored and privileged to be your student." He smiled slightly and said "Good boy! You can have a private class before my regular Sunday morning classes. We'll start at 9 AM next Sunday."

Thus, I began another 4 1/2 year period of weekly commutes from Massachusetts to New York City, arising each Sunday morning at 4:15, taking my private classes and some of Chan's public classes, and returning home late at night, after Chan's class day had ended.

The only times Chan ever reprimanded me was when I missed two of his classes (over a period of 4 1/2 years!). One time I was deathly ill with the flu and he upbraided me for not training hard enough. If I was REALLY training, said he, I would never become ill. The second time was when I stayed home during a 15-inch snowfall, rather than drive 240 miles from Massachusetts to New York. At that time, Chan said that if I was a GENUINE martial artist I would not let anything deter me from arriving at class in a timely manner.

Courage!

Somehow Chan's quote about "real students" burned in my brain throughout the years. And as I taught Taiji over more than three decades, I totally understood the wisdom and truth of Chan's observation.

Paul Gallagher with B.P. Chan, 1981
Photo Courtesy of Ray Hayward

"The Great Wall of New Jersey"
–Andy Lee Zalcman

TELEPHONE INTERVIEW EXCERPTS

Mr. Chan called Andy Lee "the Secretary."

Ron: Why did Mr. Chan call you Secretary?
ALZ: Because I was always taking notes.

Andy Lee studied ballet. Mr. Chan laughed at ballet dancing. Said "It's not work." Andy Lee and her students got him tickets to the ballet.

Ron: What did he have to say about that? Did his attitude change?
ALZ: Mr. Chan "loved" it. And his attitude changed—I paraphrase- "Movement is all the same."

A senior student argued with Mr. Chan about Tai Chi Ruler.

Ron: How did he handle that?
ALZ: How did he handle it? He just gave the class to him, as I and another student with Mr. Chan just watched. Mr. Chan said—"We are students who make teachers." He didn't seem upset. I think amused.

ON TEACHING:

- Mr. Chan created teachers even though he was a "student".
- Mr. Chan was a guide to students.
- Mr. Chan let students take over the class because he felt that some students would eventually become teachers.
- Mr. Chan said, "To be a teacher, you have to be selfless".

Mr. Chan: "Teaching is like lifting weights. When I started to teach, it was like lifting 10 pounds. Now it's like lifting 100 pounds."

Ron: Did he mean that teaching became harder and harder as the years went by, or did he mean that it was easier now than before because of his greater experiences with students?

ALZ: I believe he was stating the more you teach the MORE YOU (as the teacher) learn. WE are guides who merely point the way. He also believed you should never stop learning. By teaching, YOU are also the student.

Mr. Chan told Andy Lee that she should learn Bagua Zhang. Andy Lee told him she preferred to learn Xing-Yi. She told him that Bagua Zhang was like Israeli dancing!

ALZ: Yeah. I am embarrassed by that now. In the end - after years of Xingyiquan - he taught me Baquazhang. I said "Yes" to every art he shared. I did Qigong with Mr. Chan. I did EVERYTHING this lovely man had to offer. Push Hands, Tai Chi Ruler, —even with a Ball—Hug-a-Tree, Zhan Zhuang, In the end I said "Yes" to everything he taught. THANK GOODNESS!!!!

At the time, Andy Lee was Mr. Chan's only female student doing Xing-Yi.

ALZ: Yes, at William C.C. Chen's studio. In the other places that Mr. Chan taught, I don't know.

Mr. Chan was so open to hearing what you or ANY student— BE THEY NOVICES OR "MASTERS" — thought was a great answer or a question.

ALZ: He would say "I don't think so" if you were wrong... AND he would say "I think so" if you were right.

Andy Lee used to drive him home.

Ron: Any stories about him in the car with you?
ALZ: Too many—but I like the one about the "Great Wall of NJ"

Andy Lee and Mr. Chan were in Andy Lee's car traveling on the NJ Turnpike. Mr. Chan noticed a wall along the highway and called it the "Great Wall of New Jersey."

Mr. Chan told Andy Lee: "I'm older, so you're lucky you got me old."

ALZ: Yeah.

A student asked Mr. Chan: What do you do all day? Mr. Chan said, "I think about the questions you're going to ask me."

ALZ: I think he wanted to see "HOW" we shared. And by doing that under his watchful eye—I got to ask questions when I didn't know the answer OR thought I knew the answer; WE could investigate!

Mr. Chan never had a bad word for anyone.

On occasion, Mr. Chan would hurt himself demonstrating to students what was incorrect about their posture or movement. There were times he could bounce up and out of Andy Lee's car, other times he couldn't because he had hurt himself in class demonstrating what the student(s) were doing incorrectly.

When Andy Lee had her own studio, Mr. Chan would travel there to teach. Once when Andy Lee and Mr. Chan were together in her car on the highway, Andy gave money to the toll booth attendant to pay the toll. Mr. Chan gently reprimanded her for not saying "Thank You" to the attendant!

When learning Internal Martial Arts, you always need another set of eyes looking at you. When other Masters came to the school, the other set of eyes they wanted were Mr. Chan's. They communicated in Chinese. He was a teacher's teacher. Mr. Chan said (and other Masters said the same thing), you always need someone to look at you.

ALZ: "All Tai Chi is the same inside; it's the outside that's different." The saying is: Externally, all Tai Chi (Martial Arts) are different. Internally, all Tai Chi are the same. Then Mr. Chan would explain, we are all going to Central Park......

Mr. Chan: "We're all going to Central Park, how we get there is different."

Ron: Was he talking about death? Was he talking about attaining martial arts skills? Was he talking about being better human beings?

ALZ: He was pointing out (and let me also point out that all the Masters I have known said the same thing) "Externally different, Internally the same." This means some people go to Central Park by bus, some by train, others would walk! BUT THEY ARE ALL GOING TO CENTRAL PARK—IN TERMS OF TAI CHI/ MARTIAL ARTS—FOR UNDERSTANDING. FOR SKILL. FOR TECHNIQUE!

Mr. Chan never had a bad word for anyone.

ALZ: Sometimes Mr. Chan would take no money.

Ron: Why?
ALZ: Sorry, I don't remember.

At Andy Lee's own school, TAICHIUSA, she shared Mr. Chan's Bagua & Xing-Yi with her students.

ALZ: Not just Baguazhang and Xingyiquan, also Tai Chi Ruler, Push Hands, Applications, 5 frolicking animals, 8 Brocades.

Mr. Chan believed that the proper conveyance of words was very important. He tailored his words and his style/approach to individual students based on what he knew about them. So, if a student was a baker, he would try to explain using analogies that the student could understand.

Mr. Chan did workshops at Andy Lee's school. Based on those visits, Andy Lee's students are teaching others Qigong.

ALZ: Mr. Chan was one of the best push-hands teachers. He broke it down and used verbiage to teach; didn't use numbers.

Mr. Chan would look and search for words in English that had the equivalent physical effect on the body as the Chinese words. Like "BE CALM".

Mr. Chan made an effort to make sure that he had the language skills to be able to communicate with his students.

In 1997, Andy Lee's grandchild was born, and she took two weeks off from class. She thought she had told Mr. Chan about that, but she hadn't. Mr. Chan was very upset that she didn't tell him; he was worried about her and wanted to make sure that she was OK.

Andy Lee Zalcman and BP Chan, 1991.
Photo courtesy of Andy Lee Zalcman

"Well, Diaz, you know,
nobody's perfect."
—Andy Diaz

Real fighting martial artists in his class would show up on Sundays, right? We were all competitors, and we all had our schools, and it was a good group. It was a high-level group and Chan enjoyed it. But Mr. Chan was a stickler for details. You've got to have the details there. Okay, so this was a funny thing, right? He decides we're going to work on Eight Brocades. You know, his version of Eight Brocades and the whole thing, and the exercises.

So here this whole group came in ready to learn martial arts moves and this and that, and two people exercise, and get our timing and the whole thing. We spent a couple of weeks just doing the Eight Brocades, getting it right for the exercises. One of my peers there, who was quite good, finally gets exasperated with

Mr. Chan doing this stuff. He wanted to do the Xing-Yi, the Bagua, the applications. Finally, he turned around to Mr. Chan and goes, "Mr. Chan, these are old people exercises." And Mr. Chan said, "That's right." So, the student walks away, and then Chan walks over to me and he says, "Diaz, I think he got the wrong meaning of my words. We don't do these exercises when we're old, we're doing these exercises to become old." And I always remember that was a goodie, you know, that's the one I pass on when I teach my classes. This is the route to getting old, with mind, body, spirit, keeping the fire of martial arts, the wushu in line with it.

I'm a Karate man. My Tai Chi started with William Chen and CK Chu, and then I went to Chan because I got enamored with him when he was in the studio and teaching the Bagua. So, I wanted to learn the Bagua.

And then I finally fell in love. Of all the martial arts that I love the most is the Xing-Yi. The one that really locked me in with BP Chan was the Xing-Yi. And I got totally immersed. I really liked it because he really liked it. In the end I was considered Mr. Chan's Xing-Yi Master. You know, and you always saw, he loved it. You can see his eyes light up when he gets into that kind of a concept. But I saw him teaching Chen 3, Chen 2, this and that, he had all these different styles going on. One day I say to Mr. Chan, "Which is the best?", and I love the answer: "The one you do every day."

I got so much out of him. You walk around and basically, he ironed out a lot of my crinkles, you know, my wrinkles and crinkles, and that's really what it was. He just kept my mind going. He would give me an exercise. I had to learn the snake as one of the animals. Class would go on and he would put me on the side, keep working the snake.

Boy, I haven't had a break for months. This is on 23rd Street. An hour, an hour and a half just doing the snake. Finally, one day I'm looking out 23rd Street, right, I'm doing the snake and I stop,

I look out the window, I turn around, and in about two leaps, he moved like Michael Jordan across the floor, boom, jumped right in front of me. He says, "I saw you lose your focus and your concentration." Up to this point, he had ignored me for about a month. "Just go over there, keep working there." All of a sudden, he's right there in front of me.

He says, "I saw you lost your focus, your concentration." He looks, he starts wagging his finger. "Not good for combat, man. Not good."

Then, after years and years, I had a wife and a child. And finally, my wife was saying, "Hello!!" You get the idea. So I said to Mr. Chan, "I think I'm going to have to ease off on the Sunday classes."

I told him why. He says, "Oh yeah, yeah, wife marries a man because he combat man, then he stops doing combat and martial arts, maybe she don't fall so much in love with him." Enough guilt now, right?

I've got a million stories. I was with him for many years. I kept going in and out with him. And then you could see him aging and, you know, you start saying, thou art that. And here I'm 75 and I picture myself as other seniors. I saw him at that stage of life.

Mr. Chan was like Rubinstein, the pianist. Rubinstein, he was all over the world, you know, he was the classic. So the whole idea, when you infuse yourself so deeply into the art – and I've learned a lot along the way about that – is that there's a choice you make in life. Is it going to be the life of art or the art of life? When it comes to a life of art, that's it, baby. Nothing else matters. Mr. Chan, like Rubenstein, chose a life of art.

I mean, how much fun would it have been to be married to or be a friend to Picasso? You know what I'm saying? I don't exist unless he wants to do a picture of me. But I think that's the life of art.

The art of life is what I chose. I'm going to enjoy this experience. I've taken myself to a high level, but hey, I want a hug, a kiss, taste the food, you know? It's not all about that. It's about that. The self and the whole thing, you know? Because Mr. Chan said one time, he said, "Diaz, I've never made a perfect move."

The whole idea is you aspire to the perfect move. But I, being the ultimate number one student in the universe, said to Mr. Chan, "Yes, but your imperfections are a lot better than mine." I got a good laugh out of him from that one. I always profess to be as perfect as I can be in what I do. So, one time I'm at William Chen's up at the studio, and Chan is there. I stayed there late on a Sunday. Getting out, getting ready to go. Four o'clock, the whole thing. I left and I'm two blocks away, and I forgot my bag. First time ever, right? So, I go back, I knock on the door, I go upstairs, they open for me, and I say, "Excuse me, I forgot my bag." They're both sitting there having tea. William Chen and B.P. Chan sitting there having some tea. And they look at me, they smile, and they say "Well, Diaz, you know, nobody's perfect." They're sitting there smiling, toasting each other.

RAL: Andy, it really sounds like you must have had a wonderful relationship with Mr. Chan.

I liked him. I liked him. You know, I liked him a lot. It was nice. It was endearing. And what can you do? You know, you come, and you go, and the reality is a teacher is just a station on the train ride. There are times in life, you know, you just feel a connection - it's easy with this person. So, you know, it's like that. We can't pick our parents but the nice thing about life is you can pick your teacher.

I went to his funeral, and I met his son and one of his daughters. Very nice professional people.

"I'm Gonna Give You $5"
—Alvin Fayman

RAL: What are your thoughts about Mr. Chan as a person, or a martial arts teacher, anything stand out for you?

He was very kind to his students, especially beginning students. He knew there was a great deal that people in the West had to learn about his arts, especially the internal arts. He was very careful with his explanations about things because he wanted you to have what he called "water clear" understanding of what he was showing you. He kept things simple. He broke things down. The longer you spent time with him, the more you came to appreciate what he was showing you, and even more so, the breadth and depth of his knowledge, which was just staggering. Of course, the longer you worked with him and he got to know you, then he got tougher on you. He was always kind, but it was tough love and he made sure you did it right or he let you know that you had work to do.

RAL: You used the phrase, "water clear" understanding. Was that the phrase that he used?
His exact words.

RAL: Very interesting. I guess it doesn't get much clearer than water, right?
I guess it was as close as he would come to crystal clear, but I think water clear, depending on where you get your water, makes even more of an impression.

RAL: What years did you study with him?
I met him when I was studying at the Tai Chi Chuan Center

in New York with CK Chu. That was in the late 70s. He was teaching Bagua & Xing Yi on Saturdays and during the week he taught Qigong. I wasn't his student, but he was always very kind and polite. I would watch him demonstrate some things when he was talking to other people. His moves were just so beautiful. You could see that he was so experienced.

A lot of my friends started studying Qigong with him. A few did Bagua & Xing Yi, but it was the Qigong that intrigued me most, so that's where I started with him. I wanted to do whatever I could to improve my Tai Chi, and that looked like the best place to start, rather than another art - which I got into at a later time. And it really did open up a whole new world about standing and breathing and walking and appreciating what a strong role the basics played in everything else we would do.

RAL: You studied with him until he passed away?
Yes. There was a short period when my family first moved to New Jersey when I couldn't continue with him for transportation reasons. The bus stopped running at a certain time and so it wasn't feasible for me, but we stayed in touch by phone.

I'd speak with him periodically and I'd let him know that I was still very involved in my practice, and did get back into studying with him for a few years before he passed.

RAL: You primarily studied Qigong with him, so I would imagine that he took you through the Eight Brocades, the Ten Dao, the Eight Chi Kung, the Laying Down Set, the Sitting Meditation, and those kinds of exercises, right?
Right.

RAL: How many students were in that class, approximately? Was it a big class, small class?

My Qigong class was fairly large. We'd stand around in a circle - it had to be about a dozen people or so - and of course it varied from time to time, but usually there were quite a few of us, and the number didn't impede what he had to show us. He did give individual attention to everybody as often as he could, so that was kind of nice. Sometimes he would meet me at the door, because one of the things he did, especially with the Ten Daoist exercises, was to share the martial applications. He said we were doing this for health, but it did have a practical use. So, he'd show this move and that move, and then he'd greet me at the door with a big smile, and he would say, "Punch me" or "Do something".

RAL: Was he watching you do the exercises or was he doing them himself or was it a mixture of both?

It was a mixture. He would always do things with us, even when at some point he'd have a student lead the class after we became more experienced. He wasn't one to sit on the side and direct. He was out there on the floor demonstrating correct movements and making sure that everybody did. He would make certain corrections and he would put his hands on you gently to correct your standing posture. He would also say, "Put your hand on my spine so you can feel this movement." He was very much into demonstrating the right way to do things and to give you as vivid an idea of how it should be done and what you should feel.

RAL: Alvin, approximately how many years did you study with him?

Over 20.

RAL: If you could put your finger on one thing over those 20 plus years that made you keep coming back, what would that be?

It was his manner of instruction, his making you feel that you were the focus of his attention, and that he very much wanted you to succeed in learning whatever he had to share, which was extensive.

RAL: I would imagine that when you started studying with him, and correct me if I'm wrong, that you stopped studying with CK Chu. Is that right? Or were you studying with them both?

No, I studied with them both. I stopped studying with CK Chu only because of work responsibilities that kept me from coming to classes during the week.

Mr. Chan eventually limited his teaching to William Chen's school on Sundays. So, for that reason, I wound up going there, partly to continue a big knife class that I had been in for some time - at his invitation - through another classmate, and to see what else there was available for me. I had started Bagua at the time, so I continued in that as well.

RAL: What aspects of Bagua did he teach? I assume he taught you the Outer Palms, perhaps the Inner Palms, the Two-Person Sets, the Bagua Push-Hands?

Yes. All those. It's all basic stuff, and he always said, "I only teach kindergarten." He never claimed to lay out an entire curriculum, but mastering those basics took constant review and the word Master was not in his vocabulary; he hated that word. He didn't want to be called a Master; he said, "You're Master when you're dead."

RAL: You used the phrase big knife. Could you tell me what that was?

It's a broadsword. He referred to it as a "big knife" because it was, and we had a lot of fun with that. He taught a solo set, and three two-man sets that I learned over time with him.

RAL: With the broadsword or with other weapons?

One was broadsword against broadsword, and two of them

were broadsword against staff. I didn't take the formal staff class with him because I was doing other things, but whatever use of the staff I learned to take from the two men sets in the big knife.

RAL: Did you ever go to any workshops or go up to the Tai Chi farm in Warwick?

Yes. He invited us up there. In fact, a couple of us would go up there before the formal workshops started because he was getting some areas ready. He built the Bagua Nine Palace there. He was clearing land for that. We did get to do some informal practice there. When the formal workshops began, I went three or four times, and he was very open about, you should try what he (other instructors) has to offer, you should go and see how they do things. I know he had a pretty good relationship with Yang Jwing-Ming, certainly with Master Jou and Dr. Painter. He got along with everybody and he wanted us to experience what all these people and some of their senior students had to offer. It was a very worthwhile experience. I remember there was a Tai Chi teacher who passed away, Zhang Luping. He was kind enough to do push-hands with me. I was having quite a time trying to avoid what he could do because he was just so very accomplished. Dr. Painter was there at the time, and he wanted to illustrate the feeling of being pushed with internal energy. He put his hand on my chest and he pushed me, not hard; I didn't go flying or anything, but I was very, very aware of a sensation building up inside me that would send me back.

I very much appreciated doing what Mr. Chan said. He said that you should feel something. He really wanted you to get the feeling of whatever it is that you were involved in, whether it was a solo movement or with two people. He said it was very important that you experience it in your own body system. There are no two people alike, it's just "your body, my body, not the same."

RAL: Were you one of the students who was involved in initially clearing that whole area of all the bushes and other stuff that was there?

No, it was done by other people on a varied basis; people would go up there every weekend and work the land and do whatever building was necessary. I really didn't have those skills, anyway. At some point, when it was well along, I went up there and was amazed at all that he had put together, and I'm sure he made great use of it. What he eventually taught was week-long workshops. Just to see that these facilities were available was very heartening. You knew there was a place where people could go and learn things that they weren't able to do on a regular basis. It was very worthwhile. I'm sure it still is, but it's under different auspices now and has been for a good long time.

RAL: Did you ever teach Tai Chi or Qigong?
I taught Tai Chi Ruler for a short time.

RAL: Are you still doing any of that these days?
Oh yes, oh yes. I still practice daily.

RAL: Please give me one or two anecdotes about Mr. Chan that maybe none of his other students would know about. Anything that he did, something that he said, or something unusual?
I don't know that other students wouldn't know about things. Hard to say off the top of my head.

RAL: Fair enough. Anything else about Mr. Chan, either as a person or as a martial arts teacher, that you feel would be good for me to know?
He was certainly human. He had a temper. It wasn't pleasant to be on the receiving end of his …….. Well, first of all, if you ever heard him say "Jesus Christ," you were in trouble.
He was really exasperated with what you weren't doing, or

you were doing incorrectly continually, so it was that. If he really got annoyed with you, he would say, "I'm gonna give you five dollars," which meant he'd slap you on your right arm and it would hurt you on your left side. If he was really in a mood he would say, "Be careful or I'll give you $50." He never did that to anybody I know of because they'd be gone from this world. I know he got upset with people when they did things that they shouldn't be doing.

I knew somebody who was fasting for her own reasons, and she broke the fast improperly. She ate something she shouldn't have, and it basically immobilized her. She called him up and said, "I did this and now what?" and he got very upset. He said, "You want to kill yourself?" If you did something that was really improper, it was how he showed his concern for you.

Another friend of mine went to see him who had back issues all his life and had undergone surgery. I thought, maybe if he took some Tai Chi classes it would be helpful. Mr. Chan did meet with him and suggest, not so much that he should study movement, but that he focus on quiet sitting and things like that. He sent him back to me and said, "You can teach him this and you can teach him that," so I gave him some basic instructions. I don't know whether or not he kept it up, but I told him this is what Mr. Chan thought would be helpful, and to use it if it does help. Mr. Chan was very generous that way with his time.

He took an interest in you and if anybody you knew had a problem, you could talk to him about it. He was always very open with his knowledge and his recommendations. I know he helped me with a couple of minor issues that I had myself that turned out fine. Of course, if someone said to him, "I hurt myself doing this" he'd say, "Don't do that. That's not the best way. Don't do that."

Alvin Fayman (center) with BP Chan and Richard Raab
in Mr. Chan's Apartment, NYC
Photo Courtesy of Bruce Marcus

"Are you Buddhist?"
"What's your religion?"
He said, "My religion is kindness."

This interview was done with a direct student of BP Chan. The name of the person interviewed has been withheld at their request. The students' names mentioned have also been changed.

RAL: When did you start studying with Mr. Chan?

79

Maybe when I was 30-35 years old. I'm 56, so I don't know when that would be? 1998? 1997, 1998. Till he died. When did he die?

RAL: 2002.

Yeah, that sounds about right. I studied Tai Chi and the Tai Chi Ruler. I would go there early with John. We'd show up early and we would do standing meditation for 30 to 50 minutes.

John was like my instructor with Mr. Chan there. And then the formal Tai Chi class would start. I'd stay extra for the Tai Chi Ruler. I would stay also for a Qigong class. It depended on what I could afford. It was $25 per class. Yeah, but he really liked me.

RAL: Was that when he was at William Chen's school?

Yes. Yes, at William Chen's.

RAL: And you said your senior student/teacher at that time was someone named John?

Yeah, I forgot John's last name, but it was John who was a more senior student and so Chan would be teaching us and then he'd………… Oh, I'm sorry, we would do the standing meditation, then we would do the Tai Chi form, and then we would do Push Hands Class which he called "Feeling Hands" because he didn't like to use the term Push Hands, preferring "Feeling Hands." After that, we would do the Ruler. Those are the three classes. But John, basically, was my instructor, because it would be Mr. Chan and John and a couple of other people there.

But I would work directly with Mr. Chan, too. You want to hear one great anecdote I remember? Mr. Chan was doing Push Hands with me or Feeling Hands with me. And next to us was John doing it with somebody else. Mr. Chan would say it was like steel wrapped in cotton. And when you would do it with him, it felt like at any moment, a tidal wave could just wash you away.

It was so powerful and so subtle. I remember one time he was doing it with me and he's playing with me because I had nothing compared to what he had. He'd be looking at John and he'd be correcting them while he was doing it with me. And then he'd say to me, "Your left toe is up." And I would be like, how could he know? I had my shoes on. Then he'd make a face. "Because I could feel it." And I said, "How do you do that?"

He goes, "Take a little while." That was his little thing, which meant 20, 30 years, you know, so he could feel when you were off without even looking at you. I remember another time, a guy came in. He was pretty advanced in Feeling Hands. And so he started doing that with John and he was kind of mopping up the floor with John. Then he went with Mr. Chan. This guy was like 6'2", maybe 220. Mr. Chan was like 5'4", 140, 150. And so they started doing push hands and all of a sudden Mr. Chan did this one move where he tied up both his hands and his palm was facing up and his fingers were pointing to the guy's throat and the guy just kind of bowed to him. Looked at us and said, "Your teacher is incredible."

RAL: Your senior student/teacher was John….

Yes! John, he was really good. He's one of the top people, I think. Of course, Fred was his number one student.

Apparently, Fred spent a long time with Mr. Chan and was his top, top, top guy.

I was a student of Fred's. I started with him, and then Mr. Chan came to give us a guest workshop, and I think what sparked Mr. Chan's interest in me is I asked something about the back and that was like the Holy Grail for Mr. Chan. Everything came from the back. The kua and the yao, but also from the back. He loved that question. After that, since I moved to New York City, I studied with him for a year. I started studying with Mr. Chan every Sunday. When Mr. Chan died, I went back to Fred and I was commuting. But then I just couldn't do it anymore. I was commuting for a couple of years.

Fred is phenomenal. I mean, you know, right?

I remember Mr. Chan used to move your hand like a quarter of an inch, change the angle and he'd say, "This is the difference between life and death."

RAL: He was very good at the technical aspects, wasn't he?

Oh my God, and the feeling that he had was just phenomenal. I mean, it was like, wow, the skill level was incredible.

RAL: Do you still do any Tai Chi?

I practiced for a while, but then I stopped. Occasionally, I'll get back into it because Mr. Chan said, the standing meditation was everything. So once in a while, I'll practice it, you know, just standing 15-20-30 minutes. He felt that that was the core of everything. That's what he told me. I mean, that was it. That was the bottom line, standing.

He was a huge fan of Pa Kua and of the Ruler also, and he knew other styles. I remember this one student came in, paid a year up, a month up front, and he started telling Mr. Chan that he did Kung Fu and all this stuff. Then he asked Mr. Chan who his teacher was. He started questioning his credentials and Mr. Chan said, "Maybe school no good for you" and he gave back his money and the kid left.

I always tell my wife that Mr. Chan's favorite quote was, "100 father worth one mother." He'd always say that.

RAL: Well, what do you think he meant by that?

I guess because he had eight kids and how valuable the mother is. When I used to go in early, it was John and I before the actual class started. He'd talk to us in this little room like the locker room area and he would just give us little anecdotes. I think what he meant by that was that like a lot of times when we're doing the Qigong they say rock the baby, and he would just say see all these things.... you know your mother.... how your mother holds you, your mother taught you. We always go back to the mother.

Always, there was always some kind of reference point to the mother. He always used to say that, if they ever want to make the ultimate assassin, it would be a woman. I brought my mother one time, she wanted to meet him. She sat, and she watched him, and you know, he was so sweet to her. He told me to go over there. Let me talk to your mother, and he was so nice to her. I asked him one time, "Are you Buddhist? What's your religion?" He said, "My religion is kindness."

I used to joke with him. I knew it would make him mad. But he knew I was joking. I'd call him "Master" Chan. He goes, "Don't call me Master, only Master when I'm dead." Oh my God. I personally think he was enlightened. John and I talked about how he could teach anything. Just being around him was enough. You know, just his energy, his aura, his humility, he was funny and very charismatic. It was something else. I mean, he was special. Yeah. I mean, really special, you know, and again, extremely humble.

One time we were talking about Mike Tyson-he was a fan of Mike Tyson-and also of Steven Seagal, because their skill was real. But he'd say Mike Tyson was great because he knew how to use his body. He would show us, you don't reach out, right? You turn your body so your hand goes forward. Everything comes from the body, and he said Tyson understood that. One time I said to him, Mr. Chan, "What would you do if you got in trouble with Mike Tyson, or you got into an argument." He goes, "You run." Yeah, he'd always say to us, "You don't learn for yourself, you learn for others."

RAL: Do you teach any martial arts now?

No, I was doing a little bit on-line, because I'm a personal trainer, and an actor. I was doing some on-line Tai Chi classes, but it's not the same as classroom. Mr. Chan didn't want to have too many students because he wanted to keep an eye and he'd come, and he'd adjust you on the smallest minutiae. You know, like even when I was doing standing meditation and my eyes were closed, he'd be like, don't look down, look forward.

I'm like, how do you know I'm looking down? He goes, "Because I see your body." He'd come, his feet would be shuffling because he'd always be just with his socks on. He'd shuffle behind me and he'd adjust my pubic bone you know like my back that was slightly tucked under. He'd adjust the angle of my hands. You know when doing Feeling Hands with him or the form he'd be adjusting the slightest, slightest little thing. He was just on you. But it was in a good way, even when he yelled at you, it was fun. You were happy that you got a lot of attention from him, you know, that kind of thing.

RAL: Yeah, yeah, and that he thought enough of you to want to correct you.

Yeah. Yeah, because I remember one time he said, "Oh, I could have 100 students in here, but then how am I going to see everybody?"

He'd come and adjust the angle of your foot. He'd tell you if your toe was up, he would tell you if your elbow was too high, if your shoulders were not relaxed. I mean, just a million things. And then he would show one of his hands, I think, was a little darker. And he'd say that he put his hand in hot sand. but he said, "I'd never use this hand."

I know he spent a lot of time doing charity work at hospitals. Yeah, I think he mentioned that he used to go to some... I don't know where, but some hospital.

Mr. Chan would also teach Fridays down by Lafayette Street, he'd have a little class. He was never about money. I remember he told me that William Chen, who he owed a lot to for bringing him here, would make him charge a lot for one-on-one, and he stopped doing it because he felt bad for having to charge the students so much, so he stopped doing the one-on-one.

He would go to a hospital, that's all I know. He'd say he'd go to the hospital, and he'd help people and I remember one time my back was hurting a lot and so I went to the Friday thing and he had us do the whole Qigong sitting down. He showed me like the rocking with the hands. He was big, big on that. I showed it to my mother who has arthritis. Because I told him about that, he said, "Yeah, this helps people with arthritis a lot." He'd say stuff like "After you work out, don't wash your hands, let them cool down a little bit." "Hold your breath in when you're going from the inside to the outside, or the outside to the inside."

He was a big fan of eating garlic. He used to put garlic on everything. He didn't eat much pork. I remember one time I came to his house on 15th Street because I had busted my hand. He just gave me a little advice, and he gave me water and it was from the sink, and it was hot and cold mixed. He goes, "You never want to drink too cold or too hot."

He's on YouTube, doing the short and the long form. The guy who posted it was with him for a long time. If you put in BP Chan Tai Chi form you should be able to find it and you see him doing the short form and the long form and he's dope. He'd always say, "You see these people who are very flowery, and they have long beards and they have robes on and they make it look so beautiful but has no substance." He didn't care about the look of it, just that it was coming from your body. He always said, "It's all about principles. If the principles are correct......." What was the famous thing he said? "Shoulder follows elbow, elbow follows hand. Elbow drop, shoulder sink."

His most important tenet for me when he was doing the standing meditation, the Qigong, the Feeling Hands and the Tai Chi is the eyes always guide and guard. So the eyes are always a little bit ahead. Mr. Chan would always say with the Feeling Hand that when they push you, you turn your body and then you screw down. So you always screw in, screw out. The power had to come from the bottom of the foot, right? It would screw in. He'd say that the foot is the handle of the whip and the hand is the end of the whip. It would all come from the bottom of the foot and that's why he was a big fan of Tyson. With Tyson, it would all start from the bottom and just express itself in the hand. One time I think I asked him about weapons, and he said that "Weapon is just extension of the hand." That's all.

RAL: You have a pretty good recollection of your time with him.

Yes. I was very sad when he passed away, both for him and his family, but also, he was a light bulb, just a light bulb on any topic. I remember one time, I used to bring in the Times and he'd look at the title of the, let's say the front page, and he'd look at how they wrote it and he'd say, "See here, see how they write this?" And he'd basically say how they manipulate.... I didn't even understand him, he's not proficient in English, but he realized the way they wrote it was a kind of a manipulation of what they wanted you to look forward to reading. And I was like, damn.

I remember he used to always tell me "I'm still working on it," he says, "Cook it up a little bit, cook it up." He'd say, "Everything is one thing." That was another big thing he used to repeat over and over.

RAL: What do you think he meant by that?

I'm not sure, but I know I find myself saying it over and over, and I'm like, oh, that's what he meant. He told me a story about a guy who he showed how to crunch up a paper bag, then flatten it out, crunch it up, flatten it out, crunch it up, flatten it out. And then one time the guy was in some kind of situation, and he just flattened out his hands, right? His right hand moved from center to the right, the left went from center to the left. And it was like a move, you know? When he was teaching, he would talk to people in a language they understood. If it's a cop, you talk to him, you make everything relevant to that. If you're talking to a bricklay-er......... He helped this guy who had a problem with his back because he was loading and unloading boxes, I think for FedEx.

And Mr. Chan said, when you want to move an object, you don't look at the object, you look at the place where you're go-ing to place it. Then you look back to the object and then you place it. He was helping a guy who said he would walk really high planks, a construction worker. Mr. Chan said the standing meditation would help him. He told him that either the Qigong or Ruler, I can't remember which, would help the guy with his balance when he was up high. He talked about the Indians, how they never had fear of heights. They could go up and up and up and up and up and no problem for them.

I remember the time he talked about that character in Mortal Kombat, he goes, "That guy very mean, very tough."

His knuckles and his fingers were so calloused. He would show me how to develop your hands. For example, you would strike your right forearm with your left forearm, but on an angle, certain angle, you do it slowly, to develop it. Then you would tap a wall with your finger to make it stronger, or you could open and close jars with your fingers. But what I'm trying to get at is that everything is one thing. So, when you're doing something, somehow, I'm not explaining it well, but everything is connected. I mean, from his point of view, anyway.

He said everything's a meditation. That's what he'd say all the time.

A lot of times he'd say to me "You learn nothing" when I'd say something or do something. I used to work late at a restau-rant. I was a waiter and then would come in Sunday morning. I was exhausted, but I'd still make it and I would tell him how I got really upset because a customer yelled at me or the boss yelled at me. He said, "You learn nothing." He said, "Somebody yell at you, you smile." It was like somebody comes in hard at you, you go soft.

He learned how to yield. Life lessons. Oh, yeah. 100%. That's why I said he could have taught anything, and I would have gone to him.

I had one best of the best experiences ever. I remember standing and like Mr. Chan said, your hands are in a circle, your elbows are down there at your mid chest level. Your palms, your fingers were never touching, but it's like you were holding a book. One time I started standing like that, and then I must have drifted off and 40 minutes went by. When I looked at the clock again, I had been standing in that position for 40 minutes.

Never did that before. And I was like, WOW!

I originally started Tai Chi because my acting coach told me it's great for actors. Apparently, a lot of the big drama schools use it, as do Yale, NYU, and Juilliard for movement, so actors can learn to move and be more grounded. It's funny, because after I started doing the standing, and I would be in an audition room, my hand wouldn't shake the paper; I felt more solid.

RAL: There was a very positive impact on you on your career because of the training.

Yeah, and I use it in lifting, too. I remember the eyes guide and guard and where the eyes go the body follows, so I make sure the eyes are in the right position when I'm lifting. Mr. Chan would say when you're walking, you're looking straight as if you're looking ahead two blocks. He used to say, "Practice under a pine tree", because it was great for breathing. Also, you want to look out to the open. You don't want to look at a wall because it comes back to you. That kind of thing. He'd talk about when you're walking or whatever you're doing, your body's turning and there's a little bit of a sinking feeling in the hip area. You're a little bit sunk down. You're not chest up, you know, forward. You're sunk down. In terms of breathing, I'd ask him about breathing and he'd always say, "Natural breathing." And then he'd talk about your standing and that you're never standing double weighted, right?

I have a three-and-a-half-year-old. Talk about natural movement and squatting down. I mean, the baby can sit like an inch from the ground with her butt, her back is perfectly straight and she's almost down to the ground- like nothing. Babies do everything naturally right. You watch how the baby grabs very naturally using their whole body, everything.

And Chan was a big proponent of that, you know, using the whole body.

"Knock Knock"
—Cooper

Mr. Cooper does have a first and middle name, but he prefers to be known simply as "Cooper."

RAL: Mr. Chan was held in very high regard amongst all his students. And there has been a bit of a reluctance on the part of some of his students to talk about him, although you spoke about him on a recent podcast.

He was private about it. He never wanted anybody to know any of the names of his teachers. That was his personal thing.

Mr. Chan was very big on standing. I give him credit for building upon the standing training that I had from a previous teacher. He gave me my basic secondary movement.

RAL: You were in that first group with Frank Allen and Jan Lang?

Jan Lang and I were taught by the same person originally how to stand and basically move back and forth and then Jan discovered Mr. Chan. I was in New Mexico, and I came back from New Mexico to visit. He said you got to meet this guy. Went up to the class and stood horribly for sure. Mr. Chan looked at me after the class and said, "You got to breathe deeper in your belly," and he touched me in my belly. I felt three distinct layers of feeling. Wow. As far as I know, for our neighborhood in the East Village of New York City, Jan is the person who found him, discovered him, and then the rest of us all joined in. All of William's senior students were in the class, and initially there was Jan and I and all the senior students that William had.

RAL: And that was what, in '74, '75?

It was before the boats came in, so I think it was '76. I don't know how much before that I first met Mr. Chan. He was living on 7th Avenue between 23rd and 22nd. Not that that matters where he was living, but it was the first place I knew where he was living. Then he moved to Stuyvesant Town.

RAL: What styles did you study with Mr. Chan? Was it Tai Chi, Bagua, Xingyi?

I was in the first Chen Style class with Mr. Chan on Sundays. He started teaching when he found William C.C. Chen. Mr. Chan didn't want to teach the Yang style, which was, he said, his personal Tai Chi form. Yeah, he taught us that because he didn't want to interfere with what William CC Chen was teaching.

So, he taught us a Chen style. It doesn't look anything like the Chen Fa Ke that you see people do nowadays. You see the Chen style, it's much more flowery, you know. You can actually see in Mr. Chan's, the one that he showed us, you can actually see how the Yang style could have developed from the Chen style. Whereas nowadays, when you look at the modern Chen styles, you can't conceive of how the Yang style came out of that. My present teacher, Zhang Weidong, saw it and he told me that he thought it might be about the oldest Chen style.

Mr. Chan also taught us the fast form of that. Very few people have ever seen it. You know, there's not too many of us that have ever actually got it. And now I'm doing Yang style mostly.

RAL: So then you were exposed to this very early, very rare Chen style by Mr. Chan?

But yeah, Mr. Chan told us he was teaching us the Chen style. He never even alluded that there was another Chen style. And at the time I didn't look into stuff enough to know there was any other kind of Chen style at the time. The main one people study nowadays is called the Chen Fa Ke.

I also did the Bagua with him. I did all the courses with Mr. Chan on Sundays. I used to go up there and take four classes on Sunday. I've done push-hands. Mr. Chan was pretty good. Just as a doer of internal martial arts, he was really good.

RAL: Mr. Chan as a person and a martial arts teacher, were there any kind of life lessons that you may have taken away from him, from his teachings?

Mr. Chan is probably the first person I ever personally knew that actually had a fairly firm foundation in Taoism and Buddhism. Sometimes all I do is keep my tongue at the roof of my mouth…

As far as my own personal take, Mr. Chan's forms, the way they work, were as practical as anybody's I've ever seen. Like most of the forms you do, you learn the form and then the application and the other aspects of it. Wow, how do you even get that application out of the form moves?

Mr. Chan was just magically useful. Take Mr. Chan's Chen Style. Even though I don't consider myself at all accomplished at it, I can still use the applications having only learned the form. Wow. You know what I mean? His system just worked great. Very, very compact, very concise.

RAL: Well, you know, that's something very, very extraordinary that you took away and it's been what, 40 some odd years later.

Well, I mean, the internal system is a pretty interesting thing. It's got a spiritual connection and it's really very practical. If you bang into...... if the earth bumps into you, you can get away from getting hurt as much.

RAL: When was the last time you saw Mr. Chan?

I don't know what year he died. I know I didn't see him at the end, but I visited him while he was in the hospital at that time.

RAL: He passed away in 2002.

Okay, so the last time I saw him was sometime in 2002.

RAL: Can you fill me in on that? I mean, what were his spirits like? Were his spirits still good?

Mr. Chan was really like a Daoist. He was fine. He was pretty strong, too.

RAL: I can imagine. Did he do Iron Fist training or Iron Bell training or something like that?

Iron Palm. He told me that knowing what he knew later on that he was sorry that he had done the training. He did it in the old days when you'd start off with the gravel and the rock that was heated, and you'd sift your hand through it and then they'd keep making it smaller and you'd be sifting your hand through sands. It was a very old-fashioned way, and he only did one hand - his left hand had Iron Palm. So when he would play with us, we could do anything we wanted contacting his right hand, but his left hand, he would just put it out there totally passively. And if you want to knock wrist with him or something, he would just put it there. He wouldn't put even a lick of motion into it. I don't know how to describe that hand, but you know, the nails were like gnarly, you know, and he said he was sorry he did it that way. If you saw the guy's hand, you'd say oh what happened to his hand. Nowadays they don't do it that way anymore. Yeah, that was a pretty tough way of training. You have to withstand a lot of pain or you have to build, you have to build that up gradually. For him to have the Iron Palm was an accomplishment.

I will tell you something, just because you want a Mr. Chan story. I believe Frank (Allen) might be able to validate it. One of the most amazing things Mr. Chan ever did just nonchalantly, was when we were in Union Square Park.

It's got these big trees, where five or six people could hold hands and just get around it. Really big trees in the middle of that park there. We were circling one day around one, and Mr. Chan said, "You know, if you practice, you could maybe do this, right?" And he walked up to the tree while we were circling, and he knocked on it. You know, literally just knock, knock. As if somebody went to the door, and then knock, knock so they could walk in. We actually heard the tree sound just like it was almost a hollow door. It went knock, knock, we could all hear it, right? And the ground actually thumped. We actually felt it through our legs and we were just so blown out. He did it once, never mentioned it again, never showed it to us again. He just went knock knock on it and it was like a door. If you can go find a tree only a foot around and hit it with your knuckles, see if you can get it to go knock knock.

RAL: That's an amazing story. So you were all walking around the tree?

Yeah, we were circling around the tree. It was like the ground actually moved underneath our feet.

RAL: But you sure it wasn't a subway?

So, if it was a subway it had to be very much in tune with what was happening when he was knocking on the tree and then somehow was making the thump thumps in our legs.

RAL: Wow. That's an amazing story.

Yeah, it was one little thing, and it just blew me out.

"I'm Going to Take Energy From You"
—Mike Trombetta

The real cats are like Ken Cohen and Jim Russo. They're the real guys that know BP Chan stuff.

I only studied with Mr. Chan for about a year, off and on. I looked for my file, there's only one old flyer from 1993, from when he used to teach at the school where I took lessons from him, which was on 6th Avenue between 23rd and 24th.

Because when I found out about how great BP Chan was, it really put Grandmaster William Chen up like 10 notches to have someone that he would just bring into the school to help him out. It says a lot about Grandmaster William Chen having a teacher of that caliber come in and teach at his school.

I don't know if you ever saw the inside of the school on 6th Avenue. There was a stairwell that went up to this little raised area, which was just used for storage. This would have been about 1986. I started in 1985, went for about a year, and then took some time off, and then came back. I didn't think anything of it when I saw it happen, but then after I went home, I started thinking about what I saw, that was pretty amazing. What I saw was Grandmaster William Chen come down face forward on this ladder that went up to the top, and he was holding two boxes, one in each hand, and he delicately came down the ladder facing forward. I looked at it, as it happened, and thought, oh, it's nothing. But then as I started thinking about that, I'm thinking about the incredible balance and strength. That's one of the things that I wanted to mention, because, for Grandmaster William Chen to have BP Chan teaching at his school says a lot about Grandmaster William Chen.

I was one of those students that came in and out of BP Chan's classes. I always went to the beginner's classes. I did a couple push-hands classes. I just wanted to learn the form as best as I could.

There's an amazing thing about this guy. He was the only teacher that I've ever had in all my years of the disciplines that called me and asked me how I was doing with my practicing. It showed me a whole other degree of his personality, a whole other aspect of his personality. What a kind man.

Some funny things. First, I have to ask you, are you familiar with the Tai Chi Ruler and the 8 Chi Kung?

RAL: I did learn the 8 Chi Kung but never learned the Ruler.

There's like 10 sections of Tai Chi ruler, and I only did the first four sections, and I'll say three and a half, because we really didn't get into number four.

In the very beginning, you just do a small rocking motion, like the feet are separate, one foot is about one foot length in front of the other. You're just slowly rocking back and forth, and you're only coming up a little bit off the heels. You really feel a burn in your thighs after you're doing it for a while. After a while I was talking to him, Mr. Chan, and I asked, "Should I time my breathing with the rocking, with inhaling and exhaling?" He laughed and he said, "If you did that, we'd have to hook up an exhaust to your bottom." I didn't know Tai Chi Ruler was used for self-defense. His response was, "Now you know, and I know, but they don't know."

When I first came to Mr. Chan's classes, I was already study-ing the 60 movements with Grandmaster William Chen. But Mr. Chan demonstrated two or three different forms through their whole entirety for me, and no one had ever done that for me before. I mean, he did the whole Cannon Fist form. I'm one of these guys that believe in the Chi, and I believe when he's there, there's Chi going around, and I want to soak it up like a sponge. So, I was there as many times as I could when he was teaching.

As I said, Mr. Chan demonstrated maybe two or three forms for me. I remember one thing that he did, which I think was in the Chen Cannon Fist form. He did almost a full split. I mean, he was twisted a little to the side, so it wasn't like a total split, but it was like a 95% split. I understand that's a certain move where you're pulling someone down and you're doing that split and their face is going to hit the ground if you do it right.

The other thing that I remember was that, and I'll preface this by saying, the Tai Chi Ruler System begins with what he used to call a "foot-hole" exercise. That was just to get you rocking back and forth. That's not even listed on his chart that he gives with the sections on it. First section is what they call horizontal fishing, another one is vertical fishing, and then the fourth section is called HO Boxing. That's where Mr. Chan wanted me to build something which I never got around to; it's a board that you set up that's about the height of your body, up to your head, and it gets thinner as it goes to the top, and it's pliable. It's almost like you can push on it, and then when it responds, it's almost like push hands with a board: you're feeling that board coming back at you. I knew people that would do push hands type exercises and sensitivity exercises with hydraulic doors, those doors that have the gas and then they come back on you, and you feel the pressure. You're just sensitively touching that door as it comes in and you know you're feeling how much energy is coming at you.

One time Mr. Chan pulled me over. He was watching me doing the rocking back and forth and he said, "I like what you're doing" and said, "I want to show you something else. I'm going to transfer energy into you." And he faced me; we're both doing the rocking back and forth. I don't know if I can describe this properly. Let's say my left foot is out in front, my right foot is back. So his left foot would be in front of my right foot a little bit forward and his right foot would be behind my left foot. So, we're rocking back and forth. So, we're rocking back and forth together.

I was doing what is called the swirling fishing, the horizontal fishing. That's like making small circles while you're rocking back and forth. He put his hands on top of my hands and he said,

"Now I'm going to issue energy into you," and to be perfectly honest, I didn't feel anything. At the time, I felt nothing; I'm just trusting what was going on. He goes, "Now I'm not going to do too much, but I'm going to take energy from you." We were rocking back and forth, and then I felt something.

I said, whoa, what's going on here? This is going to sound strange, but it's true. I tried to pull my hand back and I was stuck to his hands. I said, oh man, this is what I read about. This is that stuff where you're actually stuck to the person. I don't know what it was. Then he stopped rocking and walked away. It was one of the most bizarre feelings I've ever had. I think maybe he did that to give me a little bit so I would keep coming back. I think he fed me a little something that was way beyond my knowledge. He knew that since I was doing the horizontal fishing right, and he issued energy into me, I honestly thought oh, I'm going to feel like Superman or something. I didn't feel anything. But then when he said, "I'm going to take energy from you", that was weird.

It made me think that maybe that has something to do with where your mind is at. And maybe this stuff that I'm reading about isn't "woo woo" stuff. You know what I mean? There really is something to the sticking energy. I never went to any of the Tai Chi form classes although I was invited, but I'm a musician and sometimes the musical life took over, like getting in at three in the morning, not getting to bed till five and things like that. I think that seeped over into my lack of, well, I'll just say, dedication.

By the way, when I told Mr. Chan I played saxophone, he said, "Well, why do you need Qigong? You're doing it. You're already doing it."

RAL: He was a smart guy, wasn't he?
Oh, man. Yeah. Beyond what we all realize. I'm just so envious of the time people like Jim (Russo) got to spend with Mr.

Chan, but he really got it. I mean, let me tell you something. When I see some of the videos of Jim doing just the beginning stuff that Mr. Chan showed me, he adds a whole other dimension to it because he has the same look that Mr. Chan used to have when he was doing it. I mean, there's something about the eyes and the concentration of the eyes where you're focusing and things like that.

In the 8 Chi Kung exercises, there are some similar moves that are in the Tai Chi Ruler system. Mr. Chan demonstrated these things, the first I think is called Twin Dragons in the Stream.

There are certain moves in there (the 8 Chi Kung) that are similar (to the Tai Chi Ruler), like the swirling fishing or the horizontal fishing and things like that. When you do the exercise, you go up on your toes, correct?

When you're doing the Twin Dragons, you're inhaling and you're going up on your toes, your hands are going out, and when they come out and around is when you exhale. And when you exhale, you go down, but you don't let the heels touch the ground. Your body is still supported by your toes. Your body goes down, but your heels stay off the ground. And then you go up onto the balls of your feet and then when you exhale you go down, your feet go down, the backs of your feet go down, your heels go down, but they don't touch the ground.

So, you're constantly exercising those calf muscles. And then after you do it 10 times, you hit the ground. I don't know if you were exposed to that, because I think when he first taught that, he didn't teach you to go up on your toes. I remember him teaching me just doing it flat-footed and then he taught me Tossing the Cauldron, which is the second one. That's when he showed me. He says if you want to take it to another level, you do these exercises and you never let the entire foot touch the ground. You do 10 and the heels come back to the ground, but they are only about a quarter of an inch off the ground.

Now, this was similar to what he was saying to me and why I was saying it's comparable to the Tai Chi Ruler. In the first exercise of the rocking, you go back and forth, and you only raise your heel off the ground when you're moving forward; your back heel only rises about a quarter inch off the floor. Then you rock back and your toe, your left toe - if you're doing it with the left foot forward - rises only about a quarter inch off the ground.

After you do this for a while, he said, you start rising to about a half inch. So you're starting to increase the range of the calf muscle when you're doing the rocking. He didn't directly come out and say this, but I think the 8 Chi Kung means you can start with your feet flat on the floor because it's not that much of an exercise. It's just it's more of an upper body exercise. When you bring it into full focus, you're staying off the ground and then you start really feeling some strength in the calf muscles. You're doing 10 of those repetitions, but your feet are never actually finishing touching the ground until it's all over.

When I started getting back into it again, I thought that I'm just going to do the upper part of my body because I don't have room in my house. I don't have enough room, being in Manhattan. So to me, I'm making excuses, but it was more convenient for me to just do the upper body parts of the 8 Chi Kung. But when I'm outside, I do the whole form; it's very invigorating. I can really feel it, even if I only choose to do three or four of each movement, and if I go through all eight, I feel invigorated.

Mr. Chan also alluded to - he didn't come right out and say it - but there's something very, very special about that last one, with the spirals, doing the spirals. He alluded to the fact that there was something pretty magical about that. And you're not going to get it, even if you practice it for a few months. It may take a year to get it. But it's something about that spiral motion.

You know, he was big into spirals. I remember he gave me one of the handouts. He often talked about the spiral; he said people say "Circles, circles yeah, yeah. It's the spiral." When people say "circle" he said to stop and think if they mean "spiral." That's another important thing, because I can do a circle, sure, and that wards off, but if I'm thinking of a spiral, I'm sending that sucker somewhere. He's going somewhere.

I mean, just that alone, you know, can guide someone into.... oblivion. I had a situation in the streets of New York where I almost threw somebody into traffic. It was fortunate that it worked out, that it didn't come to that. But it was a close altercation that kind of left me a little nervous, too. I was fortunate because that could have turned into a horrible situation and the police would have been called.

RAL: You mentioned the time when you felt like your hand was actually stuck to Mr. Chan's hand. Now, were you actually touching him? Was he touching you or was there space in between your hands?

No, no, no, we were touching. It was actually as I said. He laid his hands on top of my hands, and we were doing the circles, rocking back and forth and doing the circles. His hands were on top, and they were against mine. I was pressing up, and he was pressing down. Then he said he was issuing energy at that time. And then he said, "I'm going to withdraw energy." He didn't do it for a long time. I got the impression that that would have been dangerous. I don't know if that's true or not. I just got that impression, but he did a little bit and I tried to pull away. I tried to drop my hands and I couldn't. This is mysterious. This is really weird. Then he pulled away quickly. I don't know if he sensed that I was trying to pull away and he didn't want to give away too much or whatever, but it was it was uncanny. It was a very, very, very, mysterious feeling.

I recall asking Mr. Chan if he ever had to use martial arts in a real-life situation. He said that once, in a cab in the Philippines, a man reached into the cab with a knife. He said he disarmed the man with a technique we were just discussing in which you trap/break the elbow, bend/snap the wrist and roll/break the fingers. Mr. Chan added that the assailant did manage to cut his sleeve.

I just wanted to add that Mr. Chan was very knowledgeable in herbal medicine and Traditional Chinese Medicine. He looked at my tongue once and asked me if there was diabetes in my family. I explained that my mother had diabetes and he said you want to try and eat pig pancreas. And he drew the Chinese character for what it is. And for the longest time, I looked, I went to butchers and things like that, and I couldn't get it. And I found out that it's also considered a sweetbread that gourmet chefs use, but it's not one of the top organs that's used for sweetbreads. Well, I did a little more research and found out that where the pig pancreas of all the slaughtered pigs goes is to the pharmaceutical industry. And that's how they make insulin. They get it from pig pancreas.

RAL: Oh my gosh, I didn't know that. Wow.

Yes, yes, that's where the insulin comes from. So, I have asked butchers to try and order it for me, special order, and they still haven't. It's just not worth the effort for them. But I just thought that was very interesting that Mr. Chan looked at my tongue and right away his question was, is there diabetes? So we knew that I am prone to, or at least it's in my bloodline.

And the other thing was when he explained to me, the first move of the Tai Chi Ruler, he lined my fingers up with certain parts of my body that were acupuncture points. So there was more to it. I didn't get fully into knowing exactly what the points were and things like that, hard for me to describe now, it's just that there's an acupuncture point at the base of your palm that goes against your hip, and another at the tip of your middle finger that lines up with the kneecap. So there's more mysterious things going on that I didn't even get to the level of complete understanding, but I just know that he lined up acupuncture points with the foothold exercise. So that's my other information about Mr. Chan.

I think it's an incredible effort that you're making. I mean, more people should know about Mr. Chan.

"You Got to Stop Somewhere"
—Dr. Richard Chin

You actually called the right person. I know BP Chan from when he first got off the boat. He stayed with me for a while, and I also stayed with his family. We became very close. I know Mr. Chan probably more than anybody else.

It's a big story, but I'll tell you in a nutshell how I met him in 1976. My Master, Chan Mon Cheung and I had a group of masters here from China. That was a Bicentennial year, that's why I remember. 10 masters and I toured the US at that time. We did Madison Square Garden and other places. I was the host in the New York area, so I took him to all the different people here, and of course, William Chen.

So we went to visit William Chen and that's how I met BP. BP happened to just come into his school shortly before that. BP and I somehow found each other, and we got along fabulously because my school at the time was in Soho and I ran a very traditional school. We did the shrine and incense, and when he came to visit me, he felt right at home because he's very traditional. My school was very classic, old China. He felt right at home, and so he taught with me for a while at my school.

There's so much. So then what happened was I sponsored his family to come to the United States. His wife, his kids and all that. And when I stayed in the Philippines, I stayed with his family and he stayed with us here. We were very close since I've known him from 1976 on.

So yes, I know a lot about him. Most people don't know about him because he was a very private person himself. I mean, people know him for what he taught. But most people don't know the back story and there's no reason for them to know it. I'm just telling you how I know him. Okay, so that's it. So I do know him very well.

RAL: When he taught with you, that was sometime after '76 then, right?

Right, right. Yeah, you know, during that year, '76, '77, he came and asked if he could teach at my school. I said, absolutely. Now, from my school, my students who studied with him were the ones who really learned his whole system. Have you heard of the name Jeff Pascal? Have you heard of Pascal at all? Okay, Pascal was his top student. He had three students which he actually turned a lot of stuff into. And Pascal has been with me for like 50 years. So in our school, in our system, we have a very tight niche with BP. And that's where you saw the article in Inside Kung Fu.

RAL: Okay, so your school was the Asian Martial Arts Studio?

Correct. That was the name of the school.

RAL: When Mr. Chan was in your school, what was he teaching?

He taught Xing-Yi, Bagua, and he taught the Chen-style Tai Chi, because we did not want to conflict with William's school and other schools. He himself knew several different systems of Tai Chi and Xing-Yi because that was his hobby; you know he loved martial arts, so he studied many of the different systems. There was one story about a master who visited us, a famous Master Dung of LA, from China. I asked BP if he knew Master Dung. He said he didn't. I was surprised. I said, "Well, how come you don't know this particular stuff?" And he said, "You got to stop somewhere." The Qigong, fabulous Qigong. That was the life of his hobby. There are hundreds of different systems of Qigong. He knew most of them, not all of them - because nobody knows all of them - but that was his hobby. He loved it.

His early background, which people don't know, is that he started very young, as a teenager, 12, whatever it is. He studied with a very famous master in Fukien; he's from Fukien, China. Fukien to Taiwan and then to the Philippines.

In southern China, in the Fukien area, in the Philippines and Taiwan area, there is a branch of Fukien martial arts, and that's where he started. Those masters and their systems have since become famous. The style he studied was called Five Ancestor Animal System. Most people don't know that's what he did. That was his background. Because his background was Shaolin, that's why he was so good.

And most Tai Chi Masters who were good, were Shaolin martial artists, also. In other words, Yin and Yang. They came together because they fully understood what was going on. He trained in classic martial arts, classic iron palm strikes, Qigong, the classic stuff that people see in the movies. He's a product of that. From his Grandmaster and all that, which we all knew because that's going back to my Grandmaster from that period of time.

RAL: Did he ever tell you why the family left China to go to Taiwan?

Sure, sure.

RAL: What was the reason?

A thing called a revolution. In 1949, the revolution ends, Communists take over. Any master who could, who was a legitimate master, got out of town. All my teachers, myself, and all my masters, got out of town, because in China, under the Communist rule, you conformed or were "re-educated."

You're a martial artist, you're a doctor, lawyer, business owner, Professor, whatever it is. They wanted you out of there or they were going to re-educate you. Right? This is Asia, the Cultural Revolution, all that. So get out of town if you can. So the really strong martial artists left mainland China. They're in Taiwan, they're in Hong Kong, Philippines, Malaysia, any place, Vietnam even. Europe, America, not in China. Because your head would roll.

RAL: The whole family moved from Taiwan to the Philippines?

Yes.

RAL: Do you know what the reason was for the move to the Philippines?

Business, basically. Economically, socially, it was just a good move for them. They weren't forced out or anything like that. It was just the move for them, the family. And they were very well established in the Philippines. The father and the grandfather were very well to do. They were pillars of their community in the Philippines. They had many different businesses. Many, many things, the furniture store being one of them, you know.

RAL: I had sent an email to the Philippines Martial Arts Association, asking them if there were any older members who had any recollections of BP Chan. I haven't gotten a response from them.

Well, that's because they've probably all passed. Chan passed a long time ago, and they would be in their hundreds. I'm the only living one that you could probably talk to, because I was young when I knew him. They would have to be my generation to know him at all because I met him in '76! How many years ago is that? My teachers, my seniors, are all passed so there's very little that you can find that way and then there's the secrecy part -being very secretive....... now they've opened up a little bit, but during that period, you wouldn't get much information. I don't think they're around, seriously. And very Chinese, for example, they wouldn't know who BP Chan was. You would have to know his Chinese name. Okay, so that's one roadblock that you never even thought of, right? They don't know who BP Chan is. They never heard of him. This is Chinese history now. How to deal with Chinese thinking.

RAL: I see now. I didn't have a Chinese name and everyone's probably dead.

You never thought of that. Well, he was 80 when he passed; that's quite a few years ago so it would be.

Jeff Pascal is one of my senior students but is the senior student of BP Chan. He's the one who was with him the most. It was like Chan was his father, Jeff was his son. They were very close together and he learned basically everything from him, and people who really know BP Chan's system will always say refer to Jeff Pascal. He's the one that knows all this stuff. Briefly, because Jeff was young, what happened was I just put them together.

It was just one of those things, one of my strokes of genius, and they just loved each other. It just fit. And they were together their whole life. They took care of each other. Jeff took care of everything he needed, and so forth and so on.

Now, my systems are Pak Mei - white eyebrow, and Jow Ga. Those are the two systems I teach. I am a 3rd generation direct disciple of Jow Ga, and a 6th generation disciple of Pak Mei (direct lineage).

I've studied Chen Style Tai Chi from BP and some other masters.

6. BP CHAN'S 12 EXERCISES FOR HEALTH

It's now commonly known that sitting in one place for long periods of time is not good for the body. I don't know when BP Chan wrote this document, but it had to be over 20 years ago. Very, very, prescient on his part to understand how long periods of sitting can be harmful. To quote from his piece:

> "If you don't exercise and spend most of your time
> sitting in an office, your health will be
> adversely affected."
> —BP Chan

十二 健身操
TWELVE EXERCISES FOR HEALTH

IF YOU DON'T EXERCISE AND SPEND MOST OF YOUR TIME SITTING IN AN OFFICE, YOUR HEALTH WILL BE ADVERSLY AFFECTED. SOME OF THE POSSIBLE DEFECTS CAUSED BY A LACK OF EXERCISE OVER A LONG PERIOD OF TIME ARE: WEIGHT GAIN, SLOWDOWN OF THE HEART, POOR CIRCULATION, CONTRACTION OF MUSCLES, TISSUES, LIGAMENTS AND NERVES, CONTRACTION OR EXPANSION OF VEINS AND BLOOD PRESSURE-DECREASE OF BLOOD SUPPLY TO THE BRAIN CAUSING POSSIBLE DIZZINESS OR TIREDNESS.

GLOWING HEALTH SHOULD BE EVERYONES OBJECTIVE. THE SECRET IS DAILY EXERCISE. IN ORDER TO HELP YOU ATTAIN THIS THE FOLLOWING 12 EXERCISES ARE SUGGESTED.

1) WHILE SITTING RELAX THE ENTIRE BODY AND CONCENTRATE ON BREATHING WITH THE STOMACH. HOLD YOUR HEAD ERRECT AS IF SUSPENDED FROM ABOVE, RELAX YOUR SHOULDERS AND DROP YOUR ELBOWS.

2) TURN YOUR HEAD FROM LEFT TO RIGHT WITH THE EYES FOLLOWING AS FAR TO THE LEFT & RIGHT AS POSSIBLE. TURN YOUR HEAD BACKWARD AND DOWNWARD SO YOUR EYES CAN LOOK AS FAR BACK AND DOWN AS POSSIBLE. TURN YOUR HEAD & EYES CLOCKWISE THEN COUNTER-CLOCKWISE.

3) PLACE YOUR TWO HANDS ON THE BACK OF YOUR HEAD, PULL THE HANDS FORWARD AND THE HEAD BACK SIMULTANEOUSLY. (HANDS & HEAD PUSH AGAINST EACH OTHER)

4) PRESS YOUR LEFT HAND AGAINST THE LEFTSIDE OF YOUR FACE, THEN HAVE THE HEAD & HAND PRESS TOWARD EACH OTHER. REVERSE THIS ACTION IN ORDER TO DO THE RIGHT SIDE.

5) LET YOUR LEFT HAND HOLD YOUR RIGHT SHOULDER AND YOUR RIGHT HAND HOLD YOUR LEFT SHOULDER

6) PLACE YOUR TWO HANDS ON THE BACK OF YOUR NECK

7) PLACE YOUR TWO HANDS TOGETHER (WITH PALMS FACING OUT) ON YOUR BACK AND HOLD THEM THERE

8) RAISE YOUR TWO HEELS AND PRESS YOUR TOES ON THE GROUND

9) EXTEND YOUR LEFT LEG FORWARD AND FIRMLY POINT THE LEFT TOE INWARD. REPEAT THIS FOR YOUR RIGHT LEG.

10) DO EXERCISE #9 WITH BOTH LEGS SIMULTANEOUSLY

11) EMBRACE THE FRONT OF YOUR BODY WITH YOUR TWO ARMS, EXTEND YOUR LEFT LEG OUT IN FRONT OF YOU AND TURN YOUR BODY TO THE LEFT. REPEAT THIS WITH THE RIGHT LEG.

12) SIT STILL RELAX AND DO NATURAL BREATHING (STOMACH EXTEND ON INHALE, CONTRACT ON EXHALE) FOR 5 MINUTES.

THE ABOVE EXERCISES SHOULD BE DONE EIGHT (8) TIMES EACH WITH NATURAL BREATHING. AFTER EXERCISING TAKE A FEW MINUTE WALK TO LET THE BODY BECOME NORMAL. WITH YOUR HEALTH AT STAKE, I HOPE EVERYONE DOES THESE EXERCISES INDUSTRIOUSLY WITH SINCERITY AND PAITENCE.

Provided Courtesy of Rudy Curry

7. CLASS FLYERS

**CLASSES TAUGHT
BY MASTER B. P. CHAN**

Chi-Kung Meditation
6:30–7:30 p.m. Monday

Push-Hands
8:00–9:00 p.m. Monday

Tai Chi Ruler
11 a.m.–12 p.m. Sunday

Chen's Tai Chi Chuan
12–1 p.m. Sunday

Mainland Tai Chi Chuan
1:15–2:15 p.m. Sunday

Pa-Kua/Hsing-1
2:30–3:30 p.m. Sunday

Tai Chi Staff
4:00–5:00 p.m. Sunday

NEW CLASSES

Tai Chi Staff
Sunday 4 to 5 pm
Master B. P. Chan

San Shou Practice Class
Thursday 9:15pm to 10:15pm
starting March 10th 1988

also

Saturday 5:30pm to 6:30pm
starting March 12th 1988

Classes will supervised by
one of our assistant
instuctors of this school
at their special rates.

Sign-up Now!

Master B. P. Chan was born in Fu-Kien,
China. Master Chan who started his
studies of Chinese Martial Arts at the
age of 10, has been teaching the various styles of Nei Cha Chuan and
Northern Shaolin Forms in the Phillipines and now in New York.

109

8. BP CHAN MEETS TT LIANG
PART I

I'm not really a Tai Chi person, but I do know that when people talk about the great ones teaching in the United Sates in the past 40 years, the names William CC Chen and T.T. Liang are mentioned frequently. Have there been others? Sure, and I mean no disservice to them by not mentioning them here, but Chen and Liang are the most widely known for their level of skill.

T.T. Liang came to New York City in the late 70's to visit his good friend William CC Chen. At that time, he met with BP Chan. Three of BP Chan's students relate their memory of this meeting - "Cooper", Richard Raab, and Ray Hayward. Paul Gallagher describes the event as told to him by Ray Hayward.

HERE'S COOPER'S RECOLLECTION OF SOME OF THAT MEETING BETWEEN BP CHAN AND TT LIANG:

T.T. Liang was like William's martial arts buddy, a senior student, and they were taught by Cheng Man-Ching.... T.T. Liang came to one of our morning classes, and basically, Jan (Lang) and I got to stand for the full two hours of the class....and watch T.T. Liang throw Mr. Chan around....and then supposedly Mr. Chan said after T.T. Liang left that morning, he said, oh, he was very impressed that I had students who would stand. You're just standing there and you're watching Mr. Chan who you thought was as good as they get, and he's like a little bouncing ball. And he was thrilled. He'd (T.T. Liang) push him and bounce (him) off the wall. He (BP Chan) was just thrilled to be able to go back and put his hand back again and get bounced…. again. *

FROM RICHARD RAAB:

There was a time when he went to T.T. Liang, who was in town, and he visited him. He asked T. T. Liang to watch his form and give him form improvement.

FROM PAUL GALLAGHER:

I am reminded of a story told to me by my martial arts brother, Sifu Ray Hayward.

He was studying with the late B.P. Chan in New York City when T.T. Liang stopped in for a visit. After exchanging a few pleasantries, Chan promptly asked Liang to observe his Form and offer corrections. Some of his students were shocked. Chan, after all, was a master of five entire "systems" of Chinese martial arts, each "system" being roughly equivalent to a PhD in the West.

After Liang had left, Chan's students demanded to know why in the world he, an eminent master in his own right, would ask another master for "corrections." Chan replied, "What kind of teacher would I be if I failed to try to perfect myself? The best teacher must also be the most humble student."

That attitude is the hallmark of a true master, and an interesting contrast to the young student of meager experience who comes to a teacher and demands to learn the "good stuff," or advanced material, claiming that he already "knows" all about the basics. A master in any art is ALWAYS practicing and refining the "basics." **

---

* Transcribed excerpts from audio interview: "Exclusive Interview - ME Cooper", May 30, 2022. Used with permission of The Nejiaquan Podcast.

** Excerpted from: What Is a Tai Chi Master? By Paul Gallagher © Copyright Paul B Gallagher. Reprinted with permission.

FROM RAY HAYWARD:

Chan also asked Liang to push hands with him and correct his sensitivity as well!

So, what's the take-away from this? Is it that your teacher, whom you respected as a skilled practitioner and teacher, was not as skilled as you thought? Was BP Chan not challenging his guest TT Liang so Liang could save face? or is there something more significant, a lesson, to be learned here? To be continued…….

9. LETTER FROM BP CHAN TO RAY HAYWARD

In this letter, a prized possession of Ray Hayward, dated June 15, 1979, Mr. Chan requests that Ray "Please extent my best regard to Master Liang and thanks for his correction of the Pa Kua and translation of Pa Kua weapon into English."

June 15.79

Dear Hayward

Received your letter + pictures dated June 10 On this day. thanks you very much.

I know you will get it. because you are an industrious practitioner.

Here enclose two shot of pa kua + Hsing I.

Please extent my best regard to Master Liang and thanks for his correction of the Pa kua + translation of Pa kua weapon into English.

Friendly Yours

B. P. Chan

Provided courtesy of Ray Hayward and used with permission.

10. IN THEIR OWN WORDS

"Everyday life is martial arts"
—Jim Fogarty

RAL: You were at the Farm when Ron (Caruso) was there, when Michael ben Aamen was there?

Ron and I met at the Sunday class in the city. He just popped in one day and he and Chan hit it off and then he was a regular. Michael ben Aamen used to drive Mr. Chan. We would go up to the Tai Chi Farm and work for half the day and then do exercise. We worked on making different exercise areas. After lunch we would work on the form or learn other exercises.

RAL: When did you first become involved with Mr. Chan?

Sometime in the early 90's, I was living in Newburgh NY, and I saw an ad in the paper for a Tai Chi class. I began learning from Richard Satlow, who was one of Mr. Chan's senior students. He was an excellent teacher so I was hooked from that time on. Later I moved to New York City, and he introduced me to his teacher, Mr. Chan.

RAL: That was 23rd Street?

It was near 23rd Street. Maybe it was on 24th and 6th Avenue. It was above Billy's Topless. It was William Chen's studio.

RAL: It's 24th Street.

Yes, it was the studio before he moved on to 23rd. Well, the class was always on Sunday, Sunday morning.

RAL: What did you study with Mr. Chan?
Primarily Yang Tai Chi and feeling hands.

RAL: There's a Chen style I think he was teaching?
On Sundays, during that time the Tai Chi was Yang style. After that class was Pa Kua.

He taught different things, at different locations. Mr. Chan had several different groups of students. On Friday night, he had another group. He had groups around the city. And not all of them knew each other. I went to that Friday class a few times. No one knew me there because I was from the Sunday class. I walked in and did the form, and they were like, "Who's this guy, where are you from?" Well, Sunday class didn't know about the Friday class and the Friday class didn't know about the Sunday class.

Each group was like his experiment, in a way. He was all about sharing, but at the same time, he would ask you, "What did you feel this week?" And when you told him, he would sometimes say, "Okay, now I learned something." He had all these people telling him what was going on with their bodies that were different bodies than his. He had a very open mind. He was always trying to learn more and more about his art.

RAL: What personal recollections do you have of him? What memories stand out?
I have a couple. Mr. Chan would always talk about how to do one move correctly. And that's an interesting thing to think about. On many levels it is not easy to do a move correctly, I will give an example from push hands. There have been many times when I have yielded and diverted somebody, and it makes them angry. Then, they want to push you or hit you. I'm yielding and I'm being soft, but something is not correct because mentally

there is a conflict. One time I was walking with Mr. Chan in a park in Stuyvesant Town and there was a guy who did Tai Chi every morning in the middle of the park. We would walk the path, and this fellow was always there. They would wave to each other, but they never had any contact. Then one day, Chan walked over to him. I stayed where I was. Chan walked into the middle of this oval, and I watched from a distance. They shook hands and as they shook hands the fellow pulled him forward. Chan stepped forward and put his foot down and got his center on that leg and then he just folded his elbow and touched that guy right in the center line where his buttons were. Just a really light touch. You could see the man's expression sink because he realized, "Oh crap, I pulled him right into me." It was just funny to watch how the guy was like, "Oh, I'm going to pull you off center" and then a second later, he realized that he pulled Mr. Chan into him. He wasn't angry. The move was so clear. I thought at the time that that move was correct. It was very calm and gentlemanly and soft. The man just knew, clearly, he had made a mistake. He learned something right there, that gentleman.

RAL: It's a teaching moment.

Very much so. And then Chan just came back and we kept walking. I am just struck by that memory of that one move. It was simple and correct. The same thing happened again at the studio. This guy came in who was really strong and he pushed me around for a long time and I just couldn't divert him. He just pushed and pushed into my center. After that, he and Chan started doing some feeling hands. He started doing the same thing, putting on some pressure. I remember clearly seeing Mr. Chan's structure. He had clear angles in the structure, without any force. This fellow had an embracing palm that was very strong and you couldn't move it. Mr. Chan somehow pivoted over that embracing palm and the guy brought him right into his center. Chan lightly touched him. The man realized that he had just brought him directly into his center. Then the guy was like, oh, thank you and thank you for helping me. I saw him bow in gratitude. It was another teaching moment. I saw it happen two times. The man wasn't angry, he was grateful.

I always think about those things. The moves were very soft, very gentle and both people learned something. Mr. Chan would always talk about how to do one move correctly and it sounds, when you first hear it, perhaps a bit corny. But the more you think about it, the deeper the meaning goes.

RAL: What do you think he meant by that?

Lots of things. Mr. Chan always said, "Everyday life is martial arts, everyday life is martial arts." When I'm in a classroom with a bunch of 10-year-olds and they get me riled up and I lose my stuff and I am yelling "blah blah blah" and I get all upset, I realize those kids took me out of my center. It's exactly that, you know. Is a person going to take you out of center or is a kid going to take you out of your center? I know when I do a move correctly in the classroom, and of course I know when I get taken out of my center. At times, I yield, I divert, I advance. Everyday life is martial arts. I connected that to the idea of doing one move correctly. How to do a move correctly in your everyday life.

RAL: That's a nice story. Because you've brought his teachings, what you learned from him, into your profession. Into your interactions with people.

Yes. All those people you talk to that spent time with Chan, that's what it was. When you were in the class, that world was very deep. I think that's what drew people to it. He helped everybody of any level without seemingly depending on your martial arts ability. He was in my opinion a spiritual teacher. That's why so many people liked to be around him. He would just say "Tai Chi, Xing-Yi and Pa Kua for all." And that's what he did. That was his everyday world.

RAL: For all. Tai Chi, Xing-Yi and Pa Kua for all?

Yes, for all people. Bob Schefsky knows that saying too. There used to be some signs at the Tai Chi Farm about that saying.

RAL: You had mentioned that you spent some time with Mr. Chan up at the Farm.

A lot of what he did at the Farm was to beautify the area with projects. In one area we put these big logs sticking up out of the ground in the shape of an S, and you could stand on them and do feeling hands. There were several Chinese gates made from logs. There was a whole Pa Kua diagram out of logs that you could walk around and circle around. There were steps going up the hill, and fences made of logs outlining certain areas. He just took a whole area and transformed it into different practice areas. Bridges, paths, practice areas, banners, Chinese signs, stone borders, gates, and more filled the woods.

RAL: Mr. Chan used his students to do that.

Yes. We would go up there and for a few hours, in the morning, say, we'd work on fences or the gates or the steps. We'd have lunch, and in the afternoon, we would do the form or do other exercises.

RAL: Do you have any pictures of that? Because this is the first time that I've heard about an S-shaped thing with logs.

Yes, I have some, but I don't know that I have a picture of Friendly Area logs. I think it was called the Friendly Area to keep people's competitive minds down. Over time, we'd work on one spot and we'd finish up and then he would say, okay, now I have another idea- let's do this, and let's do that. And it would just spread around to different areas. After a time, I was busy on Saturdays but many other students continued working on projects for years after that.

RAL: How many people were in these groups? You probably had a group doing Pa Kua up there, right? You probably had a group doing Xing Yi, probably had a group doing Qi Gong or something.

That would have been for the workshops. A workshop would last a week, but mostly on Saturday there might be a group of five or six people. David Whitehouse used to go up there quite a bit. He traveled all the way from Vermont or New Hampshire. Peter G, Michael Driver, Ron Caruso, Tim Regan, Bob Schefsky, Ron and Gar, Helena and others helped out for a long time.

If you asked Mr. Chan about his teachers, Mr. Chan would say, "My teacher's dead. Do you want to know what I know? Or do you want to know who my teacher is?" That is not exactly the saying but that is the idea of it. To me, he didn't say much about his teachers, only a few things here and there. And often it was related to martial things like a certain move. For example, "My teacher said, 'This move can save your life'" and then he would show the move. He had great respect for his teachers. He often said, "My teachers were strong coffee, and I am weak coffee." If Mr. Chan was weak coffee, I guess that means that I am decaf, or perhaps tea!

RAL: Tim Regan told me to differentiate him from Tim Folger, that Mr. Chan used to call Tim Folger "Coffee." He had names for many of his students. One student told me that he called her "Secretary."

Chan had a lot of names for people. He would just call me James- I must have been the only James. There were several Richards, and several Michaels. Michael ben Aamen was a cab driver, so he was Michael Driver. Then another Michael was at the time a baker, that was Michael Baker. And everybody thought his name was Michael Baker. He was just super dedicated to training. There were a few people who did it the old way. Chan himself would say, he practiced 10 hours a day, and took only Chinese New Year's off. That's the kind of training needed to get to a high level. One of the Michael's said "I think you've got to sweat blood." And he wasn't joking. He practiced very, very seriously. I hope nobody minds when I tell these stories, because they're compliments. One of the Richard's had a carpet in his place and he walked that Pa Ku circle so much that when you looked down along the perimeter of the room, the wall-to-wall carpet was in folds and rolls around the perimeter because it had been stretched out all to the perimeter by walking in circles on it. Imagine how much you have to practice for that to happen to your carpet. Chan appreciated them because they had great commitment.

Suppose you want to be a concert pianist? Are you going to practice six hours or eight hours a day? Otherwise, you're not going to a very high level. It's that kind of thing. And somehow Chan, even though he came from that world of that total commitment, still seemed to have the idea that he would help people of all levels. He showed you these things. so you could have a healthy life, and share with others. That part's real. He really wanted Tai Chi, Pa Kua, and Xing-Yi for all.

I practice every day and I feel better and better. The snowball just keeps rolling and getting bigger and bigger. Just from a health standpoint, that's a big deal. But you have to be a bit crazy. My wife and my son think, "Oh, there he is, he's just standing still doing his strange exercises, day after day after day." I don't care. I just like it. But how many people are going to like it? Not many. It's the same with the Tai Chi form. Everybody's excited for six months and then after six months they think "Oh, this is not really for me."

It spreads and gets a little watered down and spreads and gets watered down. And then you wonder, is that good or is that bad? There's a lady in town and she was teaching Tai Chi and I asked, "What style do you teach?" And she said, "I don't know." It's all different levels. I just think of it like golf. Plenty of people enjoy golf and they love it. Their skill level is what it is and then it goes all the way to the people at the very top and that's the way it is.

Chan had a super concentration of all this knowledge. And it seems to me that he spread it to a ton of people. I guess that's the way knowledge goes throughout time. He spread it to a lot and you have to have faith that some people will carry it on. Several of Chan's students are at a high level. Now, I don't know how many people they will spread it to, but hopefully a few that can keep carrying it. That reminds me of another of his sayings- "If the student does not surpass the teacher, then the art will die." Good luck everyone!

RAL: Any other interesting recollections, Jim, that you have about Mr. Chan? Anything that kind of stands out, unique? Anything he said or did or the way he taught?

People talk about how he helped them and did so much for them. That's real for people who were there for six months or a few years or many years. Somehow, they all have the viewpoint of "That guy took a special interest in me and helped me out in my life." I'm going to guess that a lot of people will be telling you that same story. Which is, to me, the key, because it's beyond the martial arts, or maybe it's the high level of the arts. To me, that's the big picture. I think back over the years of all the people coming in, going out and coming in and going out, and Chan just kept on helping everybody with that kind of open mind and open heart. He kept on helping and at the same time learning more and learning more and learning more. He was a treasure. We were all lucky to have known him.

RAL: Well, you want to grab some lunch?
Sure-but let's do some brush knee first!

"Mr. Tailor"
—Gar Wang

Mr. Chan was a very private, humble man. Although I studied with him late in his life, his power and deftness as a martial artist was striking. He was as close to being an enlightened ascetic as anyone I have known and certainly one of the wisest. Despite his limited English, he was able to convey, with deliberately chosen words, elusive principles in Chinese Internal Arts and traditional Chinese philosophy. Presenting questions and cryptic phases rather than direct answers, Mr. Chan challenged practitioners to "take it home and cook it in your brain." He distinguished the brain from the mind…the brain as the organ controlling conceptualization, which modern society praises. The mind, however, serves as a sensorial conduit that, through intuition and feeling, taps into the subtle flow of energy throughout the body. When ideation supersedes, our will dominates, often with disregard for the natural way the body functions. In terms of body mechanics and movement, this often leads to injury. "Listen to your body. Be kind to your body."

According to an old Chinese proverb, "The higher the pedestal, the greater distance to fall." Mr. Chan fostered the concept of equality and community. When we practiced as a group, we would stand in a circle so that everyone was on equal footing. He did not want to be regarded as superior to the students and refused to be addressed as "Master" …it was always respectfully, "Mr. Chan." Instead of "teaching" (which connotes authority) he would say we "share the practice in order to help others."

He would pronounce the word "We" with open arms in a gesture of inclusiveness, as opposed to saying "Me" while poking at his chest repeatedly, demonstrating how this gesture of asserting one's ego was unsettling as he stumbled a few steps backwards. Often, he would reinforce a concept by sketching with a stick in the dirt or writing a few Chinese characters in lucid calligraphic strokes. In this instance, he would form the letter "M" with his thumbs and index fingers...demonstrating that by flipping his hands the "M" in "Me" became "W" in "We." Like many of his principles involving visual cues, this simple image of reversing "M" to "W" gelled in my mind's eye and became an enduring reminder of the delicate balance between the individual and humanity, between self-interest and the common good.

Likewise, his greatest gift to me was perhaps his message of "Pure Heart." Whenever I have doubt, I return to these words and the answer becomes clearer. As he would say, "So simple."

Other noteworthy principles to reflect upon:

The practice does not cure our ailments; rather, it enhances the body's ability to heal itself.

"Suspend like hanging" (for structural alignment while remaining "Song,"loose and open.)

"58 seconds" (versus 60 seconds...no locked joints, a little give)

"Let your eyes guide the body" (the optic nerve is connected to the spinal cord)

"*Shopwork*" instead of "workshop": "Come with an empty bag and shop, then go home and work."

"Too much decoration ruins the exposition."

"Mr. Tailor" – using the metaphor of a clothes maker's attention to the proportions of the human body, he would refer to these coordinates to demonstrate structural alignment as well as martial application... (the cuff, side seams of the pants, etc.)

"*Coochie Coochie Coo*"
—Rich Raab

RAL: Did Mr. Chan have a nickname for you?

Sometimes Chan called me Rich*ard* (with emphasis on the second syllable.) He said it was a strong name, Rich*ard*. I never pronounced it that way. His nickname for me was Richard Number Two. By the time he passed, there were about 15 Richards in his classes.

RAL: How did you find out about Mr. Chan?

I was interested in Tai Chi, and I was studying with Richard Shepard, a student of Chen Man - Ching. An old student of mine, from my Karate days, visited me and started talking about Chan. This student showed me some stuff he had learned, and I was interested, so I went to see Chan at C K Chu's because I wanted to learn more about what he was teaching. I couldn't afford private lessons with him at the time, so I started taking classes with him. I studied with him for about 25 years.

When Chan left Chu's and went to William's School on 23rd Street, we would go in on Sundays and take one class after another for the whole day.

I learned very quickly that he was a bottomless pit, and no matter how long I would stay with him, I would never know all that he knew.

There were a lot of people around, but Sunday was our day. Eventually, we broke up into a small group. I had a small group of classmates: Carl, who has since passed away, Alvin, Al and Jimmy. We saw him privately, you know, for years. We would rent studio space. I'd pick him up, drive him there, and drive him back. We went up to the Farm also, saw him up in the Farm. It was great, a great experience.

I can tell you, from my perspective, he was a true Master. Man was humble. He had a beautiful personality. I loved working with him. He could get angry at times. I remember once I said, "I feel stupid." He said, "That word's too severe."

Yeah, that word's too severe. That's too severe. But he was free giving. He was a giving person, you know, sharing, sharing was his thing. He'd love for people to share with each other. I could tell you a story. One day I went up to his apartment to meet with him with my cohorts and we went in. He calls me over and he's got a paper, and he shows me this guy's name. The guy's name is the same as his but spelled in a different dialect. This guy, Prof. Richard K. Tseng, apparently studied with Wang Xiang-Zhai, the guy that founded Yiquan. Mr. Chan said, "Go check him out." He wanted me to go to him. He was like that. He wasn't insecure, you know? He knew what he was about.

So I ended up going to the class and meeting the guy, and there were about ten students in the room, and the first thing we did was stand. We stood for an hour. Now, that was not a problem for me because I had stood for up to two hours over the years. For the other people, though, the next week nobody showed up. I understood that. It's like taking somebody running and they've never ran before and you take them out for a five-mile run. We did that for a few weeks. We stood, we stood, we stood, and then about the fourth week he said, "I'm doing an experiment at Queens College. Would you help me?", and I said "Yes." He met me in the halls of the college. He took my hand, walked me down; he reminded me of Chan. He had a similar build and that steel wrapped in cotton kind of feel. He was trying to show how standing and Qigong was better for the T-cells than aerobic exercise. So, they hooked me up to one of those machines with like a scuba thing in my mouth and while I was doing that, he was running on a treadmill. The guy was about 80 at the time and his daughter would take my vitals and whatever. I'd go back and report everything to Chan. Chan loved it. He was like a little kid.

He had a position there. They gave him a lab, so he asked me to help him with the experiment. It was nice. He was very thankful for my doing it, and I shared it with Chan and his group.

Chan was like that throughout the time that I studied. Towards the end of my study with him, I was also doing martial arts with another teacher, and we went to China as a group for about 21 days. It was a great experience. I came back with videos of everything. I went with Chan's blessing. He was very happy that I was pursuing things because I brought them back to the group and then we talked about it and we shared it. There are a lot of ways to do things; it depends on the application......What's your intent? As long as the principles are there. That was always Chan's big thing: the principles. He said, "I love my teacher, but I love the principles more." So as long as you follow the principles, you know, twigs on the tree. As long as the trunk is stable, it grows out, but the twigs can be different. Anyway, the sharing was part of our practice.

We used to hang out on his roof, or in his apartment, or we'd rent space, and we'd go out to eat. It was a great time. I remember he was like a father to me. My dad was killed when I was six months old. He was killed in the War, so I never had a male figure in my life. For me, it was Chan. He changed my life. I wouldn't be where I am today if it wasn't for him. I can bet my last dollar on that.

RAL: You mentioned that Mr. Chan was humble. Can you give any examples of that? Anything come to mind?

When he taught people, he would always talk based on their strengths. You know, if you were a carpenter, he would talk in carpentry terms. If you were a doctor, he would talk in doctor terms, medical terms. He would try to communicate so it had meaning to you as an individual. I don't know if that has anything to do with him being humble, but I can give another example. There was a time when he went to T.T. Liang, who was in town, and he visited him. He asked T. T. Liang to watch his form and give him form improvement.

Mr. Chan had been a martial artist for many, many, many years and I thought that was a really humble thing to do. He never said anything about it, but I know that some teachers gave respect to him. Yang, Jwing Ming, when he first started, when he came over here, paid his respects to Chan. I believe Adam Hsu also showed up once and paid his respects to Chan, because they had the same teacher, Grandmaster Liu Yun Qiao Chow. I know that Chan did study with Grandmaster Liu but he wasn't a student like Adam Hsu was. Adam Hsu was more like one of his disciples.

Chan had studied with a lot of people, because he had connections through his father.

I think his first teacher was Sigung Tan Kiong Beng, commonly known as Tai Peng, who was from Fukien, Fukien Province. Tai Peng, I think, very famous. Chan's father, from what I understand, had business connections, so he'd give a letter so that Chan could study; he ended up with a lot of interesting teachers. I know he was with the Tung family for a while. I'm not sure if it was Tung Hu Ling or Tung Yin Chieh. He picked up a lot of things from a lot of people. He was very skilled, and he had a very sharp mind.

I'll give you another for instance. I was looking at his moccasins that he had on, and he had them laced upside-down, so the bow was at the bottom. I asked, "Why do you do that?" He says, "You have to keep tying your lace when it opens. I don't have to keep tying it cause it all goes down to the bottom." It seems like something you should know innately, but he just had that kind of a mind. He said, "I'm always cooking my mind, always cooking my mind."

"Always have three answers." He said that if you're going to talk to people, always have three answers. That was one of his sayings.

RAL: Did you know his children?

Yes, his daughters. He had a daughter who was in the insurance business, another daughter may have been married to a doctor. There were some birthday parties and things like that. He used to invite us up to his apartment. His wife would cook, and he would invite people at different times. He'd tell you, 'You come at 12," to somebody else he'd say, "Come at 1:30," to somebody else...... so he always had people coming and going. There were a lot of people there. Boy, his wife was a good cook, I tell you.

I remember one of his daughters passed. It was very sad. To lose a child, I felt very bad for him, and when his wife passed, I was also very sad. The Chinese way of looking at things is interesting. He said to me, "You guys, you court, you get married, you get divorced." He said, "We get married, then we court." Everyone had their own job. He didn't know her things, he'd say, "That's her job." She had her things that she was responsible for, he had things that he was responsible for. They lived down in Stuyvesant Town. He had a room, somebody else had a room, and then they used the kitchen and living room as common ground, but they all had their own space. He said to us, "You all pay separate rents, you're crazy."

When he passed, it was very traumatic for me, as I'm sure it was for other students. We lost somebody very close, and then everybody just went their own way.

When Chan told me that I could teach and use his name, I was very honored, because I knew people who came to class just to quickly learn something. He sometimes would end the class because he didn't want these people to get the last moves because he knew where they were coming from. They only wanted to use his name. "Do you want to study with me? Or you want to know my teachers?"

Here's another saying that I always liked. He said that some of the best teachers are "behind the trees."

RAL: Some of the best teachers......., oh, like, like you can't see the forest? What do you think he meant by that?

In other words, you can't see them, but they're there. I don't think you should put this in the book, but he often said some of Yang Chengfu's classmates were more skilled than him.

RAL: Better than Yang Chengfu?

Yes, Yang Chengfu was the head and he pushed the style with the population, but supposedly some of his classmates were better. Chan said that to me, but you don't want to ruffle feathers. Everybody is crazy. Lineage, lineage, this, that, whatever. A little bit of information and everybody thinks they're a Master.

RAL: Rich, I had heard, maybe from one or two students, and I didn't get really deeply into this with them, I had heard that Mr. Chan did some work at hospitals. Did you know of any of that, or did you hear of anything like that?

I can't really say one way or the other. I wouldn't be surprised. You're talking volunteer work?

RAL: Yes.

I wouldn't be surprised. You know, he was a Buddhist as part of his total spiritual outlook. His wife was Filipino, so she was Catholic. I wouldn't be surprised if he didn't do that.

He originally was working in a shoe store. He stocked things. That was his job before he retired.

RAL: Was that Paragon Sporting Goods?

Could be, yes, that sounds familiar. Yeah, Paragon.

He used to always tell me that when they ask how long a job will take, he says, always tell them longer; then you get done and finished earlier. Smart, smart.

RAL: Tell me a little bit more about the Tai Chi Farm, and your experiences there.

I originally went up there when he was just starting to do the Friendly Area and the Dragon Gate, the places where Master Jou had said he could do whatever he wanted. He was happy as a pig in shit, you know, because he had the chance to go up there. Initially, Chan could have a certain number of guests, so I was a guest.

We used to go up there and meet Chan and then we'd wander around. I'd catch Dr. Biff Painter, John Painter, we called him Dr. Biff, and he was quite a character, but very skilled, I enjoyed his workshops. Kenny Cohen was up there, and I went to a couple of his workshops as an observer, along with Chan. It was just a wonderful place. I went up there maybe two or three years as Chan's guest. Eventually, he had so many students that we kind of decided we would go up on our own.

RAL: I've seen slightly different versions of Bagua that Mr. Chan taught. Can you tell me anything about that?

Chan taught differently to different people. I found this out when another student and I did the San Shou. He had a couple of moves that were different than what I had learned with Chan. Well, that's what he taught me, and I go, wow, that's interesting, you know? I don't even know how to explain it. It's just the way it is. I guess it shows there are just a lot of ways to do things. I was like a sponge, taking it all in. It was wonderful. It was wonderful.

RAL: Tell me a little bit about Mr. Chan's teaching style.

He liked to talk, he liked questions, especially when we were in a small group. He liked a small group. The thing that I noticed over the years was every time I went back to the class setting, they were pretty much doing the same thing, but those of us that were meeting privately with him were doing different things and more advanced things. But he always made it accessible to what the person's strength was. As I mentioned before, that was his big thing.

He had a little bit of humor he would throw in. He'd block you and then he'd tickle you under your chin and say, "Coochie Coochie Coo."

His way of getting you to relax was to use the word calm. He always liked to use the word "calm." He didn't like to use the word relax. "Relax" is too tense. So, we would think, "I'm calm. I'm calm. I'm very calm. Very, very calm." He had another one that I always liked. He would say "ha ha ha, ha ha ha," and you would have to laugh; it was infectious, you know, "ha ha ha." He had a very unique style. He wasn't a drill sergeant. I've done karate classes; it wasn't like that. It was nice and you learn things and you talk about things, and you tore it apart and you analyzed it and you learned why it was so. I think that that was his skill……. communicating, answering questions.

RAL: Rich, if there's one thing that you could put your finger on, that has stayed with you for the remainder of your life that came from his relationship with you or your relationship with him, what would that be?

To share, to be a good person, treat people with respect, understand karma. He was really important in my overall development, not just martial arts, but my development as a human being. I think that's the big thing.

Richard Raab at the Tai Chi Farm
Photo Courtesy of Richard Raab

"Empty Your Coconut"
—Cooper

Mr. Chan once said this to me and Jan (Lang), because Mr. Chan recognized he was in America and you don't bow to one teacher and have that teacher as your only teacher until they pass you on or until they get passed on, and you find somebody new. Mr. Chan said the most important thing to do if you meet another teacher is to "empty your coconut." That was exactly what he said: "You just have to empty your coconut." He said just empty your coconut, learn what you can from them, and then if it works, it's all going to be the same thing.

If you stay with them and open up to what they say and it doesn't conflict at all, it becomes part of you. You just add that to your thing. But then you always have to get the coconut fully and completely empty and never go to somebody and say, oh, but somebody else did this or that. You just make like you're there; you're taking their knowledge and then it's up to you to combine the two. That's the most important thing, because I've seen so many people come into classes, and immediately, because they know something already, tell the teacher, "I know this already," and it's really the wrong way to go about it.

To me, it was one of the most important things he said because he was showing you don't have to study only with me.

RAL: Did Bruce Frantzis have any kind of a relationship with Mr. Chan? Or was it just like two ships passing in the night, you know, they'd say "Hi" to each other maybe, but nothing more?

We introduced him to Bruce Frantzis. They never really became really friendly, but Mr. Chan never had any problem when Bruce came back and we took a couple seminars with him.

But no, he didn't really know Mr. Chan.

But yeah, so just empty the coconut. Next time you talk to anybody, do anything, just remember Mr. Chan, empty the coconut. Just let it in without the filter of saying somebody else said this or that. Don't worry about what your last teacher said right now, just listen to what this guy is saying. After you've done it, you'll be able to put it all together.

"...he was getting into all kinds of trouble, so his parents sent him to the Temple."
—Anonymous

I remember once I went up to be with Chan. I used to see him all the time. I knock on the door. No answer. I knock on the door again. No answer. I knock on the door again. No answer. Finally, he opens the door. He says, "You come back next week."

RAL: You had an appointment; it was scheduled with him, and he told you to come back?
Oh sure. He said, "You come back next week."

So, the following week I go back, knock on the door, no answer. But this time I wised up. See, you don't mind if you learn. I sat out there for close to an hour. Then he opened the door and said, "You come in."

RAL: What do you think that he was trying to tell you by that?
He was trying to tell me to have some patience, is what he's trying to tell me. Patience.

So that was one thing. There are so many things. I took him to the Intrepid (Intrepid Sea, Air & Space Museum, NYC) once.

RAL: Did he ask you to take him there or did you say...
We just decided to go.

RAL: Anything interesting about that visit that you remember?
He said "Oh, look at the planes. Look at this. Look at that." That was an old ship I was on.

RAL: You were on the Intrepid?

Yeah. When it was sailing. So, it was an interesting experience.

RAL: Yes, because you were in the Navy.

Yeah.

I used to go to his house and he would talk and talk, but I absorbed it.

RAL: What kind of things would he talk about?

Everything. Principles. I just absorbed and he would repeat the same thing sometimes, but each time it was different.

So, I used to go up on the roof, like you said. One day, he says, "Okay, we're going up on the roof. It was in the middle of February, it was winter. It was cold, nasty. I went to put my coat on. He said, "No, you leave the coat here." My God, I'm going to freeze. We go up, and you can believe this or not, but it was like a bubble came around us, came over me.

RAL: You were standing.

I was standing and I was warm. I was in a t-shirt and there was snow all around us, enveloped us. I remember that. I don't know what he showed other people. Once another student and I were standing (indicates about 8 feet apart), you know, roughly there in that distance. He just went like this (indicates a raised hand) and he almost knocked me over. Luckily, I had been studying with him for a lot of years so I could feel it. It almost got me but knocked the other student over. I don't know if he ever showed it to other people. I don't know.

I'd been reading about Pa Kua. It just grabbed me. It's just something about that art. Nobody was teaching it. One day I'm walking down 23rd Street, and I saw him in a window. There were a few students. I forgot about it. Maybe a year later or so, I went to study with Cecil Chu. I heard about Chan teaching upstairs and Cecil lost about 15 full-paying, full-time, dedicated people because we saw what Chan offered. Everybody went. Damn.

RAL: So, you didn't originally go to William C.C. Chen's school and go to Mr. Chan and transition to Mr. Chan, you were at CK Chu. Was Mr. Chan teaching at CK Chu's school at the time?

Yeah. Yeah. He taught at Williams' and he taught at CK Chu's. So, when I went up, I had to knock on the door and ask permission to observe the class. See, then it was very traditional. I think I told you for six months I just walked in a circle.

At first, I was a typical American. You know, when am I going to get the next move? When are we going to move? And he'd make... he'd make faces at me. I went off and I said to myself, you have to respect the teacher. I said to myself, do you really want to learn with this guy, or not? This is me. I really thought about it and I said to myself just shut your mouth, basically, and just do what he says. For about six months I walked in a circle. That's all I did, walk, turn, walk, walk....... Somewhere in that time period, a bond, something, it was just a bond, something developed between the two of us. I'd catch him watching me, you know, he wouldn't say anything, but he'd look. Every rare once in a while he'd come and correct something. See, you have to understand the Chinese way. I had to show him that I was worthy of this art, and that's what I did. I learned a lot from that. Just listen, and do, and when I was ready, he'd give me another thing. So that was interesting. That I won't forget. That was at Cecil's. And then Cecil threw us all out, and we went over to William.

RAL: You were in his classes, I guess, on 23rd Street?

Yeah, we were all over 23rd Street. William would move here, he'd move here, the rent would be raised, he'd move here.

RAL: The episode where you knocked on Mr. Chan's door and he told you to come back next week, where was that? Was he living in Manhattan at the time?

He lived on 14th. That's where. 14th, the Stuyvesant House. As a matter of fact, he told me, he says, you know, get your name on the list. His daughter ran it.

RAL: Stuyvesant House?

Yeah, his daughter worked for the insurance company. He said, get your name on the list and six months you'll be in.

RAL: Well, you didn't do that though.

Unfortunately, and I do mean unfortunately, I was moving upstate. I had to make a choice. I moved upstate, but every weekend I was in the city.

RAL: The reason that you initially went to him was because you were studying with C.K. Chu and you found out that he was teaching there. You asked for permission to watch the class, I guess, and that was a course you took to leave Chu and go to Mr. Chan.

Yeah. Well, I studied with Cecil about four years, three years, something like that.

RAL: Were you at CK Chu's place when Robert Smith came to visit?

I don't remember that, but I did meet a lot of the older people. I remember I was doing Xing-Yi. See, I used to come up an hour early, hour and a half early. Mr. Chan would say come up, and he'd lock the door, so it was just me and him. We'd work out for an hour and a half. One day I'm working out and there's Dr. Tao. I've met all these old people, that's what's good.

Well, anyway, he was pretty well-known. There's Dr. Tao. See, there was a balcony kind of within the school. He used to live up there for a while.

RAL: Dr. Tao?

Dr. Tao. This guy must have been in his 70s, 80s, and he's following us doing the Xing -Yi. So that was fun.

RAL: Were you ever up at the Tai Chi Farm with him?

Yeah, I was the original guy up there. Sure. I have old pictures of him standing (Shows me some pictures.) Yeah, I was up there. I haven't looked at these in a long time.

RAL: Tell me..., I had heard from other students that Master Jou basically said to Mr. Chan, here's an area, develop the area, do what you want in this area. Mr. Chan enlisted the help of the students to clear the area; there was something called a Pa Kua Garden there.

Yeah, I built it. I'm the one that cleaned it out. That's not bragging or anything. I mean it just was.

RAL: Can you tell me a little about that? About how Mr. Chan enlisted his students?

It was a small group of students. Small group. Mr. Chan went up there one day, he knew Master Jou, and he was walking and Jou said, pick any spot you want. Chan picked where the Pa Kua Gardens are. However, the damn thing was equal to the road with junk; I mean glass and metal and you name it and bushes all over the place. I think it took us two, three years to clean it out. People don't know that. That's when we originally went up there. Then we built the Pa Kua Gardens.

RAL: What exactly were the Pa Kua Gardens?

It was an area with the Nine Palaces and basically that was it. A few other things.

RAL: It's my understanding that Mr. Chan had a cabin there?

Yeah, he built a cabin. He had them build a cabin. That was later.

RAL: One time you told me something about Mr. Chan and levitation. Could you tell me a little more about that?

He told me a story, and I believe him from things I've seen that people can do. He said he looked into a cave once- you know I'm trying to remember. It was in China; he saw this monk levitating.

RAL: Did he talk much about his background to you, about his childhood?

A little bit. He told me he started studying in the Shaolin Temple at ten years old. The reason was, he was getting into all kinds of trouble, so his parents sent him to the Temple.

Chan is one of the few people that taught pure martial arts. He came from the Shaolin Temple, so the discipline. Today it's sloppy.

RAL: It's all performance art now.

Yeah, that's what you're seeing. And they're fooling other people into performance art. For example, at Williams', they put on gloves to do self-defense, because it's been so diluted that you can't go from their form to self-defense, so they put on gloves.

Have you ever been in a Shaolin temple, in a Buddhist Temple? You have to walk past those statues. They're really nasty looking. I mean, those statues are looking into your soul. Those statues were made to be scary. I mean, they scared the hell out of you. I remember him telling me he'd go to the Shaolin Temple, he'd close his eyes so he couldn't see the statues and run down there through them. His family was a martial art family. All the Chans are related in Fujian Province. It's one family. His uncle, Tai Ping, I think that was his name, gave Chan a letter, and Chan studied with the greatest living martial artists of the time. He studied with Tung Ying-Chieh in Macau. He studied with other people, other places. He had a real good background. Then, he went to the Philippines.

RAL: Why did he go to the Philippines?

Because of the war. He was in Macau. He used to tell me stories about how they'd go over the border and they'd do sword fights. Real sword fights.

RAL: In Macau?

Yeah. Macau was like a little enclave which was neutral. They used to go out and challenge the Japanese. I mean, these were rough times. I remember he told me once how he taught in the Philippines, to both the Communists and the regular guys, and he'd run to this one and that one, and he'd run between, totally neutral.

RAL: He taught martial arts to both sides?

Yeah. Yeah, in the Philippines. From the Philippines, he came over here, and he met William somehow when he was over here. Matter of fact, he went in and saw the class. That's what happened. He's just curious. So he watched William's. William said, "Why don't you come and teach a class?"

So he taught. Then he went back to the Philippines. Six months later or a year later, you know, he came back here. William set him up in the Pa Kua class.

RAL: I didn't know that he went back to the Philippines for a period of time.

Yeah, and then he spent God knows how many 10 years, 12 years, bringing his family over one-by-one. I was very close to the family, also. A few of the senior students used to eat at his house. The family had to let the guests eat first. We'd look over and the kids would be like this, Hurry Up! Hurry Up! I'm hungry! He used to give us so much food. After a while, I couldn't eat anymore.

He was a good father to me. He had an interesting relationship with his wife. The splitting of responsibilities was real and clear-cut. I remember the first time I ate there and I went to pick up the dishes. "That's my job."

RAL: The wife said this to you?
Wife said that. "You sit, it's my job."
And it wasn't looked down upon. That's what the key was. She had her job to cook and the kids and the... and he had his job. As she emptied the dishes, he would sit there. It was an interesting relationship.
(Shows me some pictures)

RAL: I've never seen a picture of her (Mrs. Chan) before.
No. I'm the only one I think that has that picture. Mama.

RAL: Is that what everyone called her? Mama?
Sure. His wife was a doll. I have one of the few pictures of her hanging on the refrigerator. She died. And he was ready to.... he lost weight. He was ready to go. I remember I was up with him all night one night. That night, I'll never forget it.

RAL: The night that his wife passed away, or after that?
The night his wife passed away, A few nights later, I was begging him, don't go, Mr. Chan, we need you. Another ten years. Give me another ten years. He said, okay, I'll give you 10 years. And it was 10 years. 10 years to the day. So, yeah.
After Chan died, students asked me to take over the class, but I wasn't in the school then. I was just doing privates with him. I think David Saltman took over the class. I don't know how long that went on for.

RAL: There was a handout that he gave his students called "How to Do One Move."
"How to Prepare to Do One Move"

RAL: Do you remember what he wrote in that?

I haven't looked at it in a long time. I'd have to read it again. Basically, he was saying, learn to prepare a move. Don't just do these moves. In other words, include the martial aspect of it, which is what you do with somebody to see whether you're doing it right or not. See, that's what's missing from everybody. Because they don't have the form. I assume there's a few people around but... So, that's basically what he was saying.

RAL: When was the last time that you saw him?

At his deathbed. We used to eat a bowl of garlic and ginger. They had to put a curtain around him (because of the odor.) They couldn't get a nurse, or any nurses to deal with him. They had a nurse from the Philippines who would deal with him because she was a friend of the family or something. Other than that, he drove them crazy.

RAL: As a martial arts teacher yourself, what were some of the important lessons that you learned from him?

The attention to detail. People would let things go. He wouldn't, unless it was really correct. We would stay on one move for months sometimes until I got it correct - instead of this dancing in air crap. So that's the most important thing. The attention to detail, and if you pay attention to the details, you just dig deeper and deeper and deeper and deeper and it doesn't end. When you don't pay attention to the details, it's gone. There's nothing there.

I remember he was in the hospital, and I just walked in, and he just died at that... I can still picture him lying there. He had just died.

RAL: He died while you were there?

Just before I came in.

RAL: So, you were saying that he was a Taoist, he came, he studied, he taught, and then he left.
When he left, he left.

RAL: You also said that he didn't want his own school.
He didn't want it. Many people offered to fund him for a school. We did. He didn't want it. He didn't want the problems. He figured he'd 50-50, he'd study at Williams School, this school, that school, that's all.

RAL: What's his relationship like with William?
It was cordial. It was okay. I mean, he wouldn't say anything bad about him. Yeah. Just wouldn't do it.

Just about everybody studied with other people. After a while, they studied this and studied that. I just stayed with Chan. I figured, why go to this person to learn grappling or Chin-Na? Why go to that person to learn kicking, and this teacher for Tae-kwondo, to learn punching, when it was all there? Why go somewhere else?

RAL: Do you know where any of his children are these days?
Nah, nah.

I ran into his son. He had two sons. One's dead. I ran into the other son, just me and him, and we had a real nice conversation for over an hour.

RAL: What did you talk about?
Everything, but it's the way we talked. I haven't spoken to someone like that in this way in a long, long time. Reminded me of Chan.

"He Lived and Breathed It"
—Dr. Richard Chin

DISCUSSING BP CHAN'S BAGUA PUSH-HANDS....

Jeff told me he had to put his hands on BP's back, just like you described to me and he had to feel BP move, and that's how he understood how to move. He couldn't understand how to do the Bagua Push-Hands so BP had to put his hands on him and when he followed BP's move, he began to get it.

I know BP's personal side. Jeff actually worked with him very closely on the energetic side. He knows Cooper very well. Jeff knows all the guys. I mean all the ones that are close to BP, because he's worked with BP. I don't know them, because I didn't know BP's students.

RAL: Tell me about what you know about BP Chan and the Philippines.

Well, they owned businesses in the Philippines, different businesses. Family business. His father was very successful. Chan himself was not a businessman. So he left the business to his brother who took over the business. And you know, they're well to do, you know, middle class in the Philippines.

RAL: Is his brother still in the Philippines?

Yes. Most of his family is still in the Philippines. BP's wife came here, and then later all his children, his daughters and his son. One son he had naturally, and one son he adopted.

RAL: I didn't realize he had two sons.

You see? Yeah, that's a fact that I don't think anyone knows about. No, most people do not know anything about him. I don't think any of the students know anything about his personal life. Only me, because I was there all the time. There's no reason for him to talk about it unless you ask him. He's not going to tell you about it.

There's no reason. He didn't socialize. I guess that's what I'm trying to say. He really didn't socialize with his students other than the very few. He went out with them, had dinner with them, and he did classes with them. And when they were with him, basically they wanted to know about Tai Chi, the energy, so he just talked about that. They were not interested in his family. Neither was I, I just happened to be there.

RAL: I asked William Chen's wife if Mr. Chan and William did anything socially together, and her answer to me was no.

Different, again I know William very well. So, different. William and I were very close when we were both single. And then when we married, we went separate ways because of family things, totally different things.

BP had friends, but not "hanging out" friends. He had me and very few friends, so that's the truth. They don't know much about his personality. Here's another reason. Now we get into the Chinese. William is Taiwanese. BP is Fukienese and I'm Cantonese.

But we got along very well because our brotherhood is the martial arts. Also, BP and I were very close because he liked the way I taught. My school was very classy. Just the old stuff. He felt right at home when he came to me. So we can talk like that. At that time, that's what it was.

So, he was here taking care of his grandchildren, basically. He was staying here, he was staying there.

So I would be with him. All he did was take care of his grandkids and me. We would have lunch every day. He'd cook, we'd have lunch every day. That's how we got close to each other.

RAL: So you were at his place for lunch?

His place. He lived right here. He lived on 23rd Street. We

spent every day together. He had nothing to do, I had nothing to do. I taught at night and that was it.

And he taught at night, but in the afternoon, it was the grandkids and me.

RAL: I think I located one of his grandchildren. And I sent her an email, never heard back, probably won't. Do you know where his children are?

No, not at all. When he passed, we sort of lost touch. It was just natural. I knew his son fairly well because when I lived in the Philippines, his family was all there. So when I lived with him in the Philippines, I got to know the family. But then when they all came here, the glue was BP. When BP passed, there was no reason... We didn't have the same interests at all.

About his oldest daughter, that's an interesting thing. His oldest daughter, we knew, because she and my mother and BP's wife were close. They hung around together. They called each other. They were close. Then everybody disappeared. I don't know the grandchildren. I knew them as babies. As an adult, I don't have any idea. I've lost complete touch with them. You know where they are? Jeff would know. because Jeff took care of the family. He would know where to find them. But they probably don't want to talk about it.

Jeff's the only one that I would know would do anything for them. So, when there was a problem with anything like Con Ed or something, Jeff would take care of it.

BP didn't know the system, didn't speak the language. Jeff would call and straighten out the bills and things like that. Because of that, we got to know the family, because he would straighten out any problem. Their daughter, Anita, I think that's her name. They worked in American corporations, I give you that, they worked corporate. They were very Americanized themselves. None of them did martial arts. None of them at all. The son wasn't interested.

The son wasn't interested and that's very common. Very common. Children don't want to do what the parents do. I don't want to do what my father did. Like William's son. I mean I know many of my master's children. None of them did what he did. The opposite. They hated it.

RAL: I have heard that his outlook changed rather dramatically or drastically after his wife passed away in 1992 and after his daughter passed away - there was a change in him.

Yeah. Yeah. Normal. You know what I mean. A normal change of anybody losing family. Let's put it this way, I didn't see a drastic change.

To me it wasn't drastic. To me it was kind of normal evolution. A loss...... Anybody who loses family... other than that, I thought he was good.

I enjoyed his type. He was very Taoist in his outlook, but he's Catholic.

RAL: I heard he had two different funerals. He had a Buddhist funeral and a... I guess a regular funeral.

That's very Chinese. We don't take a chance.

RAL: Did you know that Mr. Chan taught internationally? Do you know anything about his international travels or teaching?

As far as I knew, he didn't. Do you know about that? I mean, tell me about it.

RAL: My research has shown that he did workshops in the Netherlands.

Oh, I did not know that. He probably went because of William. William did workshops internationally.

My time with him was from the late 70's into the 80's. The whole time from 1976 to 1980, I was here with him, and after that I was in the Philippines.

Jeff was here with him the whole time. When I introduced them together around the 70's, they stayed together until he passed.

When BP was here, he wanted his wife to come over. That's the other reason he came to us. I sponsored him and William sponsored him, but that's a no go. They needed somebody in the business community as a sponsor, not martial arts. So he came to me and asked if my father would bring his family over. I asked my father, he said "Yes, absolutely." So my father was very instrumental in bringing BP's whole family over. That began the family relationship we had. My family, his family.

RAL: Were any of Mr. Chan's students at that time involved in helping to bring him over?

No. I think he kept it separate. They didn't know him. He kept it separate. Well, good reason, because he didn't know them.

RAL: For every student of Mr. Chan's that I've spoken to, I get a lead for an additional one or two people to talk to about the book. It's been really nice. Everybody's open except for the family.

No, they're private. Depending on what the aim of your book is, I don't know how much they know about his martial art background. His martial art life was very different from his family life. I'm the same way, it's business. There's family and there's business. If you're not into the arts, there's no reason to talk about it. And they were not into it.

RAL: On the dilution of martial arts in modern China....

In mainland China, there are no martial arts. It's Wushu government program. They're not martial arts. Classic martial arts are outside of China, because the masters left after 1949. For many years, none of this was allowed on the ground in China - it was non-existent. And then around the '80's it started to come again. And that's when we have the Wushu and all that, which is more gymnastics.

But classic martial arts are forbidden because of rebels and all that so there are no martial arts per se in mainland China. All the classic martial artists like BP and the top guys left China. BP's lineage, our lineage is from the original source. Everything you see in Chen style now is from the modern series. It's called the Peking form, or the Beijing style.

Around the 1920's, the master is Chen Fa Ke. He went to Beijing and was invited to teach Tai Chi. When he went to Beijing, they would say, Chen Fa Ke is coming to demonstrate because we have Tai Chi here. They call it the Chair incident. This is what happens.

He says, "I'm going to demonstrate a deeper Tai Chi. And then he demonstrates push-hands with a student and throws him across the room into a chair he had placed there, because he didn't want the student to get hurt. So, after seeing this demonstration, they started studying with him. He took Tai Chi's traditional five forms and combined the forms in his own way over many years. That's why it's called the Chen Fa Ke lineage.

RAL: Now when you talk about the five Tai Chi forms, you're talking about Wu, Chen, Yang, etc?

No, no, no, no.

Five Katas. Long form, short form, fast form.

He combined them. Here's the difference. The classic form that you consider the Yang style, see that's the solo form. We call that the old form, the original old form. And then you have the fast one, the jing, and he combined it. In classic style we never combined it. We had five separate forms. Now, when you see the original form, the slow form, everybody thinks that's Yang. No, that's the original Chen style.

The Yang came about from the original Chen style. So here's your two lineages. You have the Peking lineage, which you see today, and Mr. Chan's and our core is from the old lineage. We didn't change it. We didn't change it because of the masters. Our teachers didn't change it.

With BP, because we were colleagues. I didn't teach him any-thing, he taught me. That's what made him a teacher about life, about how to deal with Americans. In the fast form, I'm going to give you some principles here. The fast form itself in Tai Chi is exactly the same as the White Eyebrow form and when you get internalized deeper you see the Bagua because they're all the same, and you should be able to interchange them. So we have Bagua in our form and each style has it.

RAL: Bagua in Pak Mei?

In Pak Mei we have the Bagua, but it's in Advanced Form. We call it the Bagua Walk. So, what a lot of the teachers do is take what they want from a different style and put it in their own style. Which is normal, it's what you do. Every sport does this. So, it's knowing what to take, what to do, and how you yourself can enhance it. In the most advanced stage, we all end up doing Tai Chi. No matter what style, we all end up doing Tai Chi. Why? Because it's the flow. Tai Chi really is the flow. Everybody looks for center. Xing-Yi goes to the center. Bagua walks around the center. Tai Chi is the center.

So, now going back to BP. BP knew all this. He studied many styles of Xing-Yi, many styles of Bagua, many styles of Tai Chi because as he said, it's his hobby, it's his life, that's what he want-ed to do, besides all the Kung Fu styles. So he had a sense of humor, but you have to get close to him to understand. And also because we knew him. We went into his mystical stuff. We knew the day-to-day BP.

RAL: It was my understanding they were in the Philippines during the Japanese occupation during World War II?

I don't think so. My understanding is they left China like we all did in 1949, not during the Japanese occupation. They moved to Taiwan. They may have been in Taiwan during the Japanese occupation. Not Philippines.

I'll have to double check that myself. I'm going to check with Jeff on that. Let me think about that real quick.

Let's see. Hmm. No, it wasn't the Japanese occupation. Now, there's two different things here. Family is one thing, BP himself is another. I'll get to that. I think of his age. My parents were there during the invasion, during the war in Japan. Not the occupation, but during the war.

RAL: In Taiwan?

In China. I don't think he was born yet.

RAL: He was born in 22.

He was born in 22. 22 then? Mm-hmm. Let me check that. I'll tell you why.

How old was he when he died?

RAL: 80. He died in 2002.

It's possible because that's the same as my father. That's what I'm thinking. I'm thinking my father is older than him. My father died in 2007. He was like 85/87. So we were very close in age. Send me what you know, I'll double check it. I don't think he was in the Philippines. Taiwan is another story.

I think it's more Taiwan. You know, you're getting me to think now. Because, because... the Grandmaster is from Taiwan. Not from the Philippines. The Grandmaster of his style is from Taiwan. So we're talking about his original styles - Five Animal Ancestor and Fukien Shaolin. They're very famous in that Taiwan region. And they all emigrated to the Philippines. I never even thought about this, till you brought it up, because I didn't bother to ask him about this.

Send me what you know. I can trace it back to the master. If I have the master's name, I can trace it back. It's a question of timing. Because I know the guys from Taijo, the Shaolin system, Fukien system.

And BP was capable of teaching. His hobby. He loved it. He lived and breathed it. That's all he did. That's not all he did, but you know what I'm saying. That was his passion. I think that's why we got along so well. We're kindred spirits. We'd have lunch every day. All we'd do is talk about the different martial arts. and I did this, and that, and that. So, it was great. We fitted each other at that time.

You know what I mean? Somebody to talk to, that's what I'm trying to say. So, that's what I'm trying to get at. Kindred spirit. So, what happened was he couldn't get as close to them because he and they couldn't talk this way. They were his students. You know what I mean? There was no exchange. BP and I were having this exchange.

RAL: He didn't consider himself to be a grandmaster or a master.

Not at all. Not at all.

RAL: He considered himself to be a student, also. See that's the dichotomy there, that's interesting.

In the Chinese system, he's not considered a grandmaster, because he's junior. Remember we have a hierarchy, he's junior to the masters.

RAL: Who determines who is master level and grandmaster level? Is it the consensus of your peers?

Your peers. Definitely your peers. It's also family. We know who the oldest son is. We know who the youngest son is. It starts with that. And then we know who your uncle is, and so forth like that. So let's say your uncle is a grandmaster, so you're not the master but your uncle is the grandmaster. Then we know that his sons know nothing, because the master teaches nothing! But you may learn something. A perfect example, the Shuai Jiao, we're talking Taiwan now, because a lot of his training came out of Taiwan. Taiwan is like the hub of Tai Chi in Asia. It's Taiwan. Yang, everybody comes out of Taiwan. Two of them, Cheng Man Ching himself, Taiwan, Tai Chi and Shuai Jiao Grandmaster. So, grandmaster died. Find out who's the next master.

So we did an article one year. We went there under Inside Kung Fu Magazine. Our job was to find out who the lineage holder was. So we go there, we interview all the masters, and one of the hosts is his son. And all the seniors say, "Son knows nothing." Son is next in line, right? Nothing!

I knew the son; we were all together. I said, do you do Tai Chi? He said, damn, I hate it. Father makes me do everything. So, you know he's no good. You just know, I mean he hates it. At least he's honest about it. But none of these guys were going to be the master of anything.

So you ask me, how do I know? Well, that's an example. Who's the grandmaster of the Shuai Jiao? They told me exactly who it was. Among their consensus, one guy, he was the favorite student of master so and so, and master said he's the next master. There were plenty of other masters around. But that particular guy was designated as the lineage. So, then we get into the real world, it's also politics. So that's how you determine who's this and that.

But getting back to the old days, we know who's good because we can see who plays well, we can tell you. Let's talk about Tai Chi, Chen Tai Chi. We have the President now of this famous world tour. He's not considered the best among his peers. There are other masters that I've heard from other people that are much better than him, as an example. So, we know. How do we know? Like you're asking me, you would ask me, you would ask ten other people then you figure out, okay, seven out of ten say this guy is good. That's how you know, because you can't even use the writing system anymore. It's all political.

And the whole thing is, who's legitimate? By who you know. BP is not ranked in anything. But he's legitimate, you know what

I mean? You can't find him, you're not gonna find him in anything. You're not gonna find certificates on him because they didn't exist, OK? We didn't do that, OK? How do you know who he is? By talking to people.

Now, another story. BP, when he was teaching at my studio, this is more BP now, and what you were asking me. So he could teach anything he wanted at my studio. I didn't care. I said, you're not conflicting with anything. Whatever you want to teach is fine. Because first of all, I trusted him. He's from the old side. He was honest and cool, very straight, no games. So I had some visitors from other styles come in, from White Eyebrow and all that stuff. They'd drag themselves in, they'd look, and they'd go, hmm, it's all the same. And the teacher says, it's all the same.

And BP said, most people can't see that. Most people don't realize it's all the same. They'll see Bagua, they'll see Xing-Yi, don't realize it's all the same. At the core, you know what you're looking at. It's all the same. It is the principle. BP always said, every master will tell you, it's the principle.

This is what BP is saying. Do you want my name or the principle? Did you hear that? His famous quote. And you know that BP says you got to learn my principle. And very few people did. Most of them took his name. 90% of people you're going to meet took his name.

If you were sitting here, BP would say, "I have nothing to teach you. It's just the principles." Showing the principle, the rest is up to you. So he's perfectly correct when he says that. But that's deep. Most of us cannot understand the principle. And I don't mean just not get it. It's got to get inside you.

Intellectually, I can say, this is the point. You've got to feel it. I use this analogy with wine and cognac. It's got to sit there. It's got to mature. If you rush it, it's just alcohol. If you want fine wine, fine wine, it's got to sit there. When I first started teaching, I told my students "No mystery. Forget about that. You only need 20 years." So I've taught for more than that, double that, and I realize it's going to take you 20 years. Because it's got to sit with you, it's got to sit in the damn keg, it's got to ferment. There's no injection. This is what I understand in my teaching now.

BP is different in this respect. BP, I would say, is one of the most popular teachers from the Philippines and here. Not the best. Not the highest. The most popular, because he talked to you.

RAL: Is he still known in the Philippines?

No. Gone. Gone. See, the old masters didn't talk. BP would sit here and talk to you for hours. Discreet. Masters didn't talk, but now I understand them.

My teacher taught me everything and waited 20 years before I learned and felt it and they knew that. No amount of talking would have gotten anywhere. I needed to ferment, I needed to sit in the damn keg.

11. FROM THE SKETCHBOOKS OF RON GEE

Ron Gee is an artist currently living in Warwick, NY, and was an attendee at BP Chan's workshops at the Tai Chi Farm in Warwick. Although BP Chan did not encourage pictures or video being taken of him, he did permit Ron to sketch him - contemporaneously - as he was moving and teaching - at the Tai Chi Farm Workshops Ron attended. I don't know of any other person who did this with Mr. Chan's blessing. These drawings were provided to me courtesy of Ron Gee.

Ron Gee: (Here are) "Five pages from my sketchbooks dating to the time we practiced with Mr. Chan 1999-2002. I picked several that I thought would be of special interest for their illustrational value and the particular postures that capture the essence of his teaching/sharing."

BP Chan

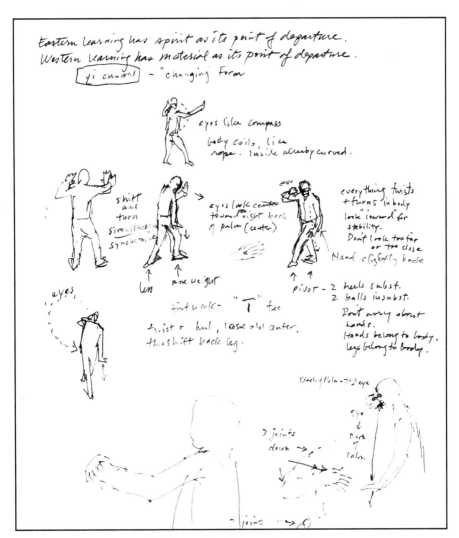

BP Chan - Tiger-Dragon Standing

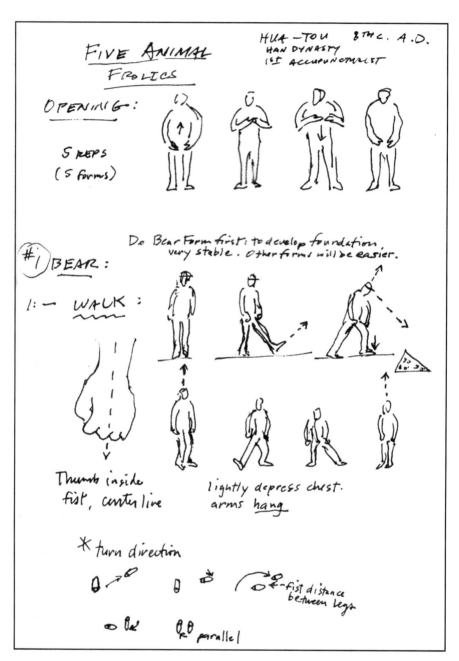

BP Chan – Bear Form

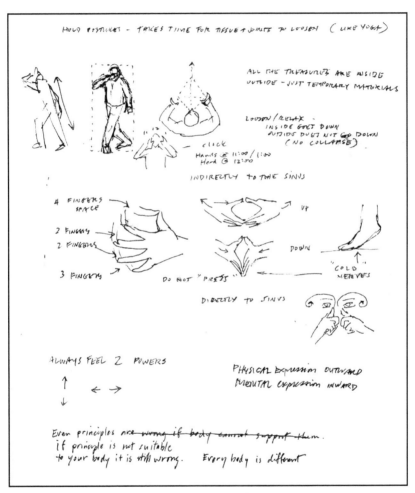

BP Chan – Postures and Sayings

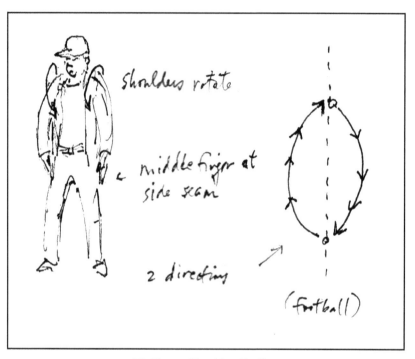

BP Chan – Shoulder Circling

12. BP CHAN – JUST FOR TODAY

BP Chan
11/94

JUST FOR TODAY

1. Just for today I will try to live through this day only, not to tackle my whole life problem at once. I can do things for 24 hours that would appall me if I had to keep them up for a lifetime.

2. Just for today I will be happy. This assumes that what Abraham Lincoln said is true, that "most folks are about as happy as they make up their minds to be." Happiness is from within; it is not a matter of externals.

3. Just for today I will try to adjust to what is, and not try to adjust everything to my own desires. I will take my family, my business, and my licks as they come and fit myself to them.

4. Just for today I will take care of my body, I will exercise it, care for it, nourish it, not abuse it nor neglect it, so that it will be a perfect machine for my bidding.

5. Just for today I will try to strengthen my mind. I will learn something useful. I will not be a mental loafer. I will read something that requires effort, thought and concentration.

6. Just for today I will exercise my soul in three ways: I will do somebody a good turn and not get found out; I will do at least two things I don't want to do, as William James sugest, just for exercise.

7. Just for today I will be agreeable: I will look as well as I can, dress as becomingly as possible, talk low, act courteously, be liberal with praise, criticize not at all, nor find fault with anything and not try to regulate or improve anyone except myself.

8. Just for today I will have a program. I will write down what I expect to do every hour. I may not follow it exactly, but I will have it. It will eliminate two pests -- hurry and indecision.

9. Just for today I will have a quiet half hour all by myself and relax. In this half hour sometime I will thank God, so as to get a little more perspective to my life.

10. Just for today I will be unafraid, specially I will not be afraid to be happy, to enjoy what is beautiful, to love, and to believe those I love, love me.

Provided Courtesy of Mark Jones

Sources say that the "Just for Today" meditations were penned by a man named Frank Crane of the Boston Globe in 1921. I don't know the circumstances under which BP Chan came to know of these meditations. I do think that there is much common ground between Mr. Chan's philosophy of life and this inspirational essay.

There's no need to reprint Frank Crane's original essay here, but take my word for it, Mr. Chan's handout is almost a word-for-word clone of Frank Crane's original essay.

Interestingly, the "Just for Today" meditations can be found in the Narcotics Anonymous and the Alcoholics Anonymous rehabilitation programs.

13. THE TAI CHI FARM

*"Master Chan and I were very good friends.
We spent many happy hours together at Tai Chi Farm."*
– John Painter, Grand Teacher of the Li Family System

Master Jou Tsung Hwa purchased an abandoned farm property in the small village of Warwick, NY, in 1984. Master Jou's vision was to promote the teaching and practice of Tai Chi. He established a Tai Chi school and a retreat there. To that end, the Farm attracted a wide group of students and a well-respected group of teachers.

Master Jou only taught Tai Chi; he did not encourage his students to study other martial arts. To his credit, though, he did allow other martial arts teachers to teach their specialties like Xing-Yi and Bagua at the Farm. BP Chan was one of those teachers.

Master Jou gave Mr. Chan an area for his teaching and instruction. Mr. Chan created the Bagua Garden, a space dedicated to Bagua. Mr. Chan used his students to help clear the area and build out the practice areas from the woods and debris there.

The Gathering of The Circle program held in 2010 after the Tai Chi Gala (the successor event to the Tai Chi Farm) lists some of the most respected Internal Arts teachers to be associated with the Farm and the Gala. BP Chan was one of them:

Through the decades, the event hosted a sampling of some of the biggest and brightest professionals in the Chinese Internal Arts, such as (listed in random order): Dr. John Painter, Dr. Yang

Jwing Ming, Master Wang Ren Gang, Master Tina Zhang, Master Wm. C.C. Chen, Sf. William C. Phillips, Master Henry Look, Master Jianye Jiang, Dr. Gary Torres, Master Ren Guangyi, Master Tchoung Ta Tchen, Sf. Pat Rice, Dr. Yang Yang, Master B.P. Chan, Master T. K. Shih, Master Fong Ha, Sf. Katy Cheng (daughter of Cheng Man Ching), Gene Ching of Kung Fu Tai Chi Magazine, Marvin Smalheiser of Tai Chi Magazine, Sf. Pedro Cepero-Yee and "Yee's Hung Ga" award-winning Lion Dance Troupe, and many, many more...

Loretta Wollering was the Operations Director of the 103-acre Tai Chi Farm from 1990 to 2000, where she produced and directed the annual Tai Chi convention "Zhang San Feng Festival."

LORETTA, ON MR. CHAN:

He was a very private guy. He was a very private fellow. He spent a lot of time on Tai Chi Farm, but he kind of spent it really in the woods, like in the back. His students helped him make a little cabin back there that was all his. He just used it. Nobody else used it. He wouldn't let anyone else in there. He was a very sort of private person in that regard. He just kind of kept to himself and his students. He was kind of quiet.

He was very friendly, you know, if somebody wanted to speak with him, he would love to show... Okay, one thing I do remember a lot of is that he would just love to show anything that they were working on. If he built a practice area with his students or different things inside of his little cabin that he built, he would just love to show them. I understood from Master Jou that Master Chan's family were Chinese in origin, but they lived in the Philippines, or they had emigrated there. They were furniture makers. So I think he had that sort of in his genes, that he liked to build, he liked to make things, you know? I remember he showed me that he made this little secret lock on the inside of his door. He was just so ecstatic to show me. You would poke some pin in this little hole. It was this secret little lock, a little latch. He was always very proud of little, just simple little things like that. In some ways, he was very simple. Little things like that just made him happy.

He loved to eat; he would cook things in a very old style. He would love it when sometimes Master Jou would give him some fatty pork, because that was a thing that he really liked to eat. Sometimes if Master Jou had extra cooked meat, he would give a portion of it to Mr. Chan, and he was just delighted to reheat it over his little fire.

He was very much like that. He had a lot of that very folksy old style Southern Chinese country way about him. He wasn't really a city person. I think people were very intrigued by that because it was just so different. It's a kind of culture that we really don't have much of here except maybe high up in Appalachia. If you would go to an herbalist or a wise man or a wise woman, they would sit you down and tell you about all these sorts of metaphysical things. They'd have their stew on the fire, and it was like that kind of feeling.

He had that very old style. He was like an uncle to his students. That's what I would say. It was like you have an old village somewhere and the wise old man would be "that's uncle so and so."

If my memory serves me correctly, Mr. Chan didn't like too many photos and things taken of him. I think that might be why I don't remember seeing or reading really about him. He was just very funny like that.

RAL: What was Master Jou and Mr. Chan's relationship like? Was it strictly professional, or did they do anything together socially?

No, it was more like neighbors. It was more like Master Jou just graciously opened his place up to Mr. Chan and he really never asked for anything. He opened it up and let Mr. Chan do his thing there. He wanted to just let him and his students be there. He let them have their privacy and he gave them their space.

The thing is, I don't think his kids had any interest in his martial arts. A lot of times what happens is when Chinese kids are in America, they may be embarrassed by their old-style culture, especially back then when it wasn't considered cool. Now it's good to be culturally aware; people enjoy that, but back then they really just wanted to bury that, and they were kind of embarrassed by it.

And I don't think any of his kids were dedicated to the martial stuff, the philosophy, and the culture. I think that's why he found that part of his family with his students. That's strongly, strongly the impression that I got.

14. THE TAI CHI FARM
IN PICTURES

"All these things were like adult toys."
-Marsha Nolan

The image above and all pictures on the next two pages
courtesy of Richard Raab

Photos Taken Circa 1993/94
Photos courtesy of Alan Stolowitz

15. IN THEIR OWN WORDS

BP Chan and Robert W. Smith
Do Push-Hands
—Rudy Curry

RAL: Do you find it hard to keep the styles that you've learned separate?

Oh, no, actually not. I used to practice them all individually, separately, so I learned how to keep them apart.

With Master Chan, the way he used to teach, he always asked you, "Why are you doing something a certain way?" I was very careful about not letting certain things creep in. I have met a few people who studied multiple systems but were not able to synthesize them effectively because they didn't know the actual differences in the styles and functions of the different forms, and how to make them work. When styles get mixed, things get lost in translation.

RAL: Again, that's the difference that a good teacher makes, you know, whether it's you or Master Chan.

I did know a lot of people who were studying with other teachers; sometimes I would end up getting them to go to Master Chan because when I was studying, I had certain advantages in some of the push hands classes. But I was progressing a little too fast. Anytime I'd have trouble, I would ask Mr. Chan, "What did I do wrong here?" And he would show me something. Sometimes it was just something simple that you should stop doing. It was his knowledge of the subtleties and techniques that made him so amazing.

One time I had a big guy in my neighborhood that was really a bruiser. I was good at breaking out of holds. He said, you won't get out of this full nelson if I put you in it, and so he did. Then I did the 3rd Bagua Palm "Take off your hat from behind your head." I could break everybody else's hold with it, but this guy ended up taking me to the ground and ended up hurting my neck. I went to Master Chan the following week. He asked me to show him what I did, and I actually shifted my weight the wrong way, so all his pressure went down on my spine instead of me twisting and breaking the force of his grip before I turned his head. I went back and did it the following week with that bruiser and the move worked. It broke his grip and twisted his head.

He taught at many locations. He taught at the Tai Chi Farm, Asian Martial Arts Studio, at Aaron Banks' school, and several other locations. He used to teach at C K Chu's school on Saturdays sometimes, which I had never known. I just knew him from studying at William CC Chen's school.

I did a little Tai Chi staff work with Master Chan, too. He had skills like the scenes in the Qing Dynasty movies - you know those scenes in the movies where one guy just takes down several guys with a sweeping move of the staff. In class, two of the other guys had staffs; I had a metal pipe because there were no more staffs left. Master Chan had only a broomstick and explained how to deflect. He told the three of us to lunge at him with our weapons. Come on, you crazy? He's only got a broomstick. We all lunged at his chest with the staffs and he took the broomstick and swept all three of our weapons down to the floor and came across and up with the broomstick and was like, wow, how'd you do that? He literally took all three of us over, it was a domino effect.

We were doing Tal Chi at that time. He was doing a demo of some of the moves. He taught many different classes periodically. One thing I still do in all my classes are the rocking and centering exercises that he taught me.

RAL: Do you have a practice routine that you do every day or every other day?

I do a few Qigong moves and things I learned from Sifu Gainey and Sam Chin along with Qigong from Master Chan and all of Master Chan's form practices. It's mostly body mechanics, sitting, and breath work. I also practice CK Chu's and William CC Chen's Tai Chi along with I Liq Chuan and occasional traditional Yang Form.

The Tai Chi form I do is mostly the one that I learned from Master Chan. The way he did the moves, it was more practical.

RAL: While you were studying with Master Chan, William Chen, and C K Chu, did you also have a full-time job?

Yes. At that time, I did, I was working day shifts. What happened in the later years was I had different jobs. I went through my little period in the streets, so I changed jobs. And then I ended up working night shifts mostly, so that's what interrupted my studies. When I had jobs where I was off on the weekends, I would get down as often as I could.

And then for a little while I learned the traditional Yang style Tai Chi from and Gim H. Won. He's a Korean guy. I studied with him for a while. I would come to class and show Master Chan that I learned this and that and so on. He would say, "So now you have more than one way to do the form." He would also correct some of my moves that I was learning from another Master named Chang who taught Fu Zhong Wen style, and he modified my I-Chuan that I learned from Y.P. Dong. Out of all the teachers, Master Chan could do applications in a seemingly effortless way and with incredible power, even for his small size. His efficiency was off the chain.

RAL: It's interesting that Master Chan was open to that because most martial arts teachers don't want you bringing technique or form that you've learned from elsewhere into their school.

Yeah, yeah. I would do stuff warming up and then he would just throw in some things and correct it, which actually helped me because I always apply something he taught me to everybody else's stuff. It made it work so much better. One of the main things he taught was keeping your elbows a certain distance from your body. He called that the "fist distance." He would say keep your elbow a fist's distance from your body.

Mr. Chan said that all your moves are measured by your bone structure. He said that if you want to know how far to keep your arm from the body, use the fist distance; this way, you're keeping your armpits open, and you can float and turn.

He used to say that we don't turn our hand, we turn the forearm.

RAL: You don't turn the hand; you turn the forearm?

You rotate everything. You rotate the forearm because the elbows are the center of the arms, the knees are the center of the legs, the hips are the center of the body. You rotate from the centers in every move. Then you've got both ends of power coming in and out. It will help you develop stable power and how to use the body to generate power all the way down to and from the foot.

He showed us another little trick, how to break holds and escape from grabs, also. He said that if you get grabbed at the wrist while your hand is closed, open the hand and rotate it. Their grip is not actually as hard as you think it is, and you rotate at specific angles against their bone depending on the grab and the direction of their force. Vice versa, if your hand is open when you get grabbed, close your hand and rotate towards their center. It takes them off balance and breaks their grip.

RAL: Right.

So now if I caught you when you're closed, you open the hand. If I caught you when your hand is open, you just do the opposite. – close the hand. That's how it makes the tendons pull and push.

Don't focus on the hand, focus on your elbow. Turn your elbow.

RAL: Fascinating. It's fascinating. Fascinating to me.

Yeah, because Mr. Chan said, the strength of the move comes from the previous section of the body. All the way back down to the foot. If you want something going on with the elbow, you have to use the shoulder, if you want something going on with the wrist, use the elbow, something going on with the fingers, use the wrist, etc.

There are many yin yang points along the body. If you want a move to work effectively, you must understand which parts are yielding and which parts are using force, in relation to your center of gravity and central axis; maintaining balance must come first. We call this the balance of power. In all moves, you have to have a foreword move directly to the opponent's center line, and angular movement that would deflect the opponent's incoming force. Your attack won't get deflected so easily and you can disrupt the opponent's balance point.

I'm in the process of writing some of this down because I was going to write a book called "The Teachings of My Teachers" where I quantify everything that they taught. A lot of the material is the same but looked at from different reference points.

Did you know Jan Lang?

RAL: No, but Frank (Allen) mentioned him a lot. Iron Man Lang?

He was one of my senior classmates along with Jim Russo and Paul Massone, too. I saw them back in the day.

At times, when I wanted to learn other things, Master Chan would ask, "What are you looking for?" I said "I just want to learn different things." He asked, "Don't you have enough?" I said "Never, I'm greedy, I want more."

Another small thing: Master Chan told us to use the eyes, lift the neck, and focus the way you aim your eyes. A lot of people look at their hand. He said that was incorrect. Your eyes must guide the hand. He said that is why people get beat up; they're following their hands. Guide and guard, yeah, that was a major principle.

RAL: What is your interpretation of that?

Well, it's similar to your eyes leading your hand where to go and seeing what's coming in so that you can deflect. The guiding and guarding at the same time mean that you must keep your defenses up at all times, meaning your guard would be projected out to the two 45-degree angles to your sides. You're also projecting straight ahead, because you're going straight, but you still have to be protected from the sides.

RAL: Right. So, would you say that what he meant by that was that the eyes are guiding the limbs or the hands to their destination?

Yes. Because one day we were doing the form and it looked like he was looking down. We were looking and asked him about that. He said "No, I'm looking past my hand."

In the books, it says eyes follow hands, which is an incorrect translation. He told us something about balance if you look inside. It disturbs your balance if you look inside. If your eyes are not in the right place, you won't be able to maintain your balance under pressure. When walking, people look down and that's why they stumble, so that's one of the first things I teach the seniors. You look ahead, not down, when you're walking. And if your head is hanging down, your momentum is going to bring you down.

RAL: And if you're looking down, it's going to pull you down.

Yeah, yeah. And then your mass is going to fall. I tell them they must learn to keep their head up and look forward. Relax your hips, so if you trip, just let the other leg swing and do what it's supposed to do. Catch it before you fall instead of using your hands on the ground to catch your fall.

Another point he taught me was there was no differentiation between grappling locks, strikes, or kicks in fighting, because it was all one. He taught us how to merge grappling locks, strikes, and kicks, because in fighting it is all one.

He used to always say the bones cross the bones and the joints cross the joints. So, whenever you were trying to do something, he said if you haven't trained your hands, don't try to grab because you won't have any control. He said you should intercept like the sword and then let your wrist slide back to catch the opponent's wrist - not try to grab the arm - and then the big will shrink onto the small. That's how you get to the joint to apply a good lock or do a twisting motion. The hand is actually a bunch of joints and tendons, so you would only use your hand against the joints. If you go for the bone, you will block or deflect and then go back to the hand. But he taught us how to spiral around the arms starting with the wrist. He also measured our stances by the size of our feet.

RAL: Have you been to BP Chan's grave?

I don't know where he's buried. I heard that at the burial site there was a problem. He was buried in a Catholic cemetery, and I had heard they didn't want to let the Buddhist monks in. Finally, the Buddhist monks were let in. I heard they did 90 minutes of chanting at his gravesite.

RAL: I had never heard that. He was a practicing Catholic, right?

He was both; he never showed his religious side in class, but he was very spiritual. One day I had an experience where my other martial arts teacher, Abu Khafra, who was into African and Egyptian religion deeply, came to Mr. Chan's class with me. He was carrying an Egyptian metal ankh that was one of their badges. One of the guys in the class walked up to Abu and asked him if he knew what that symbolized, but in an arrogant way. Abu just said, "It's an ankh. It's an African Egyptian symbol of life." He explained no more. After he left, I stayed for class and that same student asked me, "Was Abu from Africa?" Master Chan stepped in and said, "Why didn't you ask him while he was here, and why did you ask what he was carrying? Why would he be carrying something if he didn't know what it was?" Then he asked, "Can't somebody carry what they want?" He went on; it was a lecture. He said, "I don't know what is wrong with people. We all have to live together. Why do some people say, I'm this, I'm American, I'm that; some people are arrogant, they say I'm a world citizen. I am a citizen of the universe. We need to learn to live together. Next time, don't ask somebody else where he's from."

RAL: Mr. Chan was fluent in Spanish.

I think he spoke Spanish when he was in the Philippines, Tagalog Spanish.

I found out that his name, Bun Piac, meant great oak tree. I understand it was a symbol of respect when people were called BP in the Philippines. A good teacher would be referred to as an oak tree or great oak. He became Guillermo in Spanish. People would get mixed up with Chan and Chen. That's why they said he started calling himself Guillermo, the Spanish William. And then they took the "William" off and just said BP.

I have some pictures of Mr. Chan and Robert Smith and William C.C. Chen. Robert Smith came to William's school once and showed some of his old videos. Master Chan came. C K Chu was there. I took pictures of Master Chan, C K Chu and Robert, and then Master Chan, William and Robert.

RAL: I didn't know that Robert Smith knew Mr. Chan.

Yes, he did, but I guess Master Chan wouldn't allow him to write anything about him in his books. I was so surprised when Robert came. Robert and Master Chan did a couple of minutes of push-hands. Robert tried to do a little slip move and Master Chan froze him to the ground; Robert was unable to move and then he just backed up and started laughing. I was like, WOW. Robert showed us a lot of videos, some of Wang Shujin and many other Masters from his books. It was pretty nice seeing him.

Mr. Chan was an amazing guy. He taught us a lot. I went to Tompkins Square Park a few times when he was teaching there. They used to work out in the morning down there. One time it was crazy; this Kung Fu guy passed by. He just was feeling the energy. He walked past us and then he pulled out these butterfly knives and did a real mean butterfly knife routine for Mr. Chan. Everybody was thinking, "What if that guy comes over here?" Master Chan said, "He's just feeling the energy. He wants to show his kung fu." The guy just made a few moves and then moved his eyes away and kept going.

A discussion follows about the positioning of the upper hand and lower hand in the "Dragon Claw" walking posture, in some systems called the "Millstone Posture." Pictures of Mr. Chan in that posture show him with the thumb of his lower hand pointing in the vicinity of his navel, causing his lower palm to be centered. Other practitioners have their wrist in center or the middle of their forearm in center, causing themselves to be "crossed."

179

One day I asked Master Chan, "How come we don't do Bagua like everybody else?" He told me to think about it (crossing the lower palm beyond the center) and he told me it doesn't make sense. He said, "Think about it." I said, "What do you mean it doesn't make sense?" He said, "You've got this hand (the upper hand) way out here. How the hell is somebody supposed to be able to hit you? This hand (the lower hand) is the attack on him." He said, "You switch hands. That's the idea."

RAL: Also, with the lower hand to the left on the center line, you're crossing your center.

That's another one. Because he said you only cross when both cross, otherwise your back is locked, you're locking your spine when you cross.

And that's one of my big secrets in fighting. If the wrist bone crosses the midline, you're done. You either have to learn how to bend your knees quickly and then reset back to the center or move your hips and get that center line back. Otherwise, you have no strength coming from your back. I get my students with that all the time. When they cross their center, they don't realize they're off balance that way. That was one major thing I learned that you could take to the bank. I see a lot of fighters in general crossing their centerline.

On Saturdays and Sundays when I used to be with Master Chan, I would spend maybe five, six hours with him. I took the Tai Chi in the morning, the push hands sometimes, and then the Xing-Yi and Bagua.

I was studying Xing-Yi and Bagua with him and doing Tai Chi with other teachers before I started studying Master Chan's Tai Chi, learning his version of the Yang Tai Chi form, and also the Chen style with him.

Master Chan said the body is like a wrench and a bolt. You have to learn how to use the wrench and adjust it.

Mr. Chan would yell, "Just turn, just turn." Sometimes all it takes is a simple turn but turn in the right direction.

One day I felt good. I could feel the different sections of my body and I told him, "Hey, I understand the yin and yang now." And then he said, "Oh, how many?" "About 10 of them." He said," Oh, well, that's too bad. You have a long way to go. There are thousands in the body." I figured OK, forget about it.

RAL: How did Mr. Chan teach when to use the waist and when to use the hips?

They went together. He said they were connected. He pointed out that in the Chinese books, they say Yao Kua. When they say Yao Kua, the waist and the hip are actually together. The Kua itself is the inguinal crotch region, the lumbar and the waist; they are like an X and a spiral pattern. So when you turn your hip, the waist has to be turning. That's part of the reason why I say you have to move from your coccyx because once you turn your spine, all of those muscle groups in there have to move and then what you do with the feet is the feel of up, down, front, back, left, right.

The dynamics cause the muscles to actually intertwine. But it's all done to keep you in the center. Because if you coil incorrectly, you're just pulling your center over one leg, which means you still better fold and sit directly over the center of the thigh into the calf and bend over the foot at the correct angle. Otherwise, you're off. When you turn correctly, you would get the push and pull in both directions, so you can float your hip from side to side without locking. That's the key to the movement. When moving backwards, I always tell the students to move from their Ming Men, so when you move back, you're not just shifting your weight and flexing your leg muscles. Imagine the spine is going with you. When your mid back expands because your pelvis is doing this, that moves your whole center of gravity out of the way because the center of gravity is a fluid point. Depending on where you flex, even though the bones are solid the muscles are really fluid, you're shifting your center of gravity off your axis and you can't really be fully stable like that. When the core and the waist are moving correctly it will keep your center in the center no matter what move you do externally. If you stay centered, when you breathe in and pressurize and it presses your center gravity down into the dantian, you learn how to drop your center without having to physically bend your knees as much.

RAL: You were saying that after you had been doing Master Chan's styles for a while that as you got more and more into it, you said things would be "deepening."

Well, I just found that my balance and alignment was much better. I did things naturally that would just come out automatically, as opposed to trying or forcing to do certain things. Your body would teach you certain things. I started using more technique and principle over just speed and brute force. One thing about Master Chan: I used to attack him all the time when I was studying with him, and it was just amazing how easily he could stop anything. In class one day, when my student Sifu Novell (Bell) was studying with Master Chan, he told me that during a demo, Master Chan told Novell to attack him with full speed. Novell said Master Chan jump stepped towards him and knocked him across the room. His reflexes were quick.

How he centered everything became my modus operandi to this day. It's just central axis, center of gravity and how to work with your alignment. That's how all the techniques work.

RAL: Mr. Chan let you attack him?

Yes. I was kind of a raunchy kid back then. At that time, I didn't know any internal styles, push hands, or anything like that. I didn't attack him disrespectfully, but whenever he had to show something, I would step up to demonstrate. So, I said, "OK, what are you talking about?" And he'd ask, "What are YOU talking about?" Then I would swing a punch and end up tied up in some kind of wrist lock or being pushed across the room. But he never got upset. I knew some teachers that got mad. I had one teacher who would slam you and bounce you off the wall and you'd regret what you just tried to do. Master Chan was able to just stop anything. Sometimes it seemed like he was more curious about what I was trying to do, more so than how I was trying to figure out what he was doing. I wondered how he could stop me and guys two to three times my size with just a small shift and movement.

One time a friend of mine came to class. He had had a few drinks and wanted to see what I was doing. He and Master Chan were pushing, and I could tell the guy was a little bit out of it. The guy went in with an aggressive move and Master Chan hit him. He spun around like a revolving door, but he was a fighter. Master Chan just touched him on the throat and he knew to stop right there. A real fighter knows when they've been beaten. It was experiences like that that kept me there for so many years, as well as his knowledge and the way he taught the information...... the way he would explain it. He would break it down in different ways to different people. It became interesting learning about how to press your feet, align, and why you do things certain ways; he would constantly yell "Center Center Center" and how to just turn from your center and get everything rotating from your center at the same time.

RAL: What was it that first brought you to him? How did you first learn about him?

What happened was I was studying martial arts and doing Tae Kwon Do with Yun Mu Kuan. I had stumbled across Robert Smith's books in a bookstore in Jamaica, Queens. I had read about the internal, I knew about Tai Chi, but wasn't really interested. I then saw the Xing - Yi book with the old Master, Yuan Tao, on the cover. I read that book, and the information was so amazing. I said, I have to find somebody that knows this, but there was nobody around. I stumbled across Master Chan. I found him at William C. C. Chen's place. I found out there was someone teaching Xing-Yi and Bagua, so I went down there to check him out. The first day I went, I didn't really see anything that caught my interest. They had a row of people doing the Santi and I thought, well, these people aren't doing anything. What am I doing here? I left and went back and finished reading Robert's first book. I thought maybe I should have hung around for a few minutes. Let me just go back there and start studying. I thought I was strong in the legs, and when I joined the class, I didn't even know what I was looking for.

I said to Master Chan, "Look, I want to learn this style." And he said, "Why?" I said, "I just read about it. I want to learn it," and so he put me in the Santi stance and adjusted me. My lower legs never felt so much pain. I thought WOW; I really haven't been standing and my legs were not as strong as I thought they were.

RAL: Were you in high school at this time?
I was just getting out of high school.

I went there and I had seen other schools, but I had never experienced anything at those other schools. I studied the Xing Yi and then got into the Bagua with Master Chan. I didn't start the Tai Chi until later. I was studying with him and then I went to William Chen and CK Chu, so I was studying with the three of them at the same time. Master Chan was older than they were, but his information was just clearer. He was a lot more hands on than they were in a very informal environment.

On the Bagua that Mr. Chan taught:

RAL: You guys got the original stuff.
Yes, I think he started modifying some things later when a lot of people were just too lazy to really do the real training. Some went into applications.

RAL: So he may have modified the Bagua he was teaching over the years?

Yes, he may have, because he'd show you more than one way to do the same thing, but he would have his reasons why he would do it a certain way, and maybe a taller person might do something different. Even in the applications, he used to explain that most forms are done as if the two people are the same size, and he said that's not reality, so you must learn how to adjust your moves accordingly sometimes. But the main thing was to make sure you're following the principles: Your foot is the handle of the whip, keep your head suspended, you're turning from your center and learning how to rotate around your axis where everything turns and spirals at the same time. But his main thing was learning how to feel everything, because sometimes we change things around and we think it's right, but it's not quite what it should be.

He used to say that you keep studying because you never finish learning. He always said that we practice together, as if he was practicing with us. He used to tease us sometimes because we'd ask him to do something twice, and he'd say, "No, you practice." Students would ask, "How come you don't do the form with us like the rest of the teachers?" He would always say, "I don't want you copying my mistakes." I said, "Oh, well, I'd be better off with yours than mine."

He would just say, "Follow Mother Nature all the time, stay in center and keep your center still, and learn how to stay calm." He always said, "Make friends, not enemies with the martial arts; you have to learn control so you shouldn't have to hurt people," like that time I told you how he attacked me but didn't hurt me.

He said a lot of things, the main things being the centering, the turning, sitting in your stance correctly. When I first came to him, he said the main thing to do was learn how to move from the coccyx bone and breathe from the navel, using the navel to breathe. He told me to feel the navel, which I didn't realize the importance of until years later. He sat you in stance and he said, learn how to press your feet because you can't make the move happen without using your feet. That was his way of saying you make the car go forward by pressing on the gas, and subsequently, I learned to use different directions of pressing and moving your feet to push and pull the ground when you're stepping.

RAL: That's interesting. So, you said you move from the coccyx?

Yes, the turn starts in the body at the root of the spine. When you are turning your spine, you have to turn your whole spine with your axis, even though your muscles and body's rotating around the axis. Mr. Chan told us to learn how to generate movement from the spine because that controls your hips and everything else. So you keep your center with you so that when you're moving you are stabilized. If something touches you, you could spiral it off or redirect it or bounce it back, but you have to have that kind of force of yin and yang at the point of contact when you touch the person. He said that you are rolling forward like a wheel all the time.

RAL: If you practice enough, do you think you have to consciously think about turning from the lower part of your spine?

It becomes natural after a while.

RAL: Were you a fighter before you met Mr. Chan?

I was fighting a little bit. Well, I came from a rough neighborhood, so we were boxing and wrestling and fighting and getting into fights in the street regularly. My mother put me into karate school. I never liked karate. It didn't agree with me. I did it for a little while and then quit because I felt that I would probably be better off street fighting, and I used to wrestle a lot. We had a lot of martial artists around the area, and once in a while we'd see somebody that did something weird. They would tell you the secret is in the breath. They wouldn't tell you anything else. They'd say, you have to learn to meditate. Okay, teach me. No, you have to learn it as you go along and find somebody to teach you. Okay. So we didn't have anything to go on.

I was studying at a martial arts school for a while; then I said, no, I'm going straight to the internal. I did some research and found those books and ended up with Master Chan.

RAL: You purposely chose to go the "internal" route.

Yes, because I was looking for the long game, where people stayed young. I told you my first teacher sent me flying across the room with seemingly a wave of a hand. That was the end of my external days. When I started teaching teenagers, I found out that if you can be taught correct structure, you can still learn and use the internal effectively even if you don't have any external trainers. I taught a couple of students that didn't know anything, and they became pretty "hell on wheels" kind of guys from the standing. The standing builds up a certain type of solidity in the body and awareness of center and balance even though some people simply stand and they get super strong. Standing has so many, many, things to offer. Mr. Chan used to tell me to learn how to feel everything.

When Master Chan offered me a private class or wanted to show me something, I'd come early in the morning. Early for me was about eight o'clock or nine o'clock, but he meant for me to be there like four or five in the morning. Luckily for me whenever I got there, I would still be alone with him before the rest of the class started at ten or eleven o'clock. Sometimes, we would spend a half hour on just one move. We'd do the first move of the Tai Chi over and over and over. Years later, I even brought along a few teachers of mine. I had a teacher who was pretty good come to visit. Master Chan would always give them a couple of pointers, or they would just watch him and then do something that would transform their own arts.

RAL: How did it make you feel as a young man, this small, smallish stature of man who enjoyed or wanted to spend hours

with you, teaching you. How did it make you feel?

It felt great because a lot of times most teachers were all business; you would go learn and you'd go for your hour and then you'd leave when your time was up. He spent time talking with you. Once in a while, we'd go out and eat, or I'd hang out at the class and watch the rest of the classes other than the Xing-Yi and Bagua that I was doing. When I first started, I didn't like Qigong. I thought Qigong was some kind of rip-off. Luckily, I stumbled into a class one day and Master Chan invited me in because I was coming in kind of charged up. He told me to try this out. The relaxation, the feeling, and the energy just mellowed me out.

I learned other things, also. He showed how to develop parts of the body a certain way and use the Tai Chi ruler tools and the table. I have a bowling ball and now I've got to get that table someday. He had the springboard in the school and a couple of other karate tools. He studied Fukien Shaolin years before.

He knew so many things. It was almost encyclopedic. I would come in there and do things from other teachers and he would correct the form and say, "Now try it this way." Whatever he showed you was always way better. What I was learning was good, but he would always show you a way to make it just right.

He explained that if you learn how to put your wrists in the right position on the hip bone, and keep your shoulders totally loose, you can shoot your hand out like lightning, even from there. Some people might say you're too far away, but you can really fly your hand out quickly right from there and develop the shoulder tendons. A lot of people are sloppy, they pull their hands back too far or not far enough. They're just tightening everything up the wrong way when they're practicing, so then the punch actually gets slower and not as powerful. One day Master Chan told me, I call it the true chamber, where you put the wrist bone itself into the fold; it's as if you're going in your pocket, but you come from right there. If your shoulder stays light, you can shoot your hands out pretty quickly. One goes forward and one goes back. He said to pay attention to the drilling aspect, because he said the external and the internal styles are really the same thing, but that we just do things slightly differently in a way that would generate more rotational force as opposed to just strict drilling, hammering type of power.

If you do your moves right, you can develop all kinds of strength. We did applications on the Tai Chi forms. You see the textbook stuff, but he would show us the intricate turns… I mean, the moves are no joke. Tai Chi is really a deadly art if you use it correctly. And the push-hands was different, because I learned a few different push-hands and some of the Da Lus. Even when I was doing the Chen, I forgot most of the two-man form, but he was showing us a two-man set with the Chen when I was studying.

I know Master Chan was supposed to be writing a book, from what I heard. His daughter told me that, but they never finished it. At the wake, there were some pictures of him when he was young in the Philippines. There were a lot of photos showing that he was working on a book, but he just never finished it. When he was young, he was well developed, well built, and doing all the styles, the Xing-Yi, the Bagua.

On some of the other students:

I used to go to the school with many senior students such as Jim Russo, Ken Cohen, Jan Lang, Werner Ollie, etc. They would show me that wild punches don't work, and so they were very nice and kind to me. Some of them had martial arts backgrounds too, but they would always encourage me: just do it the way Master Chan is showing you, don't need to change it, no need to speed it up. They would show me how to do different things like the up-drill exercise with a heavy pipe. I still have one in the house. Master Chan had an exercise where you hold the pipe at the end, then you lift it up and down slowly while holding it by the wrist, inhaling on the way up, exhaling on the way down. It's in one of the Tai Chi staff moves we do. It builds up tremendous wrist and body strength. It gives you a soft flex throughout the whole body going up and down with it.

He came up with a lot of simple things, such as showing us how to create torque or work the whole body as one unit. For instance, body geometry: he would show two hands, one foot, understanding the upside-down triangle when you're moving, when you're taking a step, how you have to be balanced on one leg. When you're striking, you come from two feet to one hand. And everything that you want to generate still must be coming from both legs, even though it's one step.

RAL: I've never heard of that upside-down triangle.

He had a lot of things. One of my friends who took private lessons with him would be taught some things that were different than what Master Chan taught us in class. He had many ways of teaching form and technique.

I have a friend who's a bodybuilder and very strong. One time he told me that he saw Master Chan lift a full file cabinet. My friend said Master Chan pressed it with his hands and tilted it and just moved it about an inch to the side. My friend said that he then tried moving it and couldn't even budge it.

Master Chan was simply an amazing teacher.

BP Chan (R) with William CC Chen and Robert W. Smith
161 West 23rd Street, circa 1980's
Photo Courtesy of Rudy Curry

Wu Ming
—Tim Folger

Some discussion on BP Chan's Bagua form changes over the years......

I'd never worked with Frank Allen, but there was another person that I knew of, but never studied with, Jan Lang. From what I could see, his Bagua was a little different than Mr. Chan's. Even Richard's was different and maybe in more subtle ways. I guess some people tweaked it, some people might have changed it significantly. Even the two-person forms; I remember doing two-person forms with some students of other teachers - I wouldn't want to single any one out - and I felt like maybe they were missing some things. If you studied directly with Mr. Chan, you would get all these little fine-tuning details that could sometimes get lost. That's another thing that amazes me about Mr. Chan. Here I am, I mostly did three things with him, the Ruler, Xing-Yi and Bagua. I can't remember all that stuff. And somehow, he remembered all of that: the Tai Chi, the Xing-Yi, the Bagua two-person forms.........How did he do it? If you don't practice them, you forget about them.

RAL: Interestingly enough, Adam Hsu's Bagua teacher was Liu YunQiao, who was also one of Mr. Chan's Bagua teachers at some point.

Early on, when I first asked Mr. Chan who his Bagua teacher was, he would just say Master Liu. In those pre-internet days that information was hard to find. Later, through Mr. Chan's conversations and conversations with Richard and other people, I found out. I think I might have even asked Mr. Chan, "Is this your teacher?" Sometimes he (Liu YunQiao) could look kind of severe, you know. He had big glasses and a kind of serious demeanor. I read that he trained the bodyguards for Chiang Kai-Shek in Taiwan. I never really talked with Mr. Chan a lot about that.

RAL: Tell me about how you came to know Mr. Chan.

I had moved to New York in the summer of 87 from Santa Cruz, because I moved here to start graduate school in journalism at NYU, and I wanted to continue with martial arts. Ted (Mancuso) had suggested that I look into Xing-Yi teachers. He said he thought it would be a nice bridge, having studied this kind of very dynamic Northern Shaolin style. I started going to classes in Chinatown and observing people. One fantastic teacher that I met was Kenny Gong, but after a while I couldn't afford the monthly dues – I was a poor student at that time. I wanted to start studying with someone again, because my financial situation had improved after I got my first job. This was 1988. I was aware, of course, of William Chen, the world-famous Tai Chi teacher, and I'd stopped by the studio, took a few classes with William Chen, and I saw a brochure that this guy named Mr. Chan taught Bagua and Xing-Yi and Tai Chi, so I thought maybe I should check out his Bagua and Xing-Yi. I did. I went to one of his classes, and I have to say that initially, I wasn't overwhelmed because Mr. Chan was older at the time, kind of small, and his style of Bagua was pretty subtle. Kenny Gong and many teachers of styles of Bagua could be a little more flowing and dramatic looking. Chan's was very straightforward and seemingly simple, and I didn't appreciate it at first. The class was really small. Richard was kind of leading people, walking a circle. There were just a few people, maybe five or six people in the class. A Xing-Yi class was being taught at the same time, in the same space, so I was kind of dividing my attention between the two. I was chatting with Richard after the class and Richard said, "Are you interested in studying Bagua?" and I said "Yes." Richard may have then demonstrated the single palm change on me, and I thought, oh man, this guy's really strong. This guy learned what he knows from that little old man over there, so I thought that little old man must really be something. I signed up.

I wasn't smart enough to appreciate Mr. Chan's skill. It took someone like Richard to really show me. And I thought, there's something here. So that was 88, maybe the fall of 88. This class was taught once a week on Sunday, and I just kept going from 88 to 99. I thought I would just stick with Bagua, and that's mostly what I did. I did a little bit of Xing-Yi, maybe for six or seven years, and some Tai Chi Ruler for about the same amount of time, six or seven years. There was something unique about Bagua. It just felt good to your body, the twisting, the walking in the circle, and you're doing everything on both sides.

I really liked the Ruler. It really felt so fundamental. I still like doing the Ruler now, but I was never really a good practitioner, like some of Mr. Chan's other students. He had some good Ruler students.

He had so much to offer. I learned some different Qigong forms from him. It was like a fire hose.

RAL: Tell me, do you have any interesting stories or anecdotes about Mr. Chan?

Yes, the thing about Mr. Chan, of course, that strikes most people, was his humility and modesty. He was always Mr. Chan, never ("Master.") He would say that the only person who can be called a Master is lying underground; they've finished learning, they can't learn anymore. They've mastered their art, it's over. It was so genuine; there was no false modesty. At that time, there was no question about his skill and how good he was, the depth of his knowledge, and how he could correct just the smallest things that he saw you doing. You know, it's a funny example, but I think I sent you that picture of him in that shirt that says Wu Ming.

RAL: Yes. No name. Nameless.

Nameless, yes.

He would sometimes say, "I'm still trying to figure out who I am. You know, who is this person? Who is Mr. Chan?" I guess that's maybe the more spiritual side of these pursuits where you think, who is doing this practice? Who are we? There's nothing fixed about us. I think some of these arts express that so beautifully, like Bagua, when you're just constantly flowing and changing. You're not like this fixed battering ram that's attacking some opponent. He would always say, "The object exists within" and "The opponent is the guide." He would emphasize that what he taught wasn't about hitting people. He said that everyone wants to hit people. He said that's such an insane mindset. Why do you want to attack?

He had fundamentals. First was alignment; get your body aligned. This is where I guess the standing practice comes in. Once you have your alignment, you have your center. Once you're centered, you have a good posture: Alignment-Center-Posture. Once those three things are set, then your form could be okay. You start moving a little bit with all those three things starting to be developed. Once your form is okay, maybe your defense will start to be there. And if your defense is there, you would say, then you have your offense. So those six things: Alignment-Center-Posture-Form-Defense-Offense. And Offense was the very, very last thing.

That was one of the fundamental things that he taught, and it was those fundamentals that really stuck with me. As an older person now, you're not going to use your attack, the best response may be to just get away. Mr. Chan would say, "You go your way, I'll go my way. Get away as quickly as you can." Even as a young person, you never know what can happen. You can stumble on a curb, hit your head, die. It's nice to practice with people and try to get as skillful and strong as you can, but in the real world you never know what happens, and you might be liable for lawsuits.

Another thing that he said was that if you know one move, you know 1000 moves. Or he would say that he only knew three moves; he would use that in different circumstances, like with a staff exercise, or, those movements that are fundamental to Bagua and Tai Chi, (Illustrates the rise up drill fall over turn.) Those three moves.

Mr. Chan always wore his watch so that the face of the watch was on the inside of his wrist. If you wear it that way, he said, you could look at your watch by doing the "up" movement of "rise up, drill, fall, overturn." It was an example of how he used the principles of Bagua, Tai Chi, etc. to inform all aspects of his life.

I liked going to Mr. Chan's apartment, studying with Jim and practicing the single palm change and applications with two people, and Mr. Chan would say, "Okay, you do it that way, that's the way you should do it, you do it that way, just do it, there's slightly different ways to do it, just do that."

Some of the Chin-Na, the details of the Chin-Na, I think were amazing.

RAL: Can you give me an example of that?

Mr. Chan would use the little finger, the ring finger and the middle finger, and that would be like Do-Re-Mi. And he would bring that down on this little line on your forearm, Do-Re-Mi, and then the Mi-Fa-So. Do-Re-Mi would be the down part. Mi-Fa-So would be the up part. You don't use the meaty part of your fingers to hold on to your opponent's wrist, but you use that bony edge; it makes a big difference. You can do it yourself and you can feel like the hardness of the edge of your finger versus the softness of them. So just those little details.... that level of detail wasn't there with my other teachers.

When you're doing Bagua with a partner, you're kind of joined at the wrist there. Mr. Chan would say the center changes when there are two people walking the circle together. All these little subtleties. Mr. Chan would talk about the different centers of the body, and what is the main center, and you would have to think. He would sometimes tell you the answer right away, and sometimes he would try to let you figure it out on your own.

RAL: You talked about square standing. Was that a practice that Mr. Chan had you doing? Can you explain a little bit about what square standing was?

It's really interesting. It's like a radical version of walking in a circle. Imagine a square on the floor, and you put one foot along one edge of the square like that (illustrates), and then here's your other foot. The heel of one foot touches the toe of the other foot, so your feet are at right angles. So if this is the heel of one foot, the toe of the other foot would be left. It's kind of hard to describe.

RAL: Is it like L footwork? Something like that?

Yeah, exactly. It's kind of like L footwork. I'm doing the square standing right now. Your rear leg is on the bottom of the square. Then move your lighter leg forward and place your foot so it's perpendicular to the rear foot. The idea is to twist your body so that you're looking along a diagonal of the square. Instead of the center of the circle, you're looking along the diagonal of the square, so your body really twists much more than it does with circle walking. And then you can walk that square.

RAL: I have a DVD of Adam Hsu demonstrating that on a 12x12 square. It looks similar to what you're describing.

Maybe it's something that they both learned from Liu YunQiao.

The square standing is good practice because your footwork is so tight on that square your whole body has to twist a lot more. You're kind of squaring in this really small space. You can do the simple direction change on the square.

It's a little weird though, to try to do anything more than that. I've tried doing the single palm change, but it's a little too cramped, But it's not bad with just that simple palm (direction) change. Changing circling, Mr. Chan would call it, changing direction. I would do square standing a lot.

RAL: Tell me about life lessons that you've learned from the 11 years that you were with Mr. Chan. Anything that stayed with you to this day?

The opponent, let the opponent be the guide, I think is kind of a profound one. Not just in the obvious kind of martial application, where you try to follow what the opponent is doing. But more generally, whatever happens in life, you just don't present a hard, resisting surface to it. Just be very open, almost porous, receptive, attentive; all those characteristics about how to stand - the very basic standing.

Mr. Chan would say how the sounds of the Chinese language would elicit the proper physical response, like "umm," which depressed the chest slightly. I believe the character is pronounced "haum"; that's the way it's spelled on the instruction sheet that I received from Mr. Chan: "14 Characters on How to Stand". He said that very sound makes the chest naturally depressed. The first two characters of how to stand are really interesting. "Empty awareness, active alertness." That's like very meditative instruction. Empty awareness: Be really open and receptive; everything sinks; your body is relaxed, and everything is in its proper place. Your body becomes softer, the spaces in the joints open up a little bit. It took Mr. Chan, I think, to really make me appreciate it. It was just those first two characters, I think those are empty awareness, active alertness. Passive isn't the right word. There's an aliveness. You're open and aware, soft, but active and alive.

Mr. Chan said the character for active awareness was Ling. I think Mr. Chen would say that that sound had a brightening effect.

I thought that was interesting, just the way that language itself, the Chinese instructions, were integrated into the physical practice itself. That was an eye-opener for me, just how sophisticated these practices are. That really stayed with me. Just those simple things. Empty awareness, active alertness. Very first characters on how to stand.

RAL: Mr. Chan linked the sound or the tone of the Chinese word to what was going on with the body?

Yes.

Standing and being at ease and all these things are so basic. We stand, we walk, we sit, we lie down. You know, that pretty much covers everything. There's a Mr. Chan practice for all of us: lying down meditation, sitting meditation, walking meditation, standing meditation. He really covered all the basics. Incredible stuff, so seemingly simple.

He had this funny little toy that someone had given him. It was a little rubber doll. It had an alien look to it. It was really pretty small, maybe a few inches. You would squeeze the body and the head would blow up. He'd say that's what most of us were like, we're really heady - everything's up there. He would use that. For the rest of us the body was just an afterthought. So, he would sometimes say, at the end of the day when you're lying down, "Ask your body, how does it feel today? Did the mind treat the body okay today?" He just had this very gentle kind of humorous way of expressing these things. I think that that integration was really an important life lesson. And again, his modesty. He shared so many principles. He would talk about sharing, service, responsibility. I think he was talking about that with people in the hospital before he died, from what I heard. I was out here (New Mexico), so I couldn't visit him in the hospital.

RAL: What else?

Funny things, practical things. I think I mentioned these funny little practical things he would talk about for life in the city. When you're walking down the street, your swinging arms should be passing through the center of your body so that this part (demonstrates) of your wrist is kind of passing in front of your body as you're walking. If somebody is walking towards you, coming right at you, and they're not going to give way, bring your elbow up like you're brushing your hair back so that your elbow is right here (pointing forward.) Little things, like if you're carrying a heavy bag of groceries, don't let your elbows lock, just let them be soft. Don't ever lock the joints, just have them be nice and round just like you would in Bagua. So, Qigong is your daily life. And what better Qigong practice is there than just walking around outside? You're just on a much bigger circle.

RAL: The circumference of the earth.
Yeah.

RAL: Tell me a little bit about Mr. Chan's teaching style. When you were in class with him, what was his teaching style like?

199

In those 11 years I didn't really learn the Eighth Palm until the year before I left. Maybe if I'd asked him more, he would have taught me more, I don't know. But it was very slow.

If you asked him a question, he would often turn the question back on you or even your choice of words. He didn't like the word "relax".

I think the first thing I learned with Mr. Chan were the Ten Taoist exercises.

He would do them with us, but often it was another student who would lead us. Mr. Chan would be watching and offering some corrections. He would let you touch his body to see how things felt, how he moved. Really detailed and precise, like the Chin-Na; there's nothing vague. Everything was well defined. He would use very simple examples. He'd say, oh, this is where your shirt cuff is. He would talk about the placement of your arms.

If you measure the circumference from your belly button to your hips, that's one quarter of the circumference of your body, and halfway between there is one eighth. We'd always relate to simple instructions like that. Your belt loop is there, so you could use that as a guide. It wasn't hierarchical, of course, there were no belts or anything like that. It was almost disorganized, though that isn't the right word. It was... Even unstructured isn't the right word. It's kind of hard to describe his teaching method. Sometimes he would have something in mind for the day, sometimes he wouldn't. He would just watch you. Sometimes, he would do really basic things over and over again, like Do Re Mi for the Chin-Na. When you're working with a person you say, okay, now you're out of center, now you're in center. How do you get a person out of their center? It was so varied and very natural and easy and friendly. You knew that you could ask him anything and eventually you would get an answer; either he would tell you if you were lucky, or he would let you think about it for a while, or he would show you how something feels on his body using correct alignment.

In the Bagua posture, he would use a standing fist to show that this is where your lower palm should be, and the flat fist out here between your ribs and the middle of your upper arm. Your outer elbow should be in line with your solar plexus. Sometimes it would be a flat fist, and sometimes a standing fist for other distances. He would use the body itself as a measuring instrument to show you the proper position of the limbs. I think that was pretty ingenious and simple and just very graspable. His classes weren't like ABC. It wasn't kind of this linear approach to learning at all. You would start every class, every single class that I went to on Sundays, we always did Ten Daoist exercises. And then we would circle for a while. Sometimes we'd do that big figure-eight circle with a whole bunch of people. Did you ever do that?

RAL: Yes.
Yeah, yeah, that was fun.

You never really knew what any class was going to be about. But you could kind of expect maybe some of that basic structure, like I said, the Ten Taoists, walk for a while, and then something else. It might be how to correctly stand, or he would run through the eight standing exercises for Bagua, the square standing, Chin-Na, etc. It was always something a little different. I don't think I ever walked away from some class thinking, oh, I didn't really learn anything today, I never had that experience (laughs.) You know? I couldn't say that first we learned this, and then that, and that. It was so open-ended. And of course, he'd be responding to people's questions, so I don't know if he had an agenda when he came into class.

RAL: I think the thing that's the most telling about what you said was you never left a class of his not learning anything new. That speaks volumes.
Yes, yes.

On Sundays, I'd make sure to pretty much leave the whole day free, I could go there in the morning because people would be hanging out before their own class started. I go there and I'd be able to practice with other people, or I could stand, and Mr. Chan would come over and check me out, or you could practice Chin-Na with people, so I'd be there for the whole day from 10 until 3 or 4, whenever the class ended. and then you'd walk out feeling settled and connected for having been with him and done all those things for a whole day. Just a really nice experience. When I first started studying with him, his studio was on 6th Avenue between 23rd and 24th above that bar called Billy's Topless.

The studio was on the second floor, and every single Sunday when we left, when Mr. Chan closed the door.........it was an old door, an old building. Every single time Mr. Chan would close the door, it would be like a shoulder strike, then an elbow strike. Because he had to push against the door twice to make sure it was closed firmly. But every single Sunday, it was shoulder strike, elbow strike. So, he was just practicing that way, you know, in the simplest of circumstances.

RAL: Did you ever go up to the Tai Chi Farm and do any workshops with him?

That's one thing I regret. Yeah, I only went there, I think, twice at the most. I regret, you know, I really regret not doing that with Mr. Chan. I think the Farm days were often on Saturdays. I had a Friday night class of Xing Yi, and then a Sunday class of Bagua, and I would kind of be there all-day Sunday. Because of personal circumstances at that time, it was hard for me to devote my entire weekend. I would often meet with Mr. Chan at his apartment, and sometimes it would be the source of tension if I was away the whole weekend. It just made things difficult at home. So I really regret that I didn't make it up to the Farm more often than just a couple of times. I've heard stories about him sitting down, playing the harmonica, things like that, and I wish I could have been there to see that side of him. He had those Nine Palace posts, which I wish I could have practiced with. He did a little bit of that in class sometimes. He would have people in different positions, and then we'd be practicing with those people in different positions, but I really wish I could have made it up to the Farm. Mostly just to be with him more and the nice person that he was.

He was a unique person. It was like meeting an old sage. I don't want to romanticize Mr. Chan too much, but he was kind of like that. Just this old guy who was very modest, straightforward, direct, and kept a really low profile. I think back in those days, not a lot of people knew about him. I remember I went to a bookstore in Chinatown, and I was asking the clerk, because he was in a martial arts bookstore, so I said, "Do you have any recommendations for people who teach Xing Yi or Bagua?" And he said, "Well, I've heard good things about this guy named Mr. Chan." I think that was before I knew about William Chen, but I didn't know that Mr. Chan was teaching there. I think the first time I heard Mr. Chan's name was at that bookstore in Chinatown.

I really enjoy talking with you about this. It was such a nice, important part of my life, and he was such a wonderful, unique person. It's great to be able to talk about him anytime. Studying with him was a formative experience for many people, and, yeah, I guess, kind of irreplaceable. There will never be a time like that again. There will never be people who came from the sort of milieu that he came from.

I feel lucky that I stumbled across him and stayed with him. I wish I could have spent more time with him. I met good people like Richard and other students of Mr. Chan that I learned a lot from.

I'm always happy to talk about Mr. Chan.

"Push Me"
—Fran Buckelew

RAL: Well, I don't know how much Andy (Lee Zalcman) filled you in, Fran, but I'm writing a book about BP Chan. Andy said that at one time, you were a student of his, you had studied with him?

He came to our school. She used to go pick him up. He lived in Brooklyn. She'd go pick him up on Sundays and bring him to the school and he would share his knowledge. It was a little different than what we were studying. It was only supposed to be an hour, but usually three hours later, she would take him back to Brooklyn, and they'd get lunch. She did that quite a few times when we met him.

I also met him up at the Tai Chi Farm in Warwick, New York. We went up there every summer, and that's where I met him as well. I didn't understand. I was new into Tai Chi, and back then I didn't understand all the different aspects of so many styles, but things developed. I saw him quite a few summers up there teaching.

I didn't take any of his classes because I didn't know what they were, but he did come to our school later, much later. He liked to kid around. He liked to joke. He started teaching us the five frolicking animals.

RAL: Oh, Five Animal Frolics.

Right. We started with the bear, and then something happened. I don't know what happened. He didn't come for quite a while and then eventually he didn't teach it anymore to us. He just shared his basic Tai Chi with us, which was fine with me. I enjoyed listening to him.

The first time he came into our school, he was older, and he walked in like this little decrepit old man, all bent over, and walked in the room. We didn't know exactly who he was, only that Sifu had studied with him in New York. He walks in there like he's 150 years old, and I'm going, oh my God, what is he going to teach us, you know? He can hardly move and gets to the front of the room, kind of bowed to us all, and all of a sudden, he springs into action and he's walking real fast around the room and we're all going Ha Ha Ha, yeah, little joke. He only tried that once because then we knew what he was up to. He liked to kid around with us.

I guess he was probably about 5'2", 5'3", he was short. He always picked the tallest one in the class to show an exercise to or an application of the art. He always picked Rich who was 6'5". The one that stuck with me the most that I remember was Mr. Chan getting into his stance and we circled around him. There's probably about 15, 20 of us. We're watching and he brings Rich over to him and he tells him to push him. Well, he was reluctant to do that to this little old man. Rich was in his 40s and he's 6'5", 300 pounds. Mr. Chan says, "Push me." He pushed him, but Mr. Chan didn't go anywhere. He didn't move. He just stood there. He says, "Come, come, push, push." Rich didn't want to hurt him, but he couldn't do it. Suddenly Rich is standing 20 feet away. He got pushed and didn't even see how Mr. Chan did it. Mr. Chan was talking about rooting......it's all in your stance, your feet, your rooting, where you redirect your opponent's energy.

A bunch of us thought that Rich was in on it, that this was a joke, that it was a set-up. Well, each one of us eventually found out that it was for sure. You couldn't do anything with Mr. Chan, I was like, holy cow. That's when all the doubt that I had about things that I saw was removed. All the things that I saw, yeah, they're made up, that's theatrical, that's blah, blah, blah. Well, it took about 10 years until I realized, no, this is for true. This is really real. I had a whole new look at it, but that's how he did it. He joked around with it and kind of played along with us, you know, and then BAM! I want to say that he came to our school maybe four or five times and then he got ill, or something happened in the family. He couldn't come back. And then next thing we knew, he was really sick and then he passed away. First time I've ever been to a Buddhist wake. Unfortunately, quite beautiful, but not for the reason it happened.

He was quite a person. He was really quite a delight. I know it sounds disrespectful, but you didn't see him as a master. You saw him just like a regular person who did outstanding things. He didn't have that... I don't know the word...

RAL: Ego?

Yes, there's another word I was thinking of, but ego is good. He didn't show that he was this great, great thing. He was like your little grandpa that came in to kind of talk with you and discuss things with you and show you. Some other masters that I've seen and dealt with are not very humble. They let it be known that they are great, and this is who they are. He was not like that at all. The few years that we had with him were wonderful, and after he passed away, Sifu (Andy Lee), would still talk about how she was a student with him. So, his legacy kept going. I wish there had been more time. I would have liked more time with him, but it just didn't work out that way.

"Conquer inside before conquer outside." *—Ron Gee*

Mr. Chan was a most unforgettable and remarkable personality. His knowledge of meditation postures, qigong sets and martial forms was vast, his self-defense techniques masterfully effective, and his example of selfless teaching and willingness to share his wealth of insights truly admirable.

Yet he downplayed all these attributes, deflecting attention away from himself and refuting titles such as Master.
Holding up his little finger, he would declare that this was
how little he knew. He referred to himself as a guide who was
pointing out the signposts along our common path because
he was further ahead. As he put it "Principle is the teacher, instructor is the guide, just brings message." He frowned
upon display and artifice, projecting instead a demeanor that
was dignified yet plain, unassuming, commonplace and open.
Mr. Chan was a repository of ancient wisdom who in many
ways recalled Chuang-zi. Like the legendary Taoist sage, he
was both serious and lighthearted, direct and oblique, possessed of the Zen-like traits of simplicity, humility and un-
pretentiousness - qualities that stood out and endeared him
to his many students.

The Saturday group that studied with Mr. Chan in his later
years would gather by the small hut he and his "practitioners",
as he would call his students, built in the woods behind Jou
Tsung-hwa's Tai Chi Farm in Warwick, NY. Outdoor practice
typically began with a half hour or longer of standing meditation, sometimes even as snow was falling but never in windy
conditions which he cautioned blows qi away. This was followed by qigong exercises and then detailed review of the various forms. At the end of practice, it was customary to relax
for a rustic meal of soup or stew from the motley assortment of
ingredients everyone brought which had been cooking in a big
pot on the wood stove. The bowls, spoons and chopsticks we
ate with were then rinsed in the nearby stream and dried with
paper towels. But rather than being thrown away, Mr. Chan
would have us hang the paper towels on a clothesline to dry
for reuse the next weekend. This, too, was a lesson in mindful
frugality and a counter to wasteful habits.

During the few years I studied with Mr. Chan, I jotted notes
which included the following iconic sayings:

EAST / WEST:

"Eastern learning has spirit as its point of departure. Western learning has material as its point of departure."

———

"East - mind controls body but let body help the mind. West - mind controls everything."

NATURALNESS & FEELING:

"Let your body feel something...and tell your brain... if you don't feel something...there is nothing to explain."

———

"Takes a while to understand body...until you feel something."

INTERNAL / EXTERNAL:

"Conquer inside before conquer outside."

———

"Outside angular...Inside circular."

———

"All the treasures are inside...outside just temporary materials."

STANDING:

"The more we are calm...the more we are loose...the more we can feel...feel what is natural."

———

"Take a little time for mind to go with body...Take a little time for body to go with mind...gradually mind and body go together with help of the spirit."

———

"When thirty-three pieces of spinal cord open, the twelve joints open."

"Call 'Triple-A'...Aware - Alert - Active"

QIGONG:

"Just do the movement...when moment is right the breathing will coordinate and match the movement.... if interfere, then in conflict and breath becomes choked."

"Do nothing, Do something...Think Something, Do nothing."

"Everything is open and close...Blood and air, 24-hour service... Open and close continuously, like bellows."

"Don't think breathing, because we are already breathing... every time think of breathing, mind goes to chest."

"Ask, am I breathing there? Say 'breath there' is wrong...that is command."

DEFENSE / OFFENSE:

"Defense, body is a ball...Offense, body is a clock."

"When doing the form, you are like a clock. When others do it to you, you become a ball."
Precision:
"1 centimeter is 1000 miles."

"Understand clearly...not half-cooked (Chinese) / half-baked (Western.) If exercise incomplete, hurt people rather than help."

NATURALNESS:

"Body knows best…just do form so it is comfortable, if body feels comfortable then it is alright."

FALSE LEARNING:

"Go from unnatural to unnatural. "Proper, Chinese way: go from unnatural to natural."

"Study the Principle, Not the Form" *—Dr. Richard Chin*

You opened a big book here with a lot of stuff. One reason why it was hard to find me was because of the old martial art tradition where BP came from, where I came from. From the world we came from, we didn't talk at all. I'm going to explain that and why I'm talking to you now. It's a new world.

My teacher from the White Eyebrow system, Chin Dor, a very famous master, and many of us are famous within the martial art community. We know who we are. It isn't for public publication. You will not find any article on my teacher, for example. I remember somebody saying, when they realized we're still alive, let's go get your master, take him out for dinner and we'll do an article for Black Belt Magazine and all that. I said, absolutely not. Same thing with BP, he'd be appalled. There's a lot of reasons for that and we'll get into that because that's part of the BP program, part of what traditional martial arts is. So your question is who I am. I started martial arts very, very young, around 12, 13 as BP. I studied with some of the famous masters: Lum Song, who is the Grandmaster of the Southern Mantis, Chin Dor, who is the Master of the White Eyebrow System, and Jow Ga, under Grandmaster Chen Mon-Cheung. These names are famous within the martial art community.

RAL: The Asian Martial Arts community.

Okay, that's a good question because there's an Asian martial art community. There's the World martial arts community and there's the Chinese one, the Japanese one, the Korean one. Okay, so you are opening a big thing.

Like you and I talking here, you did something. You did something, that's why I asked you how you tracked me down. Did you ever see the movie Seven Samurai?

RAL: No, I've heard a lot about it.

It's a testing of the samurai. But not just combat. So, if you're any good at all, you can track me down. If you can't find me, okay, then no need to talk to you.

RAL: I feel better already.

Also, if you think about it, that's actually martial arts. What is martial arts? It's just not fighting. Martial arts is huge. It's life.

It's life and what it's about. So if I'm important to you, you should find me. And it's not that you can't find me. I didn't disappear. You just have to figure out how to find me. And I've said this to other people, my other students, if I wanted to find you, I'd find you. And if you wanted to find me, you'd find me. This is just the way life is. You just have to do it. Things will break open. And if you're not supposed to find me, you won't find me.

And it's not that I hide. What I don't do is I don't go out into the public and do stuff. But now I am. Okay, now coming back to what I'm doing now. I had a long discussion with BP about this years ago because we come from the same tradition. This is like '76, I met BP during the Bicentennial, 76, that's how I remember. Think about how long ago that was. And I was with my teacher, a grandmaster, Chan Mon-Cheung from Hong Kong. We were touring the US. It was the Bicentennial Year, it was beginning to open up, a sharing from China, from all Asian countries, bringing the real art of Kung Fu into America.

We did Madison Square Garden; we did the whole thing. Bruce Lee started this five years before, because I worked with Bruce Lee a great deal. The Chinese arts were really second to everybody else at that time.

RAL: You mean the Asian?

Yeah, the Asian martial arts. I can only talk about Asian martial arts. So, second to the Japanese and Okinawan and the reason being we were so secretive was that nobody knew what Chinese martial arts was. Bruce Lee started it. He started saying that we're going to show the world what we're about. One of the things that Bruce brought to my attention is we're letting a lot of people in who are totally phony. And the reason is that we're so secret. The public doesn't know who we are. But the phony guys were out there doing movies and writing books. People, including me, at that time, my teachers at that time, and BP at that time, refused to talk. So Bruce says, you've got to talk. You guys have got to make it known. You've got to know what's going on. So that's one reason why I'm talking.

We, including my Grandmaster, Chin Dor, were not even allowed to demonstrate the form, not even talk about it. So many of us, including Bruce and myself, we did karate. We were well-known karate fighters, because we couldn't talk about our Kung Fu background. I was then actually more known in the karate world than I was in Kung Fu. I'm more known now for Kung Fu.

Besides BP, we're talking about the whole world of Chinese martial arts, and Bruce Lee had a lot to do with opening that up. Of course, BP is part of that because he's part of the whole Chinese movement. So, going back to BP now a little bit, we couldn't talk about anything, but what I did do is compete. I was well known as a karate fighter in those days. There was a gap, it was a split right down the middle of traditional Chinese martial artists, which is what BP was, and Bruce Lee's guys, which I was part of.

RAL: What was the split about?

They did not want anything known. Total secret. So why the mystery of BP? I'm answering that question. He did not want anybody to know about it. And yet he was teaching. Tai Chi, Bagua, and Xing-Yi sort of were okay to be taught to the public. It was like the first real martial arts that were okay to be taught openly, but not the whole system. The whole system of combat and all that stuff was still retained secretly. I'm giving you the background on why only certain people like Jeff Pascal, myself, a few other people, are actually the only ones who really knew BP's system.

RAL:I had heard that BP Chan made some changes to the Bagua form he taught over the years.

I lived with him, he lived with me, he lived in my studio. We became very close. I really know probably more about BP than anybody else than maybe Jeff (Pascal.) First of all, he didn't change anything. All right, so this is where people get crazy. People would come to him and they would ask him "Explain a move, explain this, explain that" so he would explain that to you and he would just make adjustments to what he knew as a principle. Is that a change?

In other words, no. First of all, there's a lot of Bagua. There's a lot of Tai Chi, but people don't understand that. And they're all true forms. One of BP's statements, which is the truth in martial arts, is that principles are the same. Study the principle, not the form. The form is choreography. It's just choreography. So you can do anything you want, but the principles are the same in every system. You see what I mean? He didn't change anything. He may have given you an opinion. I'll give you an example, which is a true story. People came to visit BP after he got to be well known, people came to visit him, Tai Chi, Bagua, Xing -Yi, like that, American masters, not Chinatown masters, hundreds of students and asked him for class correction. He said to me one time that a famous master came to him for correction.

He asked, "Would you correct my form?" So, BP said, "Stand there," and BP made a correction, did this, pushed, the guy started shaking, fell down, he was so weak, he was so weak, so the guy says "What was that?" This is where BP would say, "Well I'm not familiar with your form, this is how I do my form. I don't know what you do. It's been very nice seeing your form. I made correction, you fell down." He would just say "I don't understand your form." So this is what he would do. People would come through and he'd look at a different form and it was terrible, and he would say, "I just don't understand it." BP said to me "How does this guy have hundreds of students? He's a master. He can't stand." These are the true stories of BP. I don't know if his students told you. I don't know if they know these stories. These are conversations I had with him.

He would say, "Your form is different. I don't understand it. That's all. But it isn't the form. It's the principles. How you're supposed to stand. There's a certain way in every form. So, if you don't hit those points, it doesn't work.

RAL: One of Mr. Chan's students that I spoke to told me that Mr. Chan would make reference to someone named Mr. Tailor, T-A-I-L-O-R, and as a tailor measures you for a suit or whatever, that's how he would make his adjustments to people. I understand fully what you're saying, all these minor corrections, sometimes major corrections.

Yes. There's two things. That's correct. But he would also say the most important is your feeling, let the energy flow. There's two things here, there's the technical part. Everything is technical, which is true. I can explain this to you. True martial art is beyond technique. A lot of people reach the technical point, but don't go beyond it. Does that make sense to you?

RAL: What in your opinion, is beyond the technical points?

Are you a musician or do you follow music? You know anything about music? I had a roommate in college, and he was a professional guitar player.

I once asked him, "What do you think of this guy?" He says, technically he's good. And I didn't understand it. Now I understand it. Technically he was perfect, but he wasn't a great musician. When you hear a great musician, it's feeling. Another story. I was at a jazz party for a very famous trumpet player, he was 80 years old, retiring. Every trumpet player in New York, we were all there, down in the village and everybody jammed. Everybody's playing. My point is this. Let's say a C, natural C. Everybody played it, but you could hear him. It was different. And I said, my God, that's master. Everybody played a C. Technically it was perfect. Technically it was the same, but it's not. Okay, does that help you a little bit?

RAL: What do you think the reason is for that? Do you think the reason is because the man who could hit the perfect C practiced more than the others? That he had an intuitive sense? I mean, maybe there was something in his hearing?

It has to do with talent.

RAL: Innate talent or developed talent?

Developed talent is technique. Innate talent, you're born with it. I don't know your background as a writer.

RAL: I have no background as a writer!

Okay. What makes a great writer? You see, that's what I'm trying to say. Yeah, yeah. Technically, technically, you can write. Are you a good writer? I'm not telling you. I'm trying to say to you, how do you learn that?

Do you go to Harvard and get your PhD in literature and write a book? No!

RAL: It's a little too late for me.

No, but I'm saying in general, no. I'm not a musician, but I know them. When I talk to my friends who are professionals, and I ask, "What do you think of guys who graduate Juilliard with their Master's?" They say, "Oh, good, they're good musicologists, they can teach at the University." Can they play? "No. No." They all practice, they all know their notes. What makes you come to the top?

That's innate talent. That's a born talent. So that's something you're born with. That's it. Now BP himself, we talked many times about that. BP himself practiced many, many years. Okay, now he never considered himself a master. He considered himself a student. Most students don't understand a word I'm trying to say because they consider him a master. I'm telling you why he'd say that. Because he didn't reach that level. He reached a high level. As I would say, he's PhD level. If you want to do Qigong and Tai Chi at the university, he's PhD level. But there's a master level. How many of us get there? That's insane. So that's why he would say that. Don't tell me I'm a master. There are masters in every profession. Whether it's poetry, whatever it is, great masters. You do the best you can. You're there. That's what I'm saying. You're a great author, a great professor, a great attorney, that's fine. Understand your ego. The ego will ruin you.

Understand that you're good and there are better. That's all, and then you're fine. That's what made BP great, that he knew that. He didn't do that; he didn't go around saying I'm a great master. See?

RAL: So, back to some questions about you. So, you were born in China, you came to the United States about when?
When I was like five or six, something like that.

RAL: Why did your family choose to come to the United States?
You want to get out, you want to come here. In China, Amer-

ica is called "Gold Mountain." I don't know if you know that.

So, everybody wants to come here. So, that's why most of us got here, including Bruce Lee. Now Bruce Lee is a fascinating character. We're going to go back and forth and refer to him because he's the one who really broke open the Chinese Wall, let's say, of martial arts, because now people are interested in what the Chinese arts are. Before then, it was just karate, judo, like that. Bruce Lee broke it open; people were looking for it now. I was already into it, being Chinese you had to be Chinese to study it and I remember, even in karate classes people would come to me and say, you know anything about this Tai Chi?

I did. I do. William Chen was the one who was teaching at the time, and I would send them over to William. William and I were both good friends because William Chen and I were of similar age. He was here as a student from Taiwan. He was looking to make a living. He was a student at NYU.

So, he started teaching Tai Chi and I was doing karate at the time, so we became friends, it was a small circle. Now let's go back to how I met BP. So in 1976, I was with my master, with 10 other masters, touring the US, famous masters like Sek Kin, a Chinese movie star of the Kung Fu genre. So, I'm the host in New York, okay, because it's my territory. Each place you go, there's a different host. Each territory has their own masters. So, I take them to William Chen.

Just so happens that BP went to William Chen and started teaching Bagua because he didn't want to conflict with William's Tai Chi. So, that's a true story. He's Tai Chi, I'll teach Bagua. We went to visit William, and I met BP. Somehow, we became good friends, we sort of connected. He asked if he could come down to visit me in my studio. So, my studio is down on SoHo, Wooster Street. That's the Asian Martial Arts Studio.

So, anyway, they gave me the ground floor because it had to be redone. It was just a hole in the wall. I fixed it up. And BP walked in, and it was just like being in China because I ran it very traditionally. I've come from a traditional background. And he's very traditional. He felt right at home, he said," Could I come here and teach?"

I said, absolutely come here and teach. And I didn't care what he taught. He taught everything he wanted. So he started teaching Chen Tai Chi there. Yes. He started teaching all this stuff that he couldn't teach at William's. And later on, we became very close. He moved in for a short time. And as I said, I moved in with his family in the Philippines. We brought them over. We brought his family over.

RAL: Tell me a little more about that piece, because I know that BP Chan had a rather large family. I think he had eight or nine children.

Yeah, yeah.

RAL: And a number of his students said that they visited him, I don't recall the exact location. And the question I asked them was, "Well, did you ever see his wife? Did you ever see his children there?" The answer that I got was, "No, not really."

No, because they (his students) weren't close to him. They didn't know him. It was very private.

RAL: Yeah, it's interesting that you say that because I was talking to a student of his who attended his funeral. One of his daughters was at the funeral, and he went to the daughter and asked the daughter, "What was it like having a father like Mr. Chan with all his martial arts accomplishments?" And her answer to him was, "We really didn't know him that well." Which is unfortunate, I think.

This is why I give you the Chinese background. They're Chinese, it's not that they didn't know him that well. It's very Chinese, okay? It's not huggy, kissy, things like that. How can I explain it? It was her way of saying "I'm not telling you anything.

Don't ask me." You must look at that. You can't look at it from an American point of view. She was just being very polite. Now, she knew that they all were raised with him. I know that very well. But none of his students knew him. That's my point. None of his students, except for very few of us, knew who he was at all.

And that's the way it's supposed to be. They weren't close to him. As any of the students you will meet later, they thought they were very close to him. They didn't know anything about him. They knew him as a teacher of martial arts. They didn't know anything about him at all. They didn't know a thing about his father, they knew nothing about his kids.

RAL: In your author's page on Amazon, you mention there that you learned Chen Tai Chi from BP Chan. One of Mr. Chan's early students told me that BP Chan was teaching a very old, legitimate Chen style, and the student said that it probably pre-dated the Yang style.

Okay. It's the lineage. Let me see if I can explain it to you. (Gets a book)

This picture may be easier to explain to you. You studied Bagua, right? So, this is your Tai Chi question. So, here's the (lineage) tree of the Chen style. So, this is the original. This is the modern branch that you see today. And out of this branch, the Yang style was created. But our branch of Chen style comes from this branch, from the original. So it didn't go through the changes that this branch went through.

That's all. In other words, it's simpler than you think. So, we have nothing to do with the Yang. So, that's what he means by old.

RAL: By old, you mean original?

You see, they're all original. They're all original. It's just that we're from that branch that didn't really change. The Yang style comes from the original style. So, when people watch me do the

Chen style, they say, well, that looks like Yang. I say, but you forget, Yang style comes from this. We don't look like them, they look like us. I try to clarify, because they see the modern Chen style, which is different from the way we do the Chen style.

Unless you understand the history of it, you don't know, okay? So that's that story. I learned from BP because we were close; there's only a few of us that actually learned the Chen style from him. He knew all the styles of Tai Chi; BP knew all the styles. And as BP and I were discussing, the same thing I'm discussing with you today, he says, the Chen style is going to disappear. That's why he started to now teach it. Because it was all disappearing. He was getting older, it was all disappearing, so let me do this stuff.

Same thing with me. I realized a few years ago, my Tai Chi, my Kung Fu styles, it ends with me. So that's why I'm teaching. I'm trying to lay it down before I can't do it anymore. Because it ends with me. Not the system itself, but my lineage. There are lineages with each system. So, like BP, we carry the BP lineage. If we don't teach it, it stops. That's it.

I don't know how much I can get through to them. It's not just form, it's the principles and how you do it. Going back to your other question, talent. So I've taught a lot of students, but none of them have actually come up to what I would consider a good level yet. They're okay, but I want them to get up to a higher level.

RAL: What styles have you been teaching them?

I teach White Eyebrow. White Eyebrow Pak Mei is one of the styles that we call the secret styles of China, and that's one of them. It's not popular because it was never pushed out. It's very well known in the martial system-secret system, it's one of the known secret systems that everybody wants to learn. And why? Because we weren't allowed to teach it. Now, my teacher passed away about 15 years ago, so I can teach it. But when he was alive, we couldn't even show it. So, you know, we're familiar with the other styles, like Bagua and Xing-Yi, but there are certain styles that are just coming into the light. And it's funny because I see it on YouTube and I say, God, they show that form. You would have been killed if you did this form (Pak Mei) years ago. Now you can just plug it in, except you don't know how to do it.

You do the Bagua and Xing-Yi, very sophisticated. As a young person coming out, it makes no sense to you. You want to punch and kick. It's only until you get more advanced at the PhD level that you realize, wow, that is really some good stuff. But you've got to be good to know that. You've got to be advanced. So a lot of what I teach, they can't see it. Yet.

RAL: It's about short hand strikes, right?

Well, we call it short range. There's long range, middle range, short range when you're in combat. So you have to know all the ranges. So, Pak Mei is known, more famous for short range.

RAL: How do you integrate that with, for instance, Chen Tai Chi in terms of mindset? With any of the so-called internal styles, my understanding is that there's more of an emphasis on muscular expansion or joint expansion. With the external styles, there is more of an emphasis on muscular contraction. How do you keep them separate? Does it depend on the opponent?

No. It's very simple. This is getting to the heart of what you are going to write about. As BP would say, it's principles. There are certain principles. The main principle is six coordinations. Six coordinations and the four forces, which are float, sink, swallow, spit. This is the result of your six coordinations. That's the gist of everything. Forget external, internal, hard, soft, you have to have six coordinations. As long as you move that way, everything is correct, everything falls in, going back to the posture. So it's not muscular, it's not extension, this and that, it all falls into place. In the classic setting, we'll go to classic, we never classified it (Pak Mei) as external, internal, hard, soft.

We follow the principles of yin-yang. Yin and yang. You can't have yin without yang. You can't have muscle without Qi. You can't have Qi without muscle. I call it total misinterpretation of Eastern and Western language. Because a very American thing is, "What is it?" Black or white? Are you doing a soft system? Are you doing a hard system? No.

I use a very common example. You play golf at all? How do you hit a golf ball? Soft. If you're hard, you can't hit the damn ball.

RAL: I think you have to be relaxed to a great extent. Alignment. You have the technical aspects, plus you have the softer aspects, like the relaxation.

The correct term is relaxation, not softness. I use golf because if you play it, if you grip it too hard, you can't hit it. If it's too soft, you can't hit the damn ball. It's hard and soft. It's "firm" relaxation. It's total alignment, total letting it go, is how you hit a ball.

RAL: Do you play golf?

I've taken lessons. I've... I had one of the best golf teachers. He explained it. He told me how to play golf, but it was pure Tai Chi. That's what he did. He said, if you do this, you have alignment. And I go, shit. It's Tai Chi.

And then I started to hit better. I didn't hit well. I'm still slicing this and that because I don't have my right swing. And I use another example, I said, you know how to throw a baseball? Throw any ball. He says, you can't, if you're rigid like that, you can't throw a ball. The throw is done when you relax, and that's power, coming right out. And if you're soft like a noodle, you can't throw the damn ball. So anything you do follows the principles. Basic physics. Basic mechanics.

So that's why when people say, you're doing soft style, hard style. That's not true.

Does that make sense to you?

RAL: Intellectually it does. Physically, I don't know if I'd be able to do it.

Oh, I didn't say you could do it. What's the tenets of martial arts? Mind, body, spirit. Mind and body. Some of my students understand perfectly what I'm trying to say. Can't do it. I have students, they can do it physically, but don't understand it. So, you're not a master. You reach a certain level. A master understands all of that. Now, understanding is one thing. Now there's another component. Can you do it? That's talent.

Okay, we go back to music. I understand music perfectly. I can play a C. I know exactly. But I can't play it like the masters. I just can't do it.

RAL: I realized many years ago that I would not have the skills that my martial arts teacher had. I might develop some different skills or I might develop some of the skills but I will never have the skills that he has. And I'm okay with that because I do what I can do.

First of all, it's enjoyment. You can have fun at it. And then, the sky's the limit. We have a goal, that's all, and like with anything you try to get the go of it. You don't get it, that's okay. That's where the ego comes in. Just sit back, relax and do it. And the whole idea is having fun at it. So now we go to another aspect of how I was trained and how BP were trained. We didn't have amateur status. You're professional, you enter the school, you were gonna be martial artists, you fought, and it's combat. You and other people are not in that phase. We're having fun here.

We're learning push-hands, we're not learning how to kill, we're having fun here. It's a totally different game. That's different training. I trained professionally, and BP trained professionally, and like any profession, different standards. So I'm not a golfer, I'm an amateur tennis player. Now why can't I become a pro? I'm not doing this three hours, six hours a day. That's why I'll never be a pro tennis player even if I wanted to on three hours a week. Martial arts, three hours a week. So my students, they train three hours a week if they're lucky. You're not going to get to a high level, because you're not putting the time in.

That's all. They're not living that way. So that's what my teacher said to me. He said, when they train, they train six hours every day. So their ten years training was ten years. He said, your guys train an hour a week! He says, so your 10-year training is like a year. So when you look at it in that context, he says, that's why you're not as good as me. You don't train like I do, and my students don't train the way I do.

I tell my students, you know, you're amateurs, get that in your head, you're an amateur. Some of them don't like that, that's ego. I said, well, if you want to be professional, you train every day.

When I was a professional, I did that. Because that was me. Just like any champion wrestler, any sport, that's what you do. And I tell my students, I said, you don't do that. You're facing a guy who does that. You're dead.

BP too, we basically didn't do anything except train. That was our whole life. I got away from it, that was my personality. I went to college and did other things. BP did his thing, you know, but in the beginning, that's how we got to be where we were. That's all we did. So, you're not supposed to be where we are. You know what I mean? Because you didn't do what we did.

RAL: I believe I read somewhere that you're into energetics. This article was in the Sunday Times. I thought maybe you'd like to read that.

Give me the summary.

RAL: To cure or ameliorate diseases by simply using the mind. Meditation, yoga, etc. This person doesn't come to a definitive answer, but apparently, he had cancer, and it was arrested.

Now, you don't cure anything. Okay. You control it. You manage it, you don't cure disease. So when people say that, they totally don't understand the process of what it is. So when you have cancer, you contain it. Any disease, you maintain it, you control it, you don't cure it. The word "cure" is not a medical term.

RAL: From what I understand, Mr. Chan used to say you don't cure anything, you heal.

That's all correct. Healing is maintaining it. Once you have cancer, you have it. Once you have a disease, you have it. So it's benign, it's under control. It can explode at any time, any given disease. That's what I'm saying, you don't cure it. Now, even if you do an operation and they cut it all out and eradicate it, there's a reason why you got cancer. It's in your body. It's in your DNA.

Okay? So, what do we do? We do the best we can. Now, we're talking about Chinese medicine and Western medicine. Chinese medicine's approach is preventative. Western medicine is good as... When you got it, what are we gonna do? Now, they come together. This is Yin and Yang, hard and soft. Okay? It's not good to have one or the other. That's stupid. So, in a Western approach, they do nothing to get you to fight it off; that's not the thinking. In Chinese medicine, we're doing everything we can so you don't get it. But you understand you need both.

And just because you do Qigong does not mean you won't get sick. Now, Qigong is like this, Qigong is energy. It's not mystery. We're running on an energy grid. It's part of the energy grid. You can have great qigong and still wither away. Again, we even get the conflict of Eastern thought: If you have Qigong, you can do everything. That's not true.

Well, you wouldn't be living if you didn't have chi. It's what you do with it, okay? So don't think in terms of that as magic. A lot of people will tell you "I have Chi, I can do magic." No, that's when you walk away. That's just as bad as somebody who doesn't believe in any of it. Again, Yin and Yang is the opposite of it. You see why it's important to have the two together?

RAL: They complement each other.

They perfectly complement each other. We had a student who has passed away. She was a great student. She was technically the best BP had. What I mean is that she was like this, two fingers, two toes, perfect. No feeling. No chi. Couldn't let go.

Okay, I'll give you one of my favorite sayings: Analysis paralysis. You become so intent on the technical stuff.

Professionally, my wife is a dancer. They would tell her not to count her steps, because now you're getting technique. So, it's the flow. Let's talk about the Japanese for a minute. Japanese karate is technical because that's customarily how it's taught.

But if you ever visit a Japanese class in karate, that's how they teach it. It isn't that it's bad, it's the approach. Karate is fine, it's an art, but if you do it that way, nothing flows.

RAL: It becomes all posture, no transition.

No transition is the key. When my students stand there, they're perfect. They take the first step, it's the transition. As they say, well, now we lost it. That's why you practice. Okay, you practice taking the first step of the whole thing, then second step, and you and my teaching approach is I want you to flow. I'm not into the posture as much as flow. If I can get you to flow, I can teach you the posture. It's my approach. Other people teach you the posture, but you can't flow. But you're not getting anywhere. That's my point.

If you have great posture, and you take a step and lose it, no good.

So now, push hands. We have to talk about push hands a little bit.

Push hands really is the essence of the expression of the Chi and how to play. I'll look at your form one of these days, we'll do that.

I used to play tennis. I remember asking my teacher "How do you slice it up?" He said, "You've got to think it." What? The mind goes there? I played a professional tennis player, a pro. He brought me right up to net. You see, when you understand push-hands, you can feel everything. I was there and I could feel everything he did. He just waited me out. What I'm talking about is in my mind, slow motion, I said, this guy's waiting me out.

I gotta move, sooner or later you gotta move. And when I moved, that's when he hit the ball the other way. There was nothing I could do, because his timing is far superior. So, what happens in the time of playing is, you're moving normal, he's at supersonic speed, he's watching everything, he's got time, he just watches. I cannot wait him out, I cannot. So that's push hands, okay? From my learning of push hands, I knew what he's doing to me..

RAL: You were able to sense.

I can sense it. I knew exactly what he was doing.

16. EUROPE

Photo Courtesy of Martin Wessels

Many of Mr. Chan's students are unaware that Mr. Chan taught workshops in Amsterdam:

> "My first workshop was in 1987 with Bun Piac Chan through the Taiji Netherlands Foundation. He taught Tai Chi stick and Qigong, among other things."
> – *Martin Wessels*

> "I moved to Germany permanently in 1983, but Mr. Chan came once to Amsterdam where I did a workshop with him."
> – *Linda Lehrhaupt*

17. FREEHAND DRAWINGS

I was always interested in seeing Mr. Chan's off-the-cuff drawings he made for his students before, during, or after class. Part of the fascination for me is seeing how he transmitted teaching via his drawings. Did his drawing style enable him to transmit movement, ideas, and even complex concepts, quickly? Are a person's freehand illustrations a view into their personality or psyche? Or maybe we just accept them for what they are......

Here are two examples of Mr. Chan's freehand illustrations, one from Tim Folger and one from Alan Stolowitz.

In this first drawing, Mr. Chan names the various footwork constructions: Outer T, Inner T, L, V, Inner V, Toe In, Toe Out, and Long L.

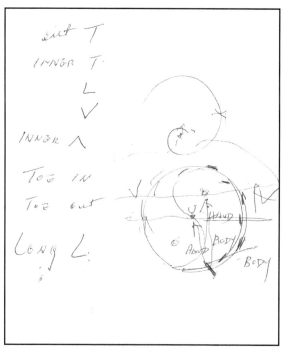

From Tim Folger - Mr. Chan's Footwork Notes

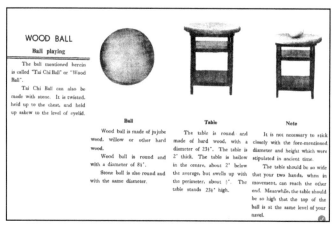

From Alan Stolowitz- Tai Chi Ball Table

From Alan Stolowitz:

In the Summer of 1992, from July 14th through the 18th, at The Tai Chi Farm, Mr Chan was giving a 5-day workshop on The Tai Chi Ruler and Bagua.

After the first day, I brought in a table I'd made a few years back for us all to use, based on the information above.

Mr. Chan looked at it and asked if I had a piece of paper, saying look at the top edge of your table. It's the drawing he did at #1 above.

He said it needs to be like this, the drawing at #2 below. No lip. (Like a wok)

In his understated, exceedingly simple way was hidden an extraordinarily precise understanding of everything he did.

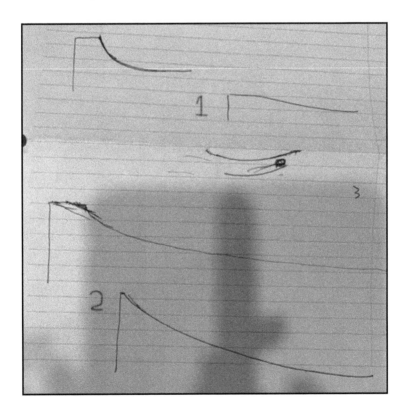

Now, as to his pronunciation of English, that took some getting used to.

In the Bagua section of the workshop I kept hearing him say "HeeBoCo..HeeBoCo.."

Huh? It was only later that I realized he was saying "Heel. Ball. Foot... Heel. Ball. Foot."

18. BP CHAN MEETS TT LIANG
PART II

In the chapter titled **BP Chan Meets TT Liang - Part I,** several students of BP Chan related their recollections of an interaction between Mr. Chan and T.T. Liang when Liang came to NYC to visit William CC Chen.

If you've been diligent and read all the good memories of Mr. Chan by his direct students, you can probably answer the question I raised in **Part I:**

SO, WHAT'S THE TAKE-AWAY FROM THIS?

Is it that your teacher, whom you respected as a skilled practitioner and teacher, was not as skilled as you thought? Or was BP Chan not challenging his guest T.T. Liang so Liang could save face? Or is there something more significant, a lesson, to be learned here?

Personally, I think there are many take-aways:

1. As Cheng Man-Ching said, "Invest in loss".
2. Learning can be a positive experience. Embrace it. Embrace the opportunity to improve yourself. Be open, or as Cooper has told us, "Empty your coconut".

3. Lose your ego. Learning is tough when your ego gets in the way. Be humble.
4. Actively seek out others who are willing to share their skills and experience with you.
5. You can improve your skills and knowledge by being around people who are more highly skilled and more experienced than you are. I'm an average chess player with a ranking of maybe 1200. The current World Champion, Magnus Carlsen, has a rating of 2829. I'll play anybody, whatever their ranking, but in game of chess with Carlsen, which I would undoubtedly lose, what a great learning experience that would be.... for me!

.......and I am sure that the reader can think of many more take-aways from this meeting between Mr. Chan and T.T. Liang.

19. IN THEIR OWN WORDS

"Crosstown, Downtown"
—Marsha Nolan

It was at the Tai Chi Farm that I was introduced to BP Chan. Any person who knows him does nothing but praise him for who he was and what he was able to share with us.

He was a Master of Bagua and Hsing-Yi; he also taught many types of Chi Gong and applications. I attended some of his classes in New York City but mostly weekly classes on the Farm property. These were small classes full of so much information.

I feel saddened that at that time I had limited knowledge of the internal portions of all those forms.

Okay, so there's a lot about me and BP Chan that had to do with the Zhang Sanfeng Festival, mostly the Tai Chi Farm. I talk about him all the time to anybody that will listen. The problem for me is that what I know now, I didn't know then. If I knew what I know now, I would understand much, much more about what he was trying to teach us.

First, I began with Master Jou (Jou Tsung Hwa) when he first started in 1971 over at the Rutgers Medical School campus. We even started the Zhang Sanfeng Festival on that campus.

I worked with him; I ran the whole thing until we started looking for property. He wanted to make a school or a farm. We finally found the one in Warwick. Suddenly, I was always going up there on the weekends. Mr. Chan started showing up with some of his students, who would drive him up there. He disliked the city, so he liked going up there on the weekends. This is my memory of him; just wanted to get away. He also liked to create things out of the natural environment. We cleared the property. It was 100 acres of not much: an old barn, an outhouse, I think, and then a bunch of old cabins and a well that often didn't work. And so, he would clear a section that was going to be his workout section for his students. Master Jou said Mr. Chan could do whatever he wanted because it was all Master Jou's property. The guys would come up and he would make them use as few store-bought things as possible. He didn't want to spend the money and we figured we could do it. It was like a playground for adults. He would cut the wood and the trees down to different heights so that you would practice jumping from one to the other, all the things that he must have used as training tools when he was in China or elsewhere. He had bricks for stepping; going forward, back, left side, right side, central equilibrium. He did all of that. All these fun things were like adult toys. His students would go there and play with all this stuff, maybe on the weekends, or when you were going to take a summer course with Mr. Chan. Sometimes he would just go up there on the weekends to simply teach and have fun. Eventually, the male students built him a little cabin of some sort, so when they went up for the weekend, they didn't have to go home. So that was fun.

I knew him more as a person, a human being, more so than as a teacher. He was very strict and thank God I wasn't his real student forever and ever because he was very strict. (laughs) I think that he learned from Masters. He did a lot of hard style stuff because if you looked at his fingers, he must have thrown them into sand or other kinds of hard training stuff. The tips of his fingers were pretty rough from doing that. I would come up to the Farm, but he didn't make me work. He'd make the guys work. I would come and then we would take a walk all around the 100 acres and he would just talk and talk. I really don't remember too much of the conversation....

He loved his wife so much. He was always careful about female energy, so I never went into the cabin, because there was only male energy in the cabin. That's the kind of guy he was. I think he had five children. I think they were all Catholic, and it was a beautiful family life. When she died, oh, it was so traumatic. He was very sick. He lost a lot of weight. He was devastated over losing her.

You could call him up if you had a health problem or some other problem. You'd call him in Manhattan at his daughter's house and he would talk you through it. Just a really beautiful man.

He knew so much. But we did not know enough about Tai Chi, about what it really was, at least for me, to benefit from all the things that Tai Chi has. He would say that you could do Tai Chi all day long because you use it in your daily life.

RAL: What do you think he meant by that?

Oh, I use it all the time now. I don't set aside time to practice right now being not too well, but these principles that I'm telling you about, I use them whenever I'm anywhere. Grocery shopping; how to open the body. I use walking around as a human being with this body of mine. The other thing he used to say was everything is 45 degrees. That was one of his. Constant. Another was how to do one move. I mean, all that stuff is just great. He'd say if you want to throw something, let's say, a beanbag, your eyes should look beyond where you think it wants to be and it'll land where you want it to be. He would show you all that; how to do the gardening, how to do anything using principles. At the Farm, one guy looked at his hands and said, "Should we quit working now?" Mr. Chan said, "Look at your hands, ask your hands. Do your hands say you should be stopping?"

RAL: Makes sense, doesn't it?

Yes, it does. He was so great. I never saw him being mean. He was tough, but maybe not so tough on me.

I don't know whether he told me or made it up, but he also told this great story that he learned to speak English through Sesame Street, watching TV, because he came from the Philippines.

One of the things that he said, and he's the only person that I ever heard this from, was if you're having trouble with a posture, you always go and check out the prior posture. In other words, that's a setup for the next move. So, if one is wrong, then the next one's going to be wrong.

I want to tell you about one of the things he wanted to do when he came here. His plan was to make everybody do standing meditation for at least a year or two before he would teach them form. But he saw the Americans, they just wouldn't do it, so he had to change his plans on that idea. Now I understand why he wanted to do that; because you learn everything you need to know with standing meditation. I can understand now why he wanted to do that. We would learn that you can connect to the ground six feet down, you can connect with the sky, you can connect with the whole space that you're in, how to get the energy to flow through your body, all those are the reasons you do all this standing. I guess that's why some of the old Masters are so good, because they did the basic work. Form is not it. It's all about principles and posture, and how to move energy around. Maybe you could learn it through meditation, because you learn how to circulate. That's probably what he meant. But you know, we didn't look at it that way. We all thought we're just standing up with our arms out and oh my God can I make it for 45 minutes? He would make us do 45 minutes.

And so, I hope I can connect with BP Chan again. I talk about him all the time when I teach my classes; he's still there.

RAL: I'm sure he's listening.
Yeah, I'm sure he is, too.

RAL: What did you study with Mr. Chan when you were up at the Farm?
Mostly what we did when we went up every week was just play around in the playground that we created. He would make us do the 45 minutes of standing. So, we did a lot of standing. That was good. I don't think at that point he was really explaining what we were supposed to be doing. I can explain that now; at that time, it was probably too much information for students. We had one lesson on different breathing, like deer breathing. I tried to do Bagua. Mr. Chan was doing the circle when we were up at the Farm. I was just playing around, but I guess I learned enough, and a man and his girlfriend said, okay, you're really good. He said, you must have done this stuff before. I thought, ah, there's Mr. Chan. He showed me how to do some stuff. I know we used to do a two-person form, and he'd say, "Crosstown," "Downtown." Did you ever do any of that? It was a prelude to Pa Kua.

You know what? I hate to tell you this. I'm not from the city. I don't know which is downtown, which is crosstown. And so, he was using the reference of the city, now that I think about it. So, we did that a lot. I tried to do a little push-hands. And then Xing-Yi, also. I kind of liked that. We would get into the stance, and then he'd say, you do this, you put your feet here, and then you go one, two, three, and then you'd get your feet in the right position. I thought that was pretty cool. He's trying to show you how you get the right positions and things like that.

The Laying Down Meditation at the Farm, that's what we did. We did a lot of meditation because we had one building that we could go inside. Mostly he liked to do that outside, but sometimes we did class inside.

He always said another concept was the five W's and one H. You probably heard about that one. We use that all the time. Not everybody uses all of those. What, Where, Why, When and How and then if you didn't know all of that about one move, forget it. People just do all this movement with their arms, moving around, nothing about how, why are you doing it, what's the application, and all the concepts. But he would. He would talk about it and show you how to try to use it. In those days, the 80's/90's, we were not push-hands people. Nobody knew much about push-hands. This was a long time ago.

Mr. Chan always had a small frame form. His arms were never these great big open wide things. You knew that that was a protection of the body and that he was a true real martial artist. Now I know. Sometimes you don't know how good you have it. I was lucky. But I'll tell you about my very last experience with him.

I was not doing too well for a while. Finally, I called Mr. Chan on the phone. He said, "Why don't you just come and try this out? No more studio in New York. I have a place in New Jersey in a library." I don't remember the location now, but it was close to the city. So, I got in the car one Saturday and I found it. I practiced with him. I went oh my gosh, I'm going to start getting better now because I found him. I'm back and he's going to be my teacher and then two weeks later, he passed away.

RAL: If you saw Mr. Chan in that New Jersey library several weeks before he passed away, that was probably in 2002.

Wow. Right. Because I was trying really hard to get back.

I didn't go to the funeral because I was not good at city driving. Today it would be so much easier to just put on Google Maps and they tell you how to get there.

But I didn't go. I know I had the memorial book somewhere at one point. I'm not sure if it was a Buddhist funeral or a Catholic one because I knew the family was all Catholic. Anyway, I felt awful because I should have been there. I loved him so much as a teacher and a person, but it was just a little bit too difficult for me to figure out how to do it.

A lot of people that I knew who came up to the Farm to study and stayed with Master Jou really didn't know Mr. Chan. They didn't study with BP Chan, but I did. I'm just so grateful. Because I talk about him, and like I said, he's just an example of things. And all his little expressions. And I really have only a limited recollection of them. I wish I had written down all the things he said.

RAL: You mentioned that you liked Xing-Yi. What about it did you find it appealing?

When people were doing Tai Chi, there was just a lot of flow. With Xing-Yi, you had a set order. You had to be close in with your hands. You took a certain step. You could feel the power. You release energy.

RAL: Fa Jin?

Right. You could feel the Fa Jin from Xing-Yi, because it was designed to emit that. I just felt this is pretty cool. I was attracted originally to Tai Chi because I took ballet as a kid and I needed peaceful, quiet things to do; I had three little kids who sometimes drove me crazy. So I liked that. I would feel all that punch. You could feel where it was coming from. Today, some people are fudging and they're not doing it correctly at all, because it's not coming from their feet, but they think they are. So that's why I like the Xing-Yi part.

RAL: Mr. Chan taught deer breathing at the Farm. The breathing methods he showed were deer breathing, turtle breathing, and crane breathing?

Yes.

He really didn't show us the Yang Style form. He did Bagua, Xing-Yi, for me anyway, and that two-person crosstown, downtown, and playing around with the Five Elements.

I heard from others that people came into the studio once. I don't know whose story is true, but you probably have heard it. There were people who came into the studio, William Chen's school. I don't know if Mr. Chan thought these people were going to challenge him or not. I don't know if my recollection of the story is exactly right, but suddenly, he seemed to disappear—like he flew. Suddenly, he jumped up on the desk and he was like disappeared. I thought about those little things that we practiced at the Farm with those trees that were cut flat. All that balancing stuff, maybe that's how he was able to do that. Hopping up from nowhere, then he's on a desk and he's not going to be challenged. I know the story is on track, but all the fine points I don't really know. But if you get somebody who went to the studio, maybe they would know that.

"You Got Lucky"
—Tim Regan

Two of Da Liu's long-time students, Reggie Jackson and Ron Caruso, were pressing Da Liu for more push-hands training, and he finally sent them down to William Chen. It was Reggie and Ron's habit to take the train down from Connecticut on Sundays when B.P. Chan was typically teaching at William Chen's old school on the West Side closer to Times Square, so they quickly discovered Chan's classes. Chan always taught on Sundays at William's School.

Both Reggie and Ron worked with William a bit, but they both got very excited about working with Chan. They really liked Chan's push-hands teaching and found it much more precise and densely detail oriented than what they had encountered in the approaches of Da Liu and the Cheng Man Ching style that was prevalent in New York at the time.

Reggie and Ron wanted to know where all this detailed information about push-hands was coming from, and Mr. Chan tells them it's straight out of the form. Okay, they decided, we have to start studying the form with you, and, pretty quickly, they weren't really Da Liu students anymore. They kept up with Da Liu, but they switched primarily to working with Chan.

Around this time, I had stopped studying with Reggie (Jackson) for a little while. I started with him when I was taking a break from my undergrad, and then I had left for a year, maybe a year or a half, before I came back. I thought, why did I stop doing that? I love this thing. So before returning, I was boning up on Da Liu's form to show I'd been practicing, but when I got back, Reggie's suddenly teaching a totally different form!

RAL: So, what was it about Mr. Chan's push hands teaching or the way that he taught that form?

It was the detail and precision. Some people would complain that Chan's approach was mechanistic. I remember Chan would say that he had come to his first classes in the US, in New York, armed with two words he'd asked his daughter to teach him. He claimed he basically didn't know a word of English before he came to this country. The two words were "axis" and "gear," to refer to how the rotation of the lumbar spine (yao) puts the whole body in motion. He was partial to metaphors around rebuilding car engines, which fit with his years in the Philippines and all those old Jeeps.

Chan came over to visit his kids in the US, and one of his daughters brought him to meet William Chen as she was living close to William's old studio. Chan's kids were moving over here one by one, and I think his daughter was thinking, "How do we hook him? We need to get him some friends." This is my inference perhaps. So, his daughter brought him to meet William and, as Chan would always say, it was "love at first sight." As soon as he met William, they just totally hit it off. And William instantly asked him, "What do you do?" And, you know, Chan, with his real, rather unique, almost intense, brand of humility admits to knowing a little Bagua. So, William offers to set up a trial class for him while he's visiting.

RAL: You mentioned that you started studying with Mr. Chan around 1992, and then after he passed away you stopped and then you spent some time with Richard #1. What do you think it was about Mr. Chan that made him such a unique human being and such a unique martial arts teacher?

I think this question dovetails with a couple of topics we've touched upon already. What attracted Reggie (Jackson) and Ron Caruso down there, I think, was they were dazzled by Chan's willingness to hold forth on detail, his precision in terms of alignment, those sorts of things. I think they are not as unusual today, although still probably to some degree. But at that time, it was practically unheard of in this country. Nobody talked that way. There weren't any books that detailed any of it. If you were a white English-speaking person on the East Coast, you didn't even know about that side of Tai Chi. You didn't know it existed. It was mind-blowing. It wasn't comparable to anything. And then the profound humility behind all this technical knowledge.

Especially in his earlier teaching career, Chan was also willing to really hold people to martial arts standards, which few people did in Taiji training. It could be kind of fluffy. It was very magical thinking based, like "Oh, I'm gonna get in touch with the Ch'i, and then I'm going to either become immortal or I'm going to become a great fighter, some kind of superhero, or both."

Just read the stories and the descriptions of Yang Lu Chan. They say this guy was built like a bull. This guy was a monster, right? And back then, those guys trained like Olympic athletes. Now you think that doing Taiji on the weekends is gonna give you some great martial power? You guys are crazy. Personally, I do this because I like it. It's interesting. I don't have these overblown fantasies of power and whatever.

Now, I shouldn't say that I didn't participate in some level of that. I mean, I remember when I got my first taste of some minuscule amount of martial ability. I hesitate to even call it that because it sounds overblown. But I was hot to get in fights for a while. I got a few fights in the street and that kind of stuff, but there was always that voice in the back of my head going, "don't kid yourself."

After I met Chan, I remember people would come in to class sometimes and say something had happened to them, some self-defense situation they'd come out of okay—"Mr. Chan, somebody came after me," and I did this or that, whatever, and I got out of it, and this and that, and Chan would just look at them and go, "You got lucky."

Which is totally different from what would happen in other schools.

Chan's classes had a unique combination of having a serious training mentality but no promises. Chan made it clear that if you want to train this stuff, this is what it's like—I'm going to bark at you, and I'm not going to be nice. I'm not going to be your pal and I'm not going to tell you how good you're doing. I'm going to tell you you're doing terrible. And Chan would make it clear he wasn't responsible for our training, only we could do that. He would say, "I'm only an instructor. The principles are the teacher." Who knows what you're going to achieve? No promises.

He would use the phrase that all this training is "just to improve your chances of getting lucky," whether it's martial arts or health. He wouldn't even promise you this is going to fix your health. But at the same time, we're really going to go at it like this is serious stuff. We're going to train seriously because that's worth doing, in and of itself without any promises.

I think, in a nutshell, that says a lot about what was unusual or special about him.

RAL: Did Mr. Chan ever use the word Ch'i? Was he a believer in ch'i?

Sometimes he would talk about Ch'i, but not often. He was clearly a believer in Ch'i, there's no question. And yes, he would talk about it. Certainly, if he was discussing ching-ch'i-shen (jing-qi-shen) like when he used to give little lectures on the three treasures at the Tai Chi Farm for the Zhang San Feng Festival.

Chan would talk about when he first came to New York all his students would ask questions and really press him about the Tan T'ian (Dantian). He thought this was both rude and over-weening. Students were throwing around a lot of words Chan didn't think they understood. They were in their heads and not in their bodies. So, he wanted to avoid that trap of using too much jargon. But bare bones terms like "yao" and "k'ua" he would use freely. But he would talk about the Tan T'ian sometimes, in the right context or if it was in the name of a standing (chan chuang) posture.

He loved car metaphors. He would say, when you're taking apart an engine, you put out the sheet, you take every piece out, you label it, and all of this. And I always thought, oh, that's just the Philippines, right? They've been building these World War II Jeeps for 50, 60 years. That a nuts-and-bolts mentality, which was his thing. It really defined him. He made it clear that this training is mechanical—that's the starting point. But it's not only mechanical, right? He was definitely a believer in Ch'i. There's something bigger than the mechanics.

But if you don't get the mechanical precision, how can you expect to get the other stuff? The mechanical comes first. And with that comes a certain training of the mind. You have to be calm and serious and a whole bunch of things to be able to focus on the mechanical stuff seriously. So, you're starting the mental training at the same time.

Chan was like, if you can't do the mechanical stuff, why do you want to talk about C'hi? None of you can even do the mechanical stuff. You're all hopeless. I remember a day he came into class; he looked around the room, and he just went, "You make me ashamed." I was a sensitive kid. So, I would hear that kind of stuff, and it would just be crushing. But at the same time, it would be motivating. I'd be like, "Oh, I've really got to earn this guy's respect. I got to train harder or at least smarter." I remember talking to Chan one day about how much training I was trying to put in, and he said to me," You don't need to put in six hours [a day], you just need a little idea." He meant the correct idea. He was also probably worried I was becoming a bit of a Tai Chi bum.

So much of Chan's older, New York crew, either resembled him a bit or came to. They're sort of irascible, like he was irascible. I should say the second and third generation of his New York students, technically, because Chan would say when he first tried to teach Bagua over here, the first group of people all quit. It was the second group who stuck.

RAL: How did Mr. Chan's teaching change from 1992 until 2002? Did you notice any changes in how he…

Oh, a tremendous amount. But this is my interpretation of things. After his wife passed, I think it was a whole new ballgame. The impression I received from the senior students was that Chan had decided to put his affairs in order. I heard that he gave himself a decade to put his affairs in order, mostly stuff to do with the children and the family.

You know, who knows how the world really works? I don't have a clue. But that seemed like Chan. He gave himself 10 years, and then that's it. What he would say is that he did not want to stick around—the world is just going to hell. Who wants to be around anymore? Not in those words exactly, but who wants to stick around and see this? He would talk about China as if China was ruined. Not so much by the communists, but by the pollution. No fan of the communists, you know, certainly not of the Cultural Revolution or any of that, but it was the pollution. It's the fact that something in his mind as pristine and big as China could become as polluted as the West.

RAL: So, was that an attitude that he espoused after his wife passed away? Do you think?

Well, most of my time was with him after. So, before his wife passed away, I'd mostly done workshops up in Connecticut when Reggie had him up, or I'd gone over to the Tai Chi Farm a couple of times. I remember quite a difference in his presentation.

When Reggie would have him up to Connecticut, he was always quite nice. He was in that general-public mode. He could be really quite open and gentle with new people. When I trained with him at the Farm, it was more like the old school Mr. Chan, which is busting people's balls, and implying most of you have no idea what it takes to learn this stuff, and you're probably not going to put in the time. I remember a week-long Pa-kua workshop with him that included standing meditation, Chan Chuang (Zhan Zhuang.)

I had never done it before. Da Liu had a Chan Chuang (Zhan Zhuang) set, but it was very light with the knees held straight. It was not strenuous the same way. So, I'm learning Chan Chuang, and I don't know how many minutes into it I'm starting to shake—you know, really shake. The wise guy next to me goes, "Oh, Mr. Chan, what's wrong with him? And Chan says, "Oh, it's just pre-Ch'i. I'll help," and he goes and pushes me deeper into the stance!

With one finger, right in the kua, he just pushes you down gently. Oh man, I think my first taste of real training was that week. I was in my early 20s.

RAL: This is on 23rd Street?

No, this is at the Tai Chi Farm.

It was just fierce. And I was like, "Okay, this is what things are like! Different from Reggie. Reggie was always a super nice guy, and again, no ego, but in a very different way from Chan, a very different manner.

And then later that week, we learned basic drills. You know Chan's three basic drills?

RAL: Were they like the Eight Chi Kung?

One of them is like the horizontal sweeping from the Eight Chi Kung. The next one is clearing the center downwards, sort of like the transition for Brush Knee. The other is that kind of spear or drilling palm, back and forth.

RAL: Not sure I was shown that specifically.

You know Chan. He often didn't like to give names to things if he could help it. If we give anything a name, then we're claiming some authority, right? We're not going to claim any authority or lineage. We're not going to let people attach to these names and think they know something now. Everything should be nameless. But then we never knew how to talk about anything. So people in class would make up new names for things sometimes for convenience, so we can discuss them and ask questions.

That's where I sometimes thought things were going a little far. If you don't want to tell us who your teachers are, that's fine. I'm not hung up on lineage. But if I don't know what to call something, I can't discuss it with other people or research it.

I remember a senior student telling me the time he once asked Mr. Chan, "What about this system? We don't learn this technique that everyone else is talking about." Mr. Chan replies, "What do you mean? We do it. It's here, and it's here."

So, so we're practicing this drill where one person is punching and the other person is cracking them on the cuff above the wrist, and Chan teams up with me. I guess I'm the newbie. I'm this skinny kid, you know? And Chan's got his metal watch band on. And I'm like, "Oh God." I mean, it's just pulping my wrist. Then after a minute or so, Chan says "Oh, sorry," takes his watch off, and puts it in his pocket. With that kind of stuff, you never know if it's done "accidentally on purpose." Then Chan starts in again, and I'm like, "Oh my God, it's worse." His forearm bone is actually harder and more painful than that metal watch band was.

So that was my introductory week to real training. I'd never gone anywhere people were really sweating and suffering. Tai Chi had been kind of nice up till then.

RAL: Welcome to the Farm, Tim.

Apparently, I liked it because I came back for more. I was really curious about Bagua, and Chan was the only person around teaching Pa-kua that I could find.

When he came to New York (well before my time), Chan had started teaching Bagua both because he liked it (I remember once he said he preferred it) but also because he didn't want to teach Tai Chi and step on anybody's toes, right?

When Chan meets William, and William says, "Oh, what do you practice?" Chan knows William does Tai Chi, and he doesn't want to intrude on William's authority. So, he says, "I do a little Pa-kua." And William invites him to teach a class.

After Chan decides to stay here, he would never teach anything anybody else in town was teaching. If somebody in town was teaching a form, Chan wouldn't teach that form. It's like for years he wouldn't teach the Yang family T'ai-chi long form. Because other people were teaching it. He initially taught what he called the "Mainland Form," the simplified 24 posture routine, but of course Chan didn't teach the postures simplified and he counted the movements much higher than 24, but he borrowed the format.

RAL: Yeah, William Chen was teaching that, right?

William was teaching a 60-move form, and Chan didn't teach any T'ai-chi for a while. When he did, Chan taught his adaptation of the official, mainland sports committee form. Which is funny, because he took just that order and put all his traditional movements in it. So, it's nothing like the standardized sports committee routine out of China. It was just his way of sort of getting around teaching anything anybody else was teaching.

RAL: I had asked one of Mr. Chan's students about how his Pa-kua changed from the early days to later days and what he said to me was that Mr. Chan simplified it greatly.

Yeah, even during my tenure, which was in the later part of Chan's teaching over here (I was like around for mostly the last 10 years of his teaching), he was simplifying things radically.

Sometimes I would come in and perform something like Mud-tread Stepping an older way, and on certain days, Chan would sort of look around and go, "Yeah, do what he's doing." Other days, you better do it just like he's currently showing you.

After that first week of training with Chan at the Farm, I knew I wanted to study with this guy. I'd been listening to other students mention classes in the city, so I asked him, "Where do you teach in New York." But Chan won't tell me. He's like, "Where are you training?", and I tell him I had been training in Connecticut with Reggie Jackson (though this was during the break I'd been taking and didn't know Reggie had started studying with Chan.) And Chan says, "Oh, that's good. Keep training, and take what you learned here, practice it," but he won't tell me where he teaches in New York.

I would have started going down to William Chen's right away, but I was too new. I was an unknown quantity, and he didn't want me getting ahead of myself. I also think part of it is Chan didn't like to mix people from different classes. If you're someone from the Tai Chi Farm workshops, you go to those workshops (unless you're already someone from one of the the New York classes). If you're a 42nd Street person, you do 42nd St. If you're an Astor Place person, you do Astor Place. Like everybody had their place. That was part of it. Also, once I did start training with him in New York, Chan made it obvious that he thought, "you're a young guy—you need to be saving your money."

I think he was conflicted about teaching for money. Because before he came to this country, I don't know that he ever did.

The story I heard him tell about teaching in the Philippines was that he'd be there early every morning and got frustrated with students showing up late. So he instituted a five-peso fee if you were late—almost nothing at all, but symbolic. This made some people feel bad. They tell him, we're trying but sometimes we're late, but you're (referring to Mr. Chan) never late. So a week later, Chan shows up late for the first time ever, and he puts his five pesos in the jar just to show them, see, I'm human too. You don't have to feel bad.

I think teaching in this country, having to always teach for money, was hard. Chan liked teaching at the Farm on weekends because it was out in the trees but also because he could teach for free there. People would pay in labor. I'm sure you've heard stories about how those guys, not so much me because I came along later, but originally those students worked like dogs, cleaning up what was basically a junkyard. I was put to work when I was there, but nothing like the labor that went on earlier. But he could teach for free. Chan used to teach in the park at Thomkins Square before the authorities told him you can't come and teach Tai Chi here.

When his daughter and his wife and he moved to Stuyvesant, they had those grounds and he wanted to teach there but again they told him no, you can't teach classes here on the property. He liked teaching for free.

After I had been an assistant teacher for Reggie, I got his approval for starting to teach some classes. At first Reggie was asking, "I don't know, are you experienced enough?" I thought I was but I knew so little. But I wasn't going to teach without his okay. Later, after I'd been teaching a few years, I had some of my students come to a workshop with Mr. Chan that Reggie was hosting. And Mr. Chan apparently told one of the women there that I shouldn't be teaching.

RAL: Mr. Chan told one of the women you shouldn't be teaching?

252

She didn't tell me until much later. She found it shocking. So I didn't know what he really said. It seems out of character, but I could certainly understand that he might have felt that way. I'm sure he would have been right. What did I know about anything at that point? On the other hand, I still knew so much more than a lot of casual Tai-chi instructors because most non-Chinese Americans really didn't know anything back then. This would have been in the 90s—just before I started going to New York to study. So, I had figured out on my own that I didn't know enough.

Reggie and Ron Caruso used to go take private lessons with Chan, and I knew they went to his apartment. So, I wheedled Chan's number out of Reggie. I just called Chan up cold with no understanding of Chinese etiquette whatsoever. I'm still in my 20s, and I've been studying some Chinese philosophy and culture, but I don't know anything from anything.

I call him up and say, "Maybe you remember me?" He does, but he's in his really nice mode that he took with outsiders. I say I'd like to do a private lesson. I haven't yet figured out you really need to be invited to do private lessons, but Chan's trying not to say no outright. He says well, it's very expensive, and where would we do it, while I'm thinking I can invite myself over to his apartment and I'll just get one lesson with so much information, so many form corrections, that I can just go practice off that. I'm a kid. I don't have any money. I don't have a real job. I'm kind of a T'ai-chi bum, and he can sense that.

So, he's insisting it's just too much money. I'm saying "No, no, I've it saved up and we could meet at your place just like Reggie does—it's fine with me." I'd be embarrassed thinking back on it if the miscommunication weren't so funny.

Once I'm down at Chan's place, he's still trying to dissuade me, telling me to keep my money, and we can just sit on the sofa and discuss martial arts. He goes to get me some tea and comes back with a cup that had a small dead roach in it then heads back to the kitchen. I'm like, Oh-ho, this is a test. Who knows if it was? So I pinch the little dried up roach out and am drinking my tea when he gets back. We chat a little but I'm not to be deterred and finally Chan agrees to take my money.

Now, I think I'm going to go through the whole Yang Family Long Form and get a bunch of corrections. I don't make it through the first move before he stops me with a shake of the head. He's clearly disappointed. He has me repeat it and keep repeating it while he goes into the kitchen. This goes on for an hour and then when it's time to go, I say, "So, should I start coming to 23rd Street on Sundays?" I've started to understand what this is going to take. Chan gives me the nod and I head off to the train.

Let me just quickly answer that question that I never quite finished. Yes, there was definitely a sense of simplification going on, even just during my tenure at Chan's classes.

Once I started Bagua on Sundays, I noticed some significant differences from when I'd met Chan years before. And when I compared notes with more senior students, it became obvious that many things had been somewhat simplified. Sometimes there was a mixing of techniques, like you would get Bagua moves in your T'ai-chi. For instance, by the time I was studying with him, in Chan's snake creeps down, the hand position had become the hand form of his Pa-kua's Purple Swallow Skims the Water.

I was not around either in New York or at the Farm at the very end. I just didn't have time for all the traveling. I had just sent one of my students down to New York to train with that group on the day the news came through that Chan had passed. So unfortunately for her, she got there and then that was it.

"Train Like Your Diapers Are Full"
—Linda Lehrhaupt

I was a regular student of Mr. Chan from 1979 until I moved to Germany in 1983. I still live in Europe to this day.

I was living in New York in those years, and I was honored to be Mr. Chan's student and attended classes regularly from 1979-1983. You have probably already realized how much of a tremendous influence he was on me, not just in terms of Tai Chi and Qi Gong, but also as a teacher.

Although in some ways I'm quite radical, in many ways I'm quite traditional. And that was something I always loved about Mr. Chan. I have tears in my eyes when I think of him because he meant so much to me.

There's that famous story of Yang Chengfu, I believe, or perhaps it was another teacher. In any case, this young man deeply wanted to study Tai Chi, but he came from the wrong side of the tracks, so to speak. He was just a poor boy. He used to watch the teachers and students doing Tai Chi through a hole in a fence. One day he got caught and was dragged into the school courtyard. They were going to punish him, but first they told him to show them what he had learned. They were so impressed with his efforts and mastery that they broke tradition and invited him to join the school. In those days, and still today in many traditional Asian Arts, the learning philosophy is basically: "Do what the teachers do. Don't ask questions. Absorb it through being in the presence of the teacher."

A lot of Western students were/are naive, especially the ones who started in the 60s, 70s, and 80s. They thought an enlightened master was also infallible and above moral reproach, which, unfortunately, was and is not true. Everyone is human. It's the same thing in the Tai Chi and Qigong world. You have teachers coming over from China who were just sports students at the university. They come to the West, put on Tai Chi outfits and start calling themselves Master So-and-so, and everyone was/is taken in.

And then you had someone like Mr. Chan who, if I tried to call him Master, would get very angry and say, "Don't call me Master." And I'd say, "May I call you Mr. Chan?" And he said,

"Yes, that's okay." I never called him BP, I never called him Bun Piac, I never called him anything except Mr. Chan.

I don't know why he refused to take on the mantle of being a Master or opening his own school. When I was studying with him, his day job was working in the stock room of the Paragon Sporting Goods Store in New York City. And he seemed content with that.

He never sought, although he deserved, Grandmaster status. He shied away from it. And when people tried to suggest it to him, he'd get quite angry. I don't know to this day why he avoided any kind of elevation.

I don't know whether it was because of experiences he had as a young man in China or when he went to the Philippines. I don't know whether he felt that keeping a low profile was important. Maybe it was a combination of this, or maybe he felt that it just wasn't him.

Mr. Chan taught in the school of Grandmaster William C.C. Chen, who was my Tai Chi teacher. I was an active student of Grandmaster Chen for 25 years. I invited him to Germany every year for 18 years and only stopped because I moved into another field of work. Mr. Chan was always the other teacher in his school, and William was respectful to him.

Mr. Chan had Saturday classes and Monday evening classes and occasionally he might have some private students.

RAL: In your emails to me you mentioned that you studied Qigong and Tai Chi saber form with Mr. Chan from 79 to 83. I did not know that he taught any kind of saber form.

Oh yes, he taught a wonderful saber form which I learned from him. And I deepened my study of it with David Pancarian, who was also a devoted student of William Chen, but who studied with Mr. Chan as well. We became friends.

I also studied the staff form of Mr. Chan with David. I invited David to come over to Europe to do a workshop, and he taught Mr. Chan's staff form.

RAL: I learned BP Chan's Eight Immortals Staff Form.

I never learned the names of the Tai Chi forms from Mr. Chan. I would say primarily I was his Qigong student.

RAL: Which of the Qigong forms did you learn from him?

Well, we did the Eight Brocade. We did what he called the Tai Chi warm-ups, which I later heard might be called the Bagua warm-ups. We did another form which I don't know the name of, but I gave it the name Playful Dragon. It was a series of eight exercises. We also did a kind of walking Qigong, which I think came from a Qigong cancer treatment program in China. We also did a lot of standing meditation.

I once asked Mr. Chan, "If I only have time to do one exercise that you've taught me, what should I do?"

He said immediately, "Stand." He was big on standing. I talked about it in one of my stories about how I first met him.

I arrived to the first night of class a bit late. People were already practicing the standing meditation, and he just said "Come, come, sit, sit." He indicated I should just watch.

I couldn't believe it: half hour later, they were all still standing. About 45 minutes later, I think, they finally stopped. I remember Mr. Chan looking at me with a kind of a glee in his eye, as if to say, "That will be you soon."

He was always very kind to me. I don't know if he taught men and women differently. But in my observation, I never saw any differences in my Qigong classes. He was always quietly, persistently, demanding. Sometimes he would just come over and say, "What are you doing? Do that." But I never ever felt put down. I felt corrected. He would make "adjustments." I think this is my term, not his.

Form was really important to him. He didn't accept sloppiness, but he also had an art of, in my opinion, accepting the best that someone was capable of. He had a way of seeing through to what the essence of a posture or movement was. He had a way of encouraging each person to do their best, their personal best, and, of course, that was different for each person. My personal best at 30 years of age is not my personal best of today.

When you were Mr. Chan's student, you never knew what you would be learning when you came to class. You might think you had finished a series like Eight Brocade or 10 Taoist exercises, and six months later, he'd begin again, from the beginning. From the very beginning.

I think my favorite story about learning with Mr. Chan is the following: When he would demonstrate a move, he would do it five times. He would say, "Watch the different parts of my body." He would point to a part of his body and say, "Look here... and then here..." and then the hip/pelvic area and the knees and the feet. You would have to watch him each time. He would do the exercise five times, and you would be observing at different body levels.

One day he was showing a move that I had seen him do many times in the years I studied regularly with him. I said out loud, "Oh!" because I finally got "it," that is, what he was trying to teach. He looked at me and chuckled a bit and said, "Finally!" It was a beautiful transmission. What I got was not so much the physical move, but the essence, which I could then translate into my body. It was like the last piece of the puzzle dropping into place. Suddenly, it just clicked.

I remember also how he would make tiny adjustments to our postures or moves. If you were standing, and maybe your elbows were drooping a half-inch or something, he would make an adjustment, and you would feel how everything just clicked into place.

Each person of course was different. He didn't insist that everybody look like a carbon copy of each other...or him. He had a way of scanning you and knowing what was right for you, for your body and for who you were.

RAL: Did he have a special name for you? Several students have told me that he had special names for them.

Not that I know of. I'm not trying to say that I was an indoor student or even close. I was just a devoted student who showed her respect. I didn't take private lessons with him. I didn't do any kind of student ritual that maybe others did.

RAL: Did you ever see him do anything unusual?

Not really. But I had a sense that if he rooted, I don't think you could have moved him.

My Qigong classes were very small, and we were a different group from the people who were doing either Chen Style Tai Chi, Bagua or Xingyi with him. I don't think we mixed very much, but that just might have been my impression.

RAL: You did the Eight Brocade; you did the 10 Taoist. Did you do the Hanging Leg Set?

I don't think so. But I did something that I called the Playful Dragon. The first exercise is two dragons swimming in a stream. The second one is also about twin dragons. It's a series of eight exercises in all. I have them in diagrams. We were lucky in those days because we had some students who would make diagrams of the exercises, and then we could follow them. We also did a Qigong exercise that was called Washing the Ligaments.

RAL: Washing the ligaments. Was this a ligament stretching exercise?

I don't know. Maybe. But he called it Washing the Ligaments.

RAL: You had mentioned that you are still a student of William Chen. He's still renowned. He's written a number of books. He probably has thousands of students, very well known. Mr. Chan never wrote any books, didn't want anything written about him. So, you've had a unique perspective in that you've had experience with both. Any thoughts on comparing and contrasting them?

I wouldn't compare them. They each had their style, way, integrity, special interests. It would just be conjecture on my part, even about their relationship. I wouldn't know how to compare them.

RAL: I think you probably hit the nail on the head. I think it's sufficient to say that they are both equally good, just different people. Different styles, different teaching styles probably.

Yes, different backgrounds. And different influences.

RAL: In Mr. Chan's classes that you attended, what was the ambiance like there?

My Qigong classes were small. I mean, it would be a huge group if there were eight of us.

Let's say for two years at a time, there might be six or seven of us. He didn't have a lot of new students coming in. We would arrive, take off our coats, put on our training shoes and then we'd go and stand.

We always began the classes with standing. Then we would practice and train. It was serious, but not unfriendly. He would be watching and looking, and he was always there, He was never late. I went to his Monday-night Qigong class for years.

He knew that I was a single mother and that sometimes it was hard for me to get a babysitter. So, if I was a bit late, he would just give me a smile. He always made me feel welcome. I felt like I was coming home when I came to his class. He was my teacher. I just felt his kindness, and I felt safe. I think the atmosphere was warm, but not in an American warm way, okay?

RAL: What do you mean by that?

Well, he wasn't American. He was Chinese and lived a long time in the Philippines. So, there was no hugging. No physical contact except for form corrections or push hands. He was very careful around women. He might touch your elbow to correct you, or he might touch your back, but in a very respectful way. Never invasive.

RAL: Did he do the exercises with you? Or just observe?
He did both.

RAL: Was this at 23rd Street?
Yes. I think it was when the school was on 23rd Street. Most of my training was there.

RAL: Did you find, in the four or five years that you were with him, that the way he taught the Qigong had changed?
He was extremely consistent. As far as I can see, he didn't innovate, in the sense that we learned what he learned and what he practiced. That's what I understood. Now, I don't know 100%, but I had a sense that we learned what he had absorbed from his teachers. I didn't even know who his teachers were. Other people did, maybe because they asked him. I found out his teachers' names through the writings of others such as Ken Cohen. I just didn't think to ask Mr. Chan too much about his past.

RAL: In one of the articles that you sent me, you mentioned that you and a group of fellow students and Mr. Chan went to Madison Square Garden, I believe.
Yes. That was wonderful. As far as I remember, it was a presentation of Chinese acrobats from China. I seem to recall it was a group of us who were Mr. Chan's Qigong students who went. There weren't many of us. But do you know the story? The story about what Master Chan said?

RAL: Yes, yes. It was so funny that I practically fell off the chair.
This was the one about "No Pretty, Just Chi."
I'll never forget that, because that was Mr. Chan through

and through. I was sitting next to him. The show started with the youngest kids, maybe seven years old. Then each time a new group would come on stage, they would be a bit older. We were all mesmerized by their performances. I turned to Mr. Chan and asked him, "What do you think, Mr. Chan?" He said immediately, "Very pretty, no Chi." Okay, I thought.

For the last performance of the evening, an elderly man came onstage. Unlike the others, he was very plainly dressed in a T-shirt and dark pants, wearing Tai Chi shoes. He walked very slowly and humbly to a seat.

He looked like he just stepped out of a Chinese village somewhere. At that point, Mr. Chan sits up ramrod straight, at full attention...eyes focused on the man on stage.

The Elder sits down in front of what looked like a large stone. He just sits there quietly, and the crowd begins to grow silent, as if realizing something is about to happen. This was in Madison Square Garden, and it was full. Thousands of people became completely silent. All of a sudden, I saw a small movement of the man's head forward, and then the stone splits apart. The crowd is stunned, and they begin clapping and expressing their excitement. I look at Master Chan and he's smiling broadly. He looks in my direction and says, "You see! No pretty, just Chi."

I'll never forget that. And that was his style, as well, "No pretty, just Chi."

RAL: And then there was the other part that you wrote about also. I think, I'm not sure if it was your child or someone else's child whose diaper was......

It was my daughter.

RAL: Her diaper was full, and Mr. Chan was talking about being rooted.

We used to practice at 6:00 am in Tompkins Square Park in the East Village of New York City. I sometimes took my daughter, who was about two years old, with me because I did not have anyone to look after her, and she loved being there with us.

One day her diaper was full, and she was walking around. I moved to change her, and Mr. Chan, who had eight children, immediately recognized the situation.

He said to me, pointing at her "You practice like that. That is good. Train like your diapers are full."

I really got it, you know. My daughter´s diaper was full of shit, and he was saying, walk and move like that, as if you are weighted down.

I would just say that he is the teacher that everyone would wish for, once they realized what it really meant to have a teacher like him. If you want to go after the stars and the flashy ones then, all power to you. But you'll never have that kind of intimate transmission that he gave.

I think, and this is just my guess, that one of the reasons why he never wanted to be called a Master was because he only saw himself as a vessel through which the teachings of his teachers flowed. That's very similar to Zen. One of the things I have been taught is that you're ready to receive dharma transmission as a teacher when you have become a vessel of the Dharma. You're not stuck, you're not clogged up, everything is flowing freely because it is not your Dharma. Mr. Chan never had the attitude, "This is my Tai Chi, this is my Qigong."

A lot of other teachers, whatever they're teaching, get stuck in the idea that they are the source of what they're doing. I think Mr. Chan saw himself very humbly as someone who could transmit what had been given to him and give further in the most non-egotistical, non-selfish way possible. He never said this, and he may not have articulated it in this way, but he lived it. That's what I believe.

And that is true humility.

You know, in Zen, we have a very famous saying, from Master Rinzai, who talked about the True Person of No Rank. That was Mr. Chan.

That's what's most inspiring about him as a teacher. And he embodied the difference between transmitting something of true worth and simply teaching a form.

Though he taught an amazing number of things, and I was grateful to learn some of them, in the end, what he really taught did not matter. There was something so much more important being taught than Tai Chi or Qigong forms. He could have just as easily been teaching me how to fold napkins, how to set a table, how to wash the dishes, how to take care of my family members. It went far beyond that.

He was impeccable in his style, his concern for form, and he was rigorous in many ways. But the most important thing he taught was respect for oneself and one another, and how to give oneself 100% to practice. He was a true master, even if he never used the title.

"I want to put him in a paper bag and take him home!" —Mark Jones

I studied Taijiquan in Mohegan Lake, NY for a few months in the early 1990's with a senior student of B.P. Chan's named Richard. Since Mr. Chan had two Richards in his early classes of the 1970's and 80's after he had recently relocated to New York, he called my teacher Richard number one and the other Richard number two, based on which Richard started with him first. In this essay, when I refer to Richard, I am referring to number one, since he was my primary teacher.

In our classes, Richard constantly would talk about "my teacher." "My teacher did this, my teacher would say that," etc. – all in superlatives. I came to realize that his teacher named Mr. B.P. Chan was still very much alive and still actively teaching in the New York metro area. It seemed obvious to me that if this living treasure was within driving distance, and he was the one who taught my teacher, I would be crazy not to seek him out as well, so I asked Richard if I would be able to meet Mr. Chan. Richard said something to the effect of "sure, he's staying at the Tai Chi Farm in Warwick, NY." So a day or two later, I looked up the location of the Farm, hopped into my car and zipped across the Hudson River toward Warwick.

When I arrived at this rural enclave, I stopped in the office where the proprietor, a tall thin Chinese gentleman named "Master Jou" directed me to walk down a trail through the woods. "Just keep going down that trail until you see a little cabin on the left. That's where you'll find Mr. Chan." Indeed, I did follow that trail and came to Chan's door. A jovial little fellow came to the door to greet me. I told Chan that I was one of Richard's students and his response was, "Richard number 1 or number 2?" He immediately invited me to have a seat at his table. It was a one room shack with a dirt floor, a bed in the corner, some martial arts magazines lying around, a hotplate….very primitive and obviously for seasonal occupancy only.

Chan offered me a bowl of cucumbers. "This very yin food. Summer very yang season so yin food balances you." He was kind of like a Jewish grandmother pushing food at me. I found that very endearing. The next thing he said was "Before you conquer opponent, you first must conquer yourself." From that moment on, I knew I had hit the jackpot. This was one of the authentic remarkable characters that legends are about. He exemplified all the Taoist, Buddhist and Confucian teachings I had been studying for over 20 years.

Next, after eating, Mr. Chan took me outside into the woods and started teaching me incredible stuff that I had never been shown before. Without going into detail, much of it had to do with mind control and visualization techniques combined with various postures. In addition, I was given instruction on guiding energy. From that time on, I would drive out to the Farm to take both private and group lessons from Chan. When I found out that he also taught at William Chen's 23rd St. studio on Sunday mornings, I began getting up early on Sundays and driving down to Manhattan.

Chan always taught in a very traditional Chinese modality which, among other things, included testing a student's commitment to learning before revealing deeper, meaningful teachings and giving indirect answers to questions so the student would have to really work at figuring out the answer to their own questions by themselves. He believed that just by giving the answer right away, the student would forget it right away because they didn't put in the work to arrive at the true, deeper meaning. He would say, "I gave you the tools. Now choose some and build something." So when I first went down there, I said "I'm here for the push hands class." Chan said, "Go over there and stand." (Standing in a Qigong context refers to standing meditation while holding several specific postures.) For most people, a statement like that would sound baffling, counterintuitive and almost obstructive. They would think, "I told him I was there to learn push-hands, so why is he telling me to go stand by myself?" But to me, I knew that it served a twofold purpose: Since I had just arrived from an hour's drive, I needed to relax, regain my central equilibrium, and cultivate my internal energy. Empty my mind so I'd have room to put something new in it. Secondly, he was testing me to see if I had enough faith in him to do whatever he told me to do without questioning it. So I stood meditating for about half an hour, then wandered over and Chan set me up with another student to push hands.

In addition to visiting and learning with Chan at the Tai Chi Farm and Sunday mornings at William Chen's studio on West 23rd St., I attended classes that he gave across the river upstairs in the Pearl River NY Library. He also came several times a year to give workshops that he called "shopworks" (you shop for what material you like then work on it) at our Mohegan Lake school.

Chan took a liking to me and we really bonded. Whenever

I arrived at a class or shopwork, he would come running across the room to greet me "Hello Mark! Hello Mark!" At the shopworks, when he demonstrated techniques in front of all the students – not only from our school but long-time senior students of his and people from other schools and walks of life, Chan would grab me and demonstrate the techniques on me in front of everyone. I served as his test dummy/punching bag. Having seen pictures of Yang Chengfu demonstrating techniques in the 1930's on the great Tung Ying-Chieh, arguably his best student, I was truly honored to get tossed around by Chan in front of everyone! In addition, after the shopworks, we'd all go out to a Chinese restaurant for lunch and Chan would park himself down next to me. I remember times I'd be eating while he told me how to get out of a choke hold or some other martial arts move!

I have never seen a more committed teacher. At one class – I think it was in Pearl River, he saw me performing a Baguazhang palm change. He yelled from across the room "NO, NO, TURN THE OTHER WAY, THE OTHER WAY." I couldn't figure out what he was getting at. He kept yelling and was furious. Eventually I got it. Later, I went into the men's room to relieve myself and Chan walked in, parked himself at the urinal next to me, and embarked on a verbal diatribe about how the move is properly done. Teaching never rests, even in a rest room! Also in Pearl River, I brought a friend along to introduce her to what Chan was teaching. After the class, I asked her how she liked it. She responded, "I want to put him in a paper bag and take him home!" Everybody loved and respected Mr. Chan. He had that special charisma.

While many have focused on Mr. Chan's teaching of martial arts, body strengthening and Qigong healing, I found that one of his most precious and unique gifts was in the philosophic and quasi-spiritual realm. I'd been studying Chinese philosophy since the early 1970's and meditating since then as well, and I found Chan to be the closest thing to the archetypal wise old sage. Kind

267

of like the Shaolin monk teachers in the Kung Fu TV show. What I will never forget is one day, at William Chen's studio, I was in the locker room after class and Chan walked in. I was very troubled and talked to him about some problems I was having with my parents back in Ohio and he gave me some really thoughtful, profound advice that resonated with me for the rest of my life. He spoke in the form of almost poetically aphoristic truths that brimmed with wisdom. I knew it was coming from a Confucian perspective, and who else nowadays thinks like that?

Although I don't believe in any paranormal jibber-jabber which is unfortunately all too prevalent in the Chinese martial arts world, I witnessed a couple of really strange events regarding Chan that I still can't figure out. First, during a "shopwork" in Mohegan Lake, this tall, hulking former student of Richard's walked up to Chan in the middle of about 20 people and asked how he would get out of a headlock. The big guy, who was at least a foot taller than Mr. Chan bent over and put his arms around Mr. Chan's neck. I was watching closely and never saw Chan's arms move at all. He just slightly jerked his body and somehow with his chin locked down on the guy's arm, tossed the big dude over his shoulder! There were many witnesses. If I hadn't seen it, I wouldn't have believed it.

Another time, I was in class at William Chen's, and I was talking to a few of the students there who I knew. They had been with him for at least a decade but were not his original senior students from back in the 70's and 80's. I knew that one of Chan's Tai Chi teachers was the great Tung Ying-Chieh. After all, Chan's picture appears in Dong's classic "Red Book" in a group photo from 1953. These long-time students mentioned that Chan never once would disclose who he learned from. I thought that was ludicrous because we up in Westchester all knew. Richard told us. Chan just wanted students to focus on the learning, not on the names of his teachers. Yet lineage is a strong component of the martial arts, as long as one isn't fixated on it. Mind you, Chan could not have heard this conversation about who his teacher was. He was in the office on the other side of the building. A few minutes later, he emerged from the office, walked across the room and asked if there were any questions. One student asked to see the Tai Chi move called "brush knee, twist step." Chan happily demonstrated, then said, "this is how I do it and this is how Yang Chengfu did it and this is how my teacher Tung Ying-Chieh did it." What are the odds?

I also found Chan to be unique in his perspective that the only thing in the martial arts or any type of movement that matters is adhering to the Principles. Alignment, posture, center. Explaining what the Principles are is far too involved for the purposes of this essay, however, suffice it to say is that it concerns various positioning of the arms, legs, head and torso that allows one to best protect oneself and most efficiently use their body to accomplish movements without getting injured. And it also includes mental and emotional elements. Often, martial arts students become accustomed to hearing their teachers criticize practitioners from other schools for what their movements looked like since they looked quite different than theirs, but Chan saw the same practitioners and gave them credit for doing things with different weight distribution but still being in center relative to their body. Adjustments were all proportionately manifested. Chan would say "everybody right, everybody wrong." He made me more open-minded when looking at practitioners of other schools and styles - as long as they adhered to the Principles and were in center, they were fine.

From what I could gather by studying with Mr. Chan in the time period I did, and talking to early senior students of his, I concluded that there were two distinct periods in his teaching career, at least in New York. The first period was from the time he arrived in New York, circa 1975 or 76. The students who began studying with him back then and remained throughout a significant amount of the 1980's were his "long term" senior students. From my many conversations with numerous of those senior students, as well as lessons from them and my 14 years with Richard, I found that back then, Chan was giving his all, being strict and detailed, and teaching his entire repertoire of arts to those who he felt deserved them. It didn't appear that any one person was given his entire repertoire, but some were given more than others. Chan taught according to who he felt was ready to receive what he was teaching. You couldn't just ask and receive. He knew who was ready for what material and who should be getting taught which things. He looked at me and told me I was best suited for Baguazhang, so he began teaching it to me.

For instance, in Taijiquan alone, there is the Yang short form, long form, two person fighting form called San Shou, Da Lu, push hands, two person sets based on various pieces of the forms, the Tung Ying-Chieh fast form, the Tung two person San Shou fighting form, the old frame Chen form, the old frame Chen cannon fist form, the Chen advance/retreat form, and various chi-na grappling exercises for all the forms. He taught all of these to his "first wave" of students in the early days. Not everyone learned everything, but most elements were given out between them.

Somewhere around the late 80's or early 90's, I believe that Chan's outlook changed. His wife passed away and from all accounts I was privy to, it devastated him. I even heard it said that people thought he was ready to join her in heaven. He may have even said something to that effect. It wouldn't surprise me because when I began studying with him, he would show me some really deep and exacting things when we were in private, but in his group classes, he seemed to water it down. It was as if he felt that he'd already given all he had to his original students, and it was now up to them to pass it on. Since he'd already done that, he was just sort of "babysitting" to keep busy. Don't get me wrong, he was teaching great stuff, only an abridged version without making sure everyone was doing it correctly. It seemed as if he was passionate about teaching and didn't feel like just sitting around at home. So many people still loved to be taught by him so he couldn't let them down. But by that time, he was just giving general instructions on things, going through the motions. I'd learned the details from Richard and other seniors, and from Chan himself in private encounters. With me he picked apart everything I did to make me better – "old school." When circle walking in Baguazhang, one's head is supposed to remain level, and when he saw mine bobbing up and down, he'd yell "Don't rising up!" But with the other late period group students, he just wanted to be around them to keep busy and do something nice for them, and rarely made any major corrections to their forms. It was more like follow the leader.

One example that bears this theory out is one day, in his Sunday morning class at William's, I was talking to some of his later "senior" students – not to be confused with his original senior students and mentioned the San Shou fighting form. This is a logical extension of the Taiji forms and I learned it from Richard in about the 3rd year of studying and found it to be one of the most useful tools for combat training. To my surprise, none of these fellows who'd been with Chan for ten years even heard of it! A little bit later, Chan walked over and asked if there were any questions. One of the guys asked, "Mr. Chan, how come you never showed us the San Shou?" Chan's face turned red and shouted, "I don't know what that is!" and turned around and stormed away. My interpretation is that he'd already given it to his first wave of students and that generation was over. It was now their responsibility to pass it on. These latter-day students weren't going to get it from him. He was only going to teach a few things that he wanted to teach until the end.

When Chan passed away, I drove into the city and attended his funeral in Chinatown. Afterward, we all drove up to Westchester for the burial ceremony at the Gate of Heaven Cemetery in Hawthorne, NY. It was a cold, muddy March Day. His family and personal friends were there, and his senior students were huddled around in the rear. I was one of the only Westchester students to attend. On the anniversary of his death, I would drive down to his grave to pay my respects. One year, I met two other former students of his and had a beautiful little commemoration in front of his grave. Then, a wonderful thing happened. As I was standing there, I heard a little voice in my head; a voice with a Chinese accent: "Suspend the crown of your head, shoulders sink, elbows drop, ask the breath to sink down below the navel. Calm the mind, loose the body." I immediately corrected my posture and felt much healthier and happier right away. He was still teaching! As Chan used to say, "You can live in heaven on earth or hell on earth. The choice is yours."

20. BP CHAN - HOW TO PREPARE TO DO ONE MOVE

"How To Prepare To Do One Move" is an essay about martial arts written by BP Chan for his students. It was not written for publication. It is most likely the longest written piece that he wrote, a philosophical discussion as well as an instructional piece. If you haven't read it before, it will take several readings to fully grasp the ideas presented. Please note that Mr. Chan called this essay "How To Prepare To Do One Move", NOT "How to Do One Move." The emphasis is on the preparation.

The philosophical areas of the essay talk about how we have lost our relationship with nature and the natural order (or disorder) of the universe. Mr. Chan advocates that in general, to bring balance back into our lives (and health and well-being), we must move closer to nature, and specifically, in our understanding of, and in the doing of, the martial arts, we must also move closer to nature.

Mr. Chan tells us that the way to achieve strength in the Internal Arts is through standing meditation. To move properly/correctly, and be in tune with nature, we must first learn how to be still through standing meditation. That is how Mr. Chan is telling us "How To Prepare To Do One Move." The preparation is in learning to be still. And, of course, just like the processes in nature, Mr. Chan explains that attaining stillness that leads to strength in the Internal Arts takes time. Mr. Chan then specifically lays out the 65 points (Yes, there are 65, I counted them) associated with Standing Meditation.

Here is Mark Jones' understanding of this essay:

My commentary on Mr. Chan's essay, "How to Prepare to do One Move" is that he liked to discourage expectations, so he would represent various moves as only preparatory in nature, so we would focus solely on building a foundation for what we thought we wanted to achieve later. By presenting it this way, he sort of tricked us into focusing on the now, yet in actuality, he was giving us the moves we were looking for without us realizing it. We were learning things we didn't know we were learning and in doing so, learned them on a deeper level without labels or expectations getting in our way to block us.

As far as preparing to do one move goes, it is only logical that if one doesn't even know how to stand still and breathe properly, i.e., according to the principles of body and mind mechanics, how is one expected to move properly? In order to build stillness into motion, the foundation has to be sound, and learning to first stand instills us with this skill. It is, in my opinion, the best way to prepare.

Just follow the principle. The principle is:
The Law Of Nature."
-BP Chan, from "How To Prepare To Do One Move"

The essay "How To Prepare To Do One Move" follows. The final page, in Mr. Chan's writing, after the last typewritten page, looks like a diagrammatic description of some content from page 1 of "How to Prepare To Do One Move."

HOW TO PREPARE TO DO ONE MOVE

In every activity of human endeavor, we have one goal. Whatever one may say, the true goal of any activity is to make us happier in some way. And if, as the wise men say, ultimate happiness is coming to the ultimate truth, then truth should be the goal of everything we do.

The true martial arts of the East were not created by men. The old masters who first practiced these arts discovered their source in nature. From the blowing of the wind and the flowing of the river, from the force of the typhoon and the swaying of the bamboo, from the flight of the crane and the strike of the snake, from the leap of the tiger and the tricks of the monkey, they studied the ways of nature; and tried to understand the principles that guide the universe. They studied the ways of nature that others take for granted, how the soft, liquid water ate away the hard rock or how the insubstantial air uprooted a great oak tree. And from their study they discovered certain principles, certain rules that nature followed. Then, they began to search for ways to help their bodies, their minds and their spirits to understand and practice these principles until they would become at one with these principles and thereby at one with nature which acted by these principles. The ways in which they trained to comprehend these principles, were the martial arts.

Thus, since these martial arts came from nature, they must take us back to nature - if we practice them the right way. And, the correct way to practice them is also the way that nature shows us. When, these arts take us back to nature, they take us back to our original inborn strength & abilities - which mother nature & our human mothers gave us. This power is what the ancient Chinese sages call PRENATAL ENERGY. The energy that nature bestows on everything in her universe. And since we men became so civilized and wise, that we no longer feel the sun in our hair, the wind in our face or the earth between our feet, we have to relearn the ways of nature to go back to what nature created us to be. When a baby is born, it comes from its prenatal state of existence in the mother's womb, out into the world. It has a hard time adjusting to the outside environment, the climate, the weather. So, the first week of a baby's life is a time of danger. Again, when a child goes to school, at around 5 years, the teachers further change its natural, inborn abilities. The child is taught to expand the chest, neglecting the natural, diaphragmatic breathing of an infant, throw its buttocks out & curve its spine like a bow. The martial artists who discovered these laws of nature, found ways that would take us back to our natural, inborn, prenatal state of pure energy, by using the help of our POSTNATAL ENERGY (the energy that makes us dash around in the modern world like mad dogs trying to destroy ourselves & the universe that creates and nurtures us). This POSTNATAL ENERGY is the energy of the Sun, the Moon, the Stars. The energy of the mountains & trees, of water & rock, of food and of the Earth; and this gift of nature that we call intelligence, which mother nature gives us as we approach adulthood, freely & undeservedly like a good mother, leaving it to us to use it as we will - for good or evil, this energy we egotistical humans take & in our arrogance, use to harm the very universe that sustains us. These old sages, disciples of nature, uncovered ways that would use this active postnatal energy to lead us back to uncover & cultivate the concealed prenatal energy that would unite us & make us one again with nature. This use of the postnatal energy to spark the flame of the prenatal energy, is like the hot ashes & cinders they always kept in the old fireplaces or, like in China, in a clay jar. Whenever one needed a fire for heat or cooking, the old people would stack fresh firewood over the smoldering embers & strike up a blazing new fire from the old.

We have spoken of principles, &, everybody knows, or thinks they know, what is meant by a principle. For those humble enough to ask again, the Eastern sages defined what they understood to be a principle. To them, a principle was a truth, that stood by itself. Not a man-made law that could be changed or revoked at the whim of some demented human, but a truth that stood firm & true - whatever came against it. A rule as true as day following night or death following life. Shakyamuni Buddha called such a principle a 'Dhamma'; and the Chinese called it 'YUANG' (i). Knowing the frailty & laziness of man, the martial artists further analyzed these principles. To them there were two kinds of 'Yuang' - the YUANG LI (ii) or theoretical principle one knew by the intellect & the YUANG CH'E (iii) or principle that one knew by practicing it. It was this ancient pragmatism & unanswerable logic that made the Communist Government of China, send their ivory-towered intellectuals into the mud of the fields & the grime of the workshop. How, they asked, could a Philosopher talk about planting rice - if he did not know what end of the plant went into the mud. How could a Professor teach the meaning of the words 'sawing wood', if he did not know how to hold a saw? It would be like making a person sit & watch a training film on swimming for four years, then throwing him into a river and expecting him to swim like an expert. And, it was a two-way street. Because, not only did the Professor learn how to saw wood, but the Carpenter in turn, learned how to read & write. Just so, in the martial arts reading a book or memorizing a form does not make one understand the meaning of the art. In the same way, one cannot just practice sparring or fighting and hope to reach the purpose of the martial arts. One must have both sides of the coin to use it. Otherwise, it is a useless piece of junk.

(i) 原   (ii) 原理   (iii) 原則

It is because these arts are from nature, that the first principle of the Chinese Martial Arts tells us that we must practice the martial arts for health, not to hurt. One practices to change one's own temperament and to make friends, not to make enemies. To put it another way, one studies these arts to get back, preserve and increase one's health, never to attack and destroy another being. Even when one is compelled to use these arts in self defense, one uses them to preserve one's own health, or the health of loved ones when under attack by an outside force; the intention is always to preserve the health of family, friends & self, not to hurt another. The aggressor - by attacking another - puts himself out of harmony with the universe, and, if he is hurt in the course of his attack being avoided by the martial artist, has only his own disharmony to blame. His hurt is caused by himself, and by nature as a way of bringing him back into balance with the rest of the universe. This is literally as well as figuratively true. Literally because, when an assailant attacks, the martial artist merely moves his body out of the way of the assailant and substitutes his hand or his foot to satisfy the attacker's desire for contact and the attacker causes his own energy to recoil and hurt himself.

When we talk of changing our temperament by practicing the martial arts, what we mean is that we try to remove the distorting mask of our own ego and try to go back to what we truly are. When we start our practice of the martial arts, before we comprehend, we call our dawning understanding SKILL; after we truly understand and absorb, it is just our NATURE. Once, someone asked the great sculptor Michelangelo just how he was able to pick the correct stone for his wondrous sculptures; his answer was that he never picked a stone for his sculptures; he merely took a stone & chipped away the extra fragments on the outside until the beauty already at the heart of the stone appeared. Just as a master jeweler cuts away the extraneous parts of a Gemstone until the radiant jewel at it's heart is revealed, is how we must practice the true martial arts. Chipping away at each ugly, obscuring piece of our ego, until our true nature stands revealed. It is then, when we become truly what nature created us to be, that we develop into pure beings that, like Tibet's great Yogi - Milarepa, live off the light of the sun & the breath of the wind & the touch of the earth, not dependent on outside things but sustained & nurtured by the power of Nature within ourselves.

Because these ancient arts are of nature, nobody can teach them to us. Only nature's principles can teach you these arts. So principle is the teacher; an instructor is just a guide. A guide who has been down the path before you and can help you along the way; but he cannot carry you with his strength or his will or his ability. Only you, yourself, can do that. You can take a horse to the brook, but you can not make him drink. The instructor, from his experience, his practice and his training, can explain the principles to you. He can explain and guide and help you, from what he sees and hears and feels of you from the outside. But only you, yourself, can know whether you are - in truth - operating by the principles of nature within yourself. An instructor can tell you of the truth he sees inside you, but, only you yourself can chip away at the obstructing ego and let nature stand revealed. And, the martial arts are a tool, a sculptor's chisel, that - used correctly - will help you cut away the obscuring concealment of your ego & let your true nature shine through. Only unremitting, sincere, hard work and study and practice of these principles, by yourself, can lead you to rediscover these truths and finally the way of nature, the Tao, in your own body and mind and spirit.

277

And, as a warning, like nature, these arts have no mercy, no charity. If you go after them with greed and desire and selfishness they will run away from you. But if you practice diligently, with no thought of gain, but just put in time and effort, expecting nothing & going on even if nothing comes of it - like a plant in the desert whose buds keep withering in the merciless rays of the Sun, still keeps trying to flower, with no thoughts of self-pity or anger or despair - when the time is right, like a flower blooming in the desert sand, nature will reveal itself within you. One must always be vigilant against arrogance & pride. It took the ancient masters a lifetime to understand one thing; how can we have the effrontery to think that one month, or one year, of practice can make us experts in everything? How can we even hope that we will understand the universe, in a single lifetime?

One fundamental principle that the ancient masters saw (like Isaac Newton, much later) was that every force had a complementary, yet opposite force. The rule of negative & positive, Yin & Yang. This was a very profound truth. The inventors of the modern binary computer, used the theory to bring about the dawn of the computer age. The martial artists found this pervasive principle had many applications in their art. They found that these forces were opposite but complementary. Where there was positive there was negative. But, an excess of positive would destroy the negative; or, vice versa. And, if one took either positive or negative to the extreme, it would give way to the other. The ways in which this principle operated, had many applications to the martial arts. As a very basic example, if an attacker struck you with all his strength & you moved out of the way, he would throw himself to the ground. Or, if he pulled you hard and, instead of resisting, you added your own impetus to the pull, you could hit him with the combined force of both your energies.

The masters found that a certain force could be applied from the internal natural sources of a human being, that far surpassed ordinary physical strength. They used the term Ch'i to describe this force. This was the same force of nature that enables a mother to defend her cub with the ferocity of a cyclone. The same force that once helped a father lift up a car that weighed thousands of pounds, which had pinned his son to the ground - to free him. They found that cultivation of this chi is enhanced by standing meditation. They found that training the inner mind would help to develop the internal force. They discovered certain ways of training mental effort:
    Keeping physical effort to the minimum required.
    Using abstract thinking, concepts, imagination.
    Concentration (by feeling, not by thought).
    Patience, persistence.
    Visualization.
When one practices standing meditation, the physical forces that operate in movement should be on vacation. This helps one to feel and cultivate the inner energy, the internal force, that the masters call the ch'i, the vital essence of the universe.

In the process of practicing the martial arts - when one practices by oneself, one uses the simple formula: THINKING, WILLING, FEELING: when practicing in a group: TALKING, WILLING, FEELING. This means that we think over a process or a movement in our minds or within our group; then we will our bodies. order our bodies. to carry out the movement; and, when our bodies do the movement, we let ourselves feel the activity and experience it - without interfering or controlling the move with our thoughts.

The masters discovered that the forces we call MIND, ENERGY & STRENGTH - the forces that make our thoughts, our feelings and our actions - are flowing throughout the Universe. During our brief, pain-filled stay on this planet, we are loaned this bag of fire & water & earth & air, we call a body, as a vehicle for our SPIRIT - the Energy of Nature that makes us what we are. The natural forces of MIND or THOUGHT we put in the container of our HEAD & BRAIN. ENERGY we store in our BODY (TRUNK); & STRENGTH goes into our FUNCTIONS with the LIMBS, our arms & legs. When we commence to practice the martial arts, we START EMPTY with SCATTERED thought, energy & strength. We Train - THOUGHT, ENERGY, STRENGTH, in the form of our MIND, our BODY and our FUNCTIONS USING OUR LIMBS with the help of our SPIRIT. By correct practice, we take our SPIRIT to a state of EMPTINESS with ALERTNESS, AWARENESS & ACTIVENESS (not inactive); a state that is MINDLESS, BODILESS & OBJECTLESS; a state where the MIND is TRAINED to be CLEAR & CALM, so that the messages of the SPIRIT (which the Chinese Sages call the HEART-MIND & which is the MESSENGER OF NATURE WITHIN OURSELVES) can come through without the interference of our mind-created ego.

The Spirit is the Owner (Thus the right orders from nature come through: do what is good for oneself, family, friends, country, nature. That is: Person, Family, Society, Universe. However, again a warning. As the opposing forces of Positive & Negative thread the skein of the Universe, so does Good & Evil run through our Spirit. Sometimes, through countless ages, our Spirits have been shaped so strong by our egos, that the good in them is overpowered by evil & we become truly demonic beings. Perhaps strong & powerful, but devoid of Love & Kindness & Compassion. This is why the Chinese say "Evil is Ten Feet High; but the Tao is only one foot".)

The Mind is the Manager (planning Strategy: to Run or to Fight. Again, some words of warning. The Mind is Creator & Destroyer. Also, if the Manager does not stick to his own job but interferes in the duties of the Supervisor, the business will soon go bankrupt.)

The Body is the Supervisor (Tactics: move left. block with right arm, kick with leg)

The Arms & Feet are the Workers (Take the Energy and Movement [the goods] from the production workers [the feet] and send it through the salesmen [the arms] to the delivery-men [the hands] to give to the customer.

279

Now, it is time to go - like nature - from the general to the particular. "How to do one move right?" is more than an empty question. It is everything of the martial arts; the beginning, the end, the on-the-way and the in-between. And, it is to nature that we must go - to find out how we must start. Most people who start learning something want to become expert, instantly. That is human nature. But it is a fact of NATURE, that one can not get anything of value in a hurry. Nature shows us in all it's facets, that anything of beauty & merit has a process to go through, before it reaches maturity. A river starts as a trickle of water on the mountainside, before it can become a mighty current, flowing & thrusting deep into the ocean. A Redwood starts as a little bud sprouting from the side of a seed, before it grows into a giant tree reaching for the heavens. A human must crawl on all fours, before he can stand on two feet. He must learn to stand before he can walk. He must be able to walk before he can run. So, in answer to our first question as beginners "How to do one move?", nature says: before one can move - one must learn how to stand still. Before the bamboo can wave in the wind, it must have roots that can withstand a gale. Thus, in the martial arts, one must prepare to move - by learning how to stand: like an oak tree or a mountain. Very simply, one must learn how to stand like a child of nature, not a disjointed puppet. The first written references to the practice of Standing Meditation are to be found in the Yellow Emperor, HUANG TI's Classic of Internal Medicine. The masters saw how the Mother Earth generated & nourished the great trees of the jungle and held them rooted in her bosom, while the Sun & the Heavens made them grow and stretch their crests towards the life-giving light. To help all humans to understand and develop their true nature, the Chinese martial artists tried to set down the laws of the Tao in simple formulas & principles, in poems & songs, that make it easy for our cluttered minds to remember & our uncontrolled bodies to practice.

The most important of these, with regard to the practice of standing can be stated in some 65 characters or statements.

A. The 6 appearances
    (1) Alignment
    (2) Center
    (3) Posture
    (4) Form
    (5) Defense
    (6) Offense

    Some words on Alignment, Center & Posture:

    "SOONG" (iv) is an important point in dealing with posture, that is loosely translated as: Relax & Sink. "SOONG" is like sitting in a Sofa. A sofa is soft & sinks-in when you sit on it. Yet it is elastic & maintains its shape, returning to its original state when you stand up.

    正

When sinking into the Crease, the Thighs automatically spread into a natural arch. The knees are vertically above the instep & the Bubbling Well acupuncture point. The knees should not go forward beyond the Toes.

The eyes, shoulders & crease maintain 3 horizontal levels. In the martial arts the spinal column is considered to be the main beam of the body which supports it, in the same way that the main beam of a house carries its roof & therefore its sheltering function (which is the whole purpose of a home). The Chinese martial artists deem the body's movement to be generated & directed by the Axis (or Waist), which they call the YAO (v). The YAO consists of the 5 pieces of the Lumbar vertebrae. Associated with the YAO is the QUA (vi). The QUA encompasses the HIPS, the THIGHS & the CREASE between the hips & the thighs. In any movement of the martial arts, 2 Arms & 1 Leg are moved by the Axis (YAO). At the same time, the whole Body moves as one. It is like a car, in which the axis of the steering column directs the car, but the whole car runs in one piece when the gas is pressed. All the spare parts which make up the car, must move as one object. Otherwise the car will fall apart.

(v) 腰   (vi) 胯

Furthermore, Substantial & Insubstantial must be clearly distinguished.

B. The 5 "W's" & 1 "H"
   (1) Who is doing it & who it is done to
   (2) What to do
   (3) Why do it
   (4) When to do it
   (5) Where to do it
   (6) How to do it

C. The 13 Joints
   (1) 2 Shoulders
   (2) 2 Elbows
   (3) 2 Wrists
   (4) 2 Hips
   (5) 2 Knees
   (6) 2 Ankles
   (7) 1 Spinal Column

A Note on the Spinal Column

The spinal column consists of 33 vertebrae. 7 cervical, 12 thoracic, 5 lumbar, 5 sacral & 4 coccyx. It is sometimes counted as 26 vertebrae, with the 5 sacral (fused into 1) as the sacrum & the 4 coccyx (fused into 1) as the coccyx.

D. The 14 Characters on standing

(1) Sser 虚 (Empty,)
(2) Ling 灵 (active, alert.)
(3) Ting 頂 (Suspend the neck)
(4) Ching 勁 (with intrinsic force.)

(5) Haum 含 (Relax, depress slightly,)
(6) Shian 胸 (the chest.)
(7) Fut 拔 (Pull up, round)
(8) Pei 背 (the back.)

(9) Wei 尾 {(The
(10) Lu 閭 { Coccyx)
(11) Ti 提 (lifted.)

(12) Ting 頂 (Suspend)
(13) Tou 頭 (the head,)
(14) Shiang 懸, (like hanging.)

E. The Eyes: with the help of the EYES, as GUIDE & GUARD

F. The 6 coordinations

 (a) The 3 inner coordinations
    (1) Heart -> Thought
    (2) Thought -> Energy
    (3) Energy -> Strength

 (b) The 3 outer, upper-lower coordinations
    (1) Shoulder -> Hip
    (2) Elbow -> Knees
    (3) Hand -> Foot

G. The 5 essences: FORM, MIND, ENERGY, STRENGTH, SPIRIT
 (Mental & Physical with the help of the Spirit)

H. 5 ways to train the inner mind - to develop internal force. To train mental effort:
1. Keep physical effort to the minimum.
2. Using abstract thinking, concepts, imagination.
3. Concentration (by feeling, not by thought).
4. Patience, persistence.
5. Visualization.

I. The 6 processes of practicing the martial arts
- when one practices by oneself:
THINKING, WILLING, FEELING.
- when practicing in a group:
TALKING, WILLING, FEELING.

J. The 3 stages of training:

We START EMPTY WITH SCATTERED thoughts, energy & strength (Thought force is in the Mind/Head; Energy is in the Body [Trunk]; Strength is in the Functions carried out with the help of the Limbs)

We TRAIN - MIND, ENERGY & STRENGTH with the help of the SPIRIT. We calm & clear the Mind. We preserve & develop the Energy of the Body. We practice the Functioning & delivery of Strength, with the help of the Limbs.

When we achieve the fruits of training, the SPIRIT reaches a state of EMPTINESS with ALERTNESS, AWARENESS & ACTIVENESS (not inactive). A state where we are MINDLESS, BODILESS & OBJECTLESS. Where the Spirit guides the Mind, Body & Limbs to carry out their natural functions, uncluttered, unclouded & unencumbered by the ego.

Thus we go from Empty Chaos through the Martial Arts to the Emptiness of the Tao.

When we learn the martial arts, practice together, everybody is right & everybody is wrong. Who is right, who is wrong - nobody knows. How do we solve this riddle? Just follow the principle. The principle is: The Law Of Nature.

— end ---

SUN
MOON stars

Shen   EARS Kidio
Chi   eyes — spirit
Ching   Mouth postnatal chi

WIND
Fire
WATER

21. BRIEF, BUT FULL OF SUBSTANCE AND MEANING

BP Chan was a master of conveying important concepts in a few words. For Mr. Chan, in both his personal and martial arts life, less was more. Below are some wonderful examples of what I mean. There's a lot of wisdom there. I keep reminding myself of many of these from time to time.

Ron Gee, who was a student of Mr. Chan's at the Tai Chi Farm, made contemporaneous sketches of Mr. Chan as he taught. In his sketchbook, he also compiled numerous "sayings" by Mr. Chan. The list that he compiled is many pages long; I asked Ron to winnow down the voluminous sayings he took down into a smaller set that resonated with him.

Here's what Ron chose, and why:

"....I finally was able to put together a selection for your book of what I think are the most representative, intriguing and profound sayings that I jotted down during the years I studied with Mr. Chan. It will be interesting to see if others who studied and practiced with this wonderful teacher recognize his voice, manner and wisdom in these spare words."

BP CHAN - RON GEE'S NOTES (SELECTIONS)

1.
Qigong
Original meaning:
How to breathe
—

Breathing in abdomen
Do not force {command} –
That is wrong
Guide to destination -
Following natural tendency-
—

When you open the door
It will come in
It will happen

2.
Intent - to think what to do
Use yi
Don't use qi
If you think qi
Then it leaves
—

Mind (Intent -yi)
Mental expression inward
Body (Form-xing)
Physical expression outward

3.
Call AAA - Aware, Alert, Active
Ask yourself:
Does mind understand the body?
—

Conquer inside
Before conquer outside
Body knows best

4.
Principles
Help us to reach
Same goal
—

Even Principles
Are not always right
If principle Is not suitable
To your body
It is still wrong
Every body is different

5.
Feeling is stronger
Than action
—

Let your body feel something
And tell your brain
If you don't feel anything
There is nothing to explain

6.
The inside
Determines the outside
The outside
Supports the inside
—

Six Co-ordinations:
INNER
Heart - Thought

Thought - Energy
Energy – Strength
OUTER
Shoulder - Hip
Elbow - Knee
Hand – Foot

7.
Outside angular
Inside circular
—

Loosen / Relax
Inside goes down
Outside does not go down
No collapse

8.
Chin out / chest out / coccyx out
- Wrong
Chin in / chest in / coccyx in
- Correct

9.
Spirit of the eyes
—

Use of eyes
When eyes guide
Nervous system is active
—

Body open joints - not enough
Eyes help body to open joints
Eyes cause nervous system to open

10.
Axis turns
Everything else happens
—

Waistline turns the axis
Forget two hands
—

Move the torso
But controlled by the axis
Where eyes look
Controls axis

11.
Keep door a little open
(60 seconds in a minute
but we only want to use 58
If we use all 60
we become locked)
—

Just do the movement
When movement is right
Then breathing will coordinate and match movement
If interfere
Then in conflict
Become choked

12.
Chinese way
Of teaching:
Indirect answers
To questions
Never answer directly
Spoil him
Then you give him spare parts only

Tell him indirectly
He goes home, cooks (in) his mind
—

Eastern learning has spirit
As its point of departure
Western learning has material
As its point of departure
—

The goal
Of our practice
Is to attain
The Void
—

Object-less
Body-less
Mind-less
—

Things just happen

AUTHOR COMMENT:

Look at section 3 above, and specifically "Call AAA - Aware, Alert, Active." What did folks do in the 70's and 80's when their car broke down? Call AAA, of course. I know I did! Mr. Chan is using the familiar AAA (American Automobile Association) as a mnemonic (sorry-just had to use that word) to help students remember information - a memory aid. This points directly to Mr. Chan's ability to communicate and help his students so they could remember important concepts. This is beautiful stuff.

22. THE 5 WISDOMS OF B. P. CHAN

Frank Allen

1. "It's all the same banana - There's no bones here.."
2. "Everyone asks, how many years do you study? The question shouldn't be how many years do you study - the question should be - How many hours do you practice?"
3. "If the students don't become better than their teachers - There will be no progress in the art."
4. "Who has the Best Tai Chi? Who is Old & Happy? HE has THE BEST TAI CHI ..."
5. "Everyone gets the invitation - but we do our exercises so ours comes a little later."

Reprinted with permission of Frank Allen

23. IN THEIR OWN WORDS

"You know what I'm thinking about?
Ticketing jackets"
– Jeff Pascal

RAL: I was reading that in 2000 you were named an instructor of the year by the U.S. Martial Arts Hall of Fame.

Hang on a second. I think I have it here. (Shows me the trophy)

RAL: Wow. That's a wonderful accomplishment.

Yes, I was surprised and pleased by it. People way above my pay grade make decisions, so I'm just happy to have it.

RAL: Do you have to be nominated for that or how does it work?

I have no idea. All I know is Sifu (Dr. Richard) Chin showed up with that for me and said "Here."

RAL: Thank you for taking the time with me tonight. I realize that you're giving up some of your personal time, and I really appreciate it.

It's for Mr. Chan, so of course, you know, anything I can do for him, I'm happy to do.

RAL: I appreciate that. Thank you. And I'm sure that he appreciates it too, wherever he is right now.

I hope so.

RAL: So, why don't we start from the beginning? What was it that brought you initially to Mr. Chan?

It's a long story. My first introduction to martial arts was in 1956. I took Judo. And then in about 1960, I studied with what was called at that point the Dream Team. They had four or five of the top Judoka from Japan come over here with to work with Jerry Mackey, and I took classes there. I started with falling, throwing, choking, and grappling.

Then in 1971, the beginning of the year, I had blown my knee out for the umpteenth time doing Judo and skiing and I said, this is ridiculous. I met someone who knew Sifu Chin in a Wing Chun class I was taking and got to meet him through her. Then, once my knee went out doing mat work, I started studying Kung Fu with Sifu Chin. Mr. Chan began at the Asian Martial Arts Studio in 1975 or 1976. The first class was memorable for me. We had a heavy bag hanging in the class and Mr. Chan came in, lit incense, and then walked over to the bag, looked at the two two-by-fours supporting the front end of it, took his fingers, slams the two-by-fours, and the two-by-fours quivered. Since this was a contact school, I just looked at it and I said to myself "I'm gonna die." When class started, he first demonstrated a defense against a front kick, with me throwing a front kick at him. He sidestepped, scooped my foot, slammed me on the bottom of my heel, and my head popped; the feeling was electric. Everybody yelled, "Oh Mr. Chan, would you do that again, please?" And he said "No, no, no" and proceeded to teach the four position post-standing.

And as we're just standing there in the first position and the first 10-15 minutes goes by and I'm thinking, oh my god, as long as we're standing, I might survive. Then he switched to second position. Now, we were used to standing. The longer we stood, the less likely we were to spar, and I assumed everyone was thinking the same thing, because we were all smiling, and our smiles broadened as we continued through the first four positions. That was the class. Everybody was so relieved and happy, and Mr. Chan was really impressed because we did that for an hour and did not complain. Due to our stance training nobody's legs were shaking and all of us were smiling. After that he said, yes, he would come teach us. And that was my first class with Mr. Chan.

RAL: This was at Sifu Chin's school?
Yes.

I had studied with him (Mr. Chan) about six years, when Sifu Chin spoke with Mr. Chan and then talked with me about learning the Yi Jin Jing, because I always loved the internal arts. I always wanted to learn more about them. I studied bodywork at that time with Sifu Chin. I had heard rumors that the Yi Jin Jing existed, so when Sifu proposed this to me, I was thrilled. I talked to Mr. Chan, and he said, "Okay," and he showed me alternate lung breathing and said "Now, you work on that, and then you show me." I said, Okay, I thought to myself, what the hell is this? But none-the-less, I worked on it. Two weeks later, he asked me if I'm able to demonstrate it, and I did. He said, "I will teach you," and this is after we had known each other for six years. We then spent six months talking about what I was about to learn and then he started the lessons. They were hard - Did you do the Yi Jin Jing with the bamboo and coat hangers?

RAL: No.
This is the other part of it. Frequently just the internal breathing and exercises are taught. But with traditional training, there is not just the breathing and stance, but the use of bamboo to learn how to bounce off strikes, and more importantly, how to direct focus to all parts of the body. To start off, you go up and down your meridians with bundled bamboo. He demonstrated the breathing, which eventually slows down to three breaths a minute.

Directing the breath was the next step. He said, you breathe up the inside, and down the outside of the arms and the legs. I said, "Oh, you imagine the path." He said, "No. Put your hand on my arm and my leg." So, I put a hand on his arm, the other on his leg, and he breathed. One side of his arm swelled, and then the other, one side of his leg swelled, and then the other. I said to myself, "Oh my God, I'm not in Kansas anymore." At that point, I said to myself, "I must learn this." I had heard rumors about this, but now I was going to get a chance to learn it. One of the reasons you do the Yi Jin Jing is because this kind of phases into Iron Shirt. If somebody hits you, you can bounce off the blows; it's like medicine-ball training in boxing. The breathing itself is wonderful and it's healthful, but the whole system of internal dynamics that underlies it is mind-boggling. I'm finally beginning to see its relationship to everything else there is in the martial arts. A key has been the first position in the Yi Jin Jing where you press down at the sides.

RAL: Yes.

The fingers come back, and the palms extend. When you breathe, the joints expand, so you can feel the joints separate over one breath cycle. This is palpable to others if they cup a knee while it is being done. The same breathing and breath direction can be done with explosive force to generate short range and fast punches. This is part of that. This is how it works. The Yi Jin Jing slows the internal breathing dynamics down so that you can see how it is supposed to be expressed when it's done quickly. You get a chance to study the internal dynamics of it. I just had not been able to put the two together really until recently. It just had not clicked in in that sense. I knew the breathing, but now I see how it specifically relates to any technique at any speed. That, for me, was the connection between the internal and the external. It is one of the major connections.

The other thing I did want to show you is the alternate lung breathing and if this is not helpful to you, just let me know.

RAL: You mentioned that to me when we spoke on the phone; I had never been shown that or learned that. So I said to myself, let me see if I can just breathe into one side at a time. And I think that I may have been able to do it. The left side was easier for me, which I found kind of strange because the heart is on the left side. But I found breathing into my left side easier than breathing into my right side. But I'm sure that I'm looking at it too simplistically.

I can see you're nearsighted, which eye is dominant?

RAL: Right.

The right eye is dominant. The eye sees directly but the brain crosses over so the left side and the right eye and the right eye and the left side are the ones that are joined so the eye is opposite from the rest of the body.

The reason I mention this is because I just, again, my eyesight is probably like yours used to be, or was like yours used to be.

Mr. Chan showed me the eight-diagonal breathing eye set: Look up, look down, right, left, and then diagonally across.

RAL: In one of the Eight Brocades I was taught to make intentional eye movements where you actually are looking in specific directions with the eyes. But the eight directional thing that you're talking about, no, I'm not acquainted with that.

All you do is look up with breathing, up, down, left, right, upper left, lower right, upper right, lower left. What I did from that was to look at the four muscles around the eye. And all you're doing is you're using them alternately. So, and this is quite a while ago, I realized, what if I did them all at once? Because I knew if you're nearsighted, your eyeball is too long. I'll inhale and you should be able to see my eyes go in.

RAL: Yes.

And then out. And then you can see I can move them independently of each other, and this is just by use of the eyes directed by the breathing. What I did is essentially I came up with pull-ups for the eyeballs.

RAL: So how did you know which muscles needed more activation and which muscles needed less activation to correct your vision?

The near-sighted eyeball looks like this (makes an elongated shape with hands.) If it sees correctly, it looks as if it's round. Otherwise, it's oblong. We should have round eyeballs. I figured; I want the muscles to tighten up. What I just did was like pull-ups for my eyeballs, that's all. I realized what they were from the exercises that Mr. Chan gave me and then I looked up the muscles in the eye so I could get an idea. I showed the exercise to Mr. Chan, and he said, "Ah, good.", one of the few times he said "Good" to me (laughs).

I remember I was with Mr. Chan once and he was just busting my chops because I wasn't moving properly. I was so frustrated. So, on my way over to his house, I just said to myself, "Screw this. I'm just going to do the form. Forget that he's there. Only form. That's it. I'm going to shut up. That's it." I went in and began our class. I started doing the form and about maybe five minutes into it, he hadn't said anything yet. And I just said to myself, oh my God, he didn't say anything. And then the little voice in me said, "shut the hell up and do the form." I went and did the whole form and he said nothing. And at the end he goes, "Hao, good, now you're soft enough to work on your own."

RAL: Oh, nice, nice, nice.

And that was about 20 years into my study with him! It just took me a long time to get to that point, that's all.

RAL: Yeah, I know. With all the internal stuff, it takes years. It takes years and years and years. Most people can't or don't want to stick with something that long.

It's so hard to explain the inner stuff. Explain it so that you can do it. Now, I ask myself, how would I explain this to myself if I were six or eight years old? And it's not easy. I can barely explain this to myself. I came from an artistic, Western background, and this doesn't easily cross-translate.

I mean, I love the surrealists and impressionists, and that's similar to what's going on inside. It's one of the reasons I love Escher. I think he's fantastic. He's very precise and yet he understands how dimensions work. His use of exponents and exponential change in his work is amazing. And you can see how that works. When you look at hands, and how and why the angles change in martial arts, it's the same and it's remarkable.

If you look at Western anatomy, when you compress a bone, the bone becomes ten times stronger. Also, a piezoelectric field sets up inside the bone, and that strengthens your bone. When Sandy Koufax, the well-known pitcher had his arms X-Rayed, his right arm was four times denser than his left arm. The baseball pitch is pure martial art and that's part of the way it changes the internal dynamics. When you punch or strike, that is how that works. And what the Yi Jin Jing does is, it allows you to feel that slowly and softly so you can really see what's going on. You can work on how the internal dynamics go, how the internal alignment goes, how you are going to get your body into position? Everything lines up with the way the body is designed, which is what I think is one of the major benefits of Yi Jin Jing study, aside from health. To me, it is an endless source of wonder. I go back and go over it again and again because each position works with a different tendino-muscular meridian.

RAL: Did you take a lot of private lessons with Mr. Chan?

Yes, I would just go over to his house every week. I would study with him. I'd come over and he would normally cook me a little mung bean stew. And we would do...... oh, the other important meditation is motion seeks stillness as stillness seeks motion; it starts off with basic sitting, which is how you can approach stillness. Tai Chi, and all movement is the motion seeking stillness. In the basic sitting, you slow down the sitting, you slow down completely until you can feel what is happening inside your body. You will feel the whole body expand. And one thing that I focused on was balance and alignment. This is what Mr. Chan used to stress, but it's really, he said, like stacking coins. The vertebrae in your spine are like a stack of coins. You can hit a point where you're just sitting; you can just sit there, and you don't have to do anything with your discs just resting in a stack. You can be completely at rest while you are still sitting upright. Just come to a complete stop. This allows everything else to turn off and the more you become aware of that, the more you will become aware of your breathing, then you can feel the motion that goes on inside. That is the steppingstone to getting into the walking and moving parts. But how do you get there? If you see how slowly, slightly, rocking back-and-forth comes back to the center, you'll feel how the body can move without effort. And that is the whole internal point. My understanding is that transition is imperative because you have to know how to be still, and you have to know how to move, and yet have the two work together. That is in the "Tao Te Ching": "These two things, although named differently, are the same." That, I believe, is the point they're trying to make.

RAL: Yeah. I think it was Mr. Chan who said that stillness is the mother of movement.

Yes, it is. Yes, that's exactly it.

RAL: I'd like to go back to a question I asked you a little while ago about private lessons. You mentioned that you used to go to his house to do work with him. Was that when he was in Stuyvesant Town or ....?

Yes.

RAL: Okay. How many years in total did you study with him, approximately?

Oh, well, I started in 76. I started in 1976 with him and I was with him steadily ever since, until he passed away, was it 2002, I guess?

RAL: 2002, yes.

Another time he showed me a sitting meditation at his apartment. He had, I remember, a TV on in one room, there's a radio on in the back, there were neighbors fighting in the hallway, and there were garbage trucks loading out on the river outside. So, I'm supposed to meditate? I figured, all right, he's doing it; I'll shut up and meditate. And suddenly, the noise just became sound, and it just didn't matter. It just was. It was so good being there with him, because most of the time, there's nobody else there, just he and I. We'd go over whatever, and then I'd go to work.

RAL: You were doing this early in the morning then?

Yeah, early. He would have had me over there at 5 or 6, knowing Mr. Chan. I didn't do that.

RAL: What anecdotes can you tell me about Mr. Chan. Words of wisdom from him, things that he said to you that you remember to this day, memories.

Have I got a bunch for you. "It already exists within."

RAL: Yes. What do you think he meant by that?

"It already exists within."

Everything is already there. You just must find it. It's what I'm learning now from the Yi Jin Jing. All the subtleties that happen, how actually to connect the muscles up to the spine. This is recent. I just figured out how to isolate the muscles, for example, in my lower back because I have herniated and bulging discs. It is already there, everything you need is already there, you just must be able to access it.

"Even a point is a circle."

Everything is circular, everything is a spiral, which is important because that's how all your strikes work. If you're working on acupressure, that's how your fingers work. With a needle it's the same, you circle the needle in. I was watching a Chinese guitarist, Xue'er Jin, and you watch her on the guitar playing classical guitar; her fingers would just circle and vibrate in on a chord. It was fantastic.

"It must be perfectly clear."

If you're going to explain something, you must be able to explain it to someone, preferably simply.

Another one of my favorites is, "Is that your arm?"

When I was first doing coiling silk, I did not move how I should have been moving. How do you move? The movement comes from circling within the body and then the arm is moved from the ground up or from your center up depending on how you combine them. That is what is important.

Mr. Chan also worked for Hudson's Sporting Goods in NYC. I got him a job there. He was just doing stock work, ticketing jackets - hundreds of jackets. And he's standing there with a little ticket gun, and just... (makes rapid clicking sounds) Jacket, jacket, jacket, shot, shot, shot. He did not miss a stroke, didn't stick his finger, and got exactly what he was aiming for.

So, I asked him, Mr. Chan, "What do you think about when you're doing that?" He turned to me and said, "You know what I'm thinking about? Ticketing jackets."

RAL: Simplicity at its core.

Yes. And that was pure Mr. Chan. I have a whole bunch of little aphorisms that I look through. Those are the ones that really stuck with me.

RAL: I'm interested in hearing about some of the personal interaction that is meaningful to you that you had with Mr. Chan.

The simplest of things, eating out in Chinatown or all the little things he showed me, such as standing-rocking, which you can do unnoticed while waiting for a bus, or his perpetual awareness. These little things became part of my life.

His passing was such a loss to me, you know. I remember when he died. I was thankful to be in New York because I was just out literally wailing in the streets and hanging on to lampposts and stuff and no one batted an eye. He kind of re-fathered me. He was like a parent to me, and he still teaches me inside to this day.

RAL: It's wonderful to have a relationship like that with someone, especially with a teacher. There were two sides to him. Mr. Chan, the person, and Mr. Chan, the martial arts teacher. What do you think made him unique as Mr. Chan, the person?

He had a wicked sense of humor. With some of this stuff, it was kind of an absurdist martial arts humor maybe.

We were doing a Tai Chi exercise, and in the opening, you bring both hands up like this (brings hands up in front of body, palms facing down.) He was showing me this, and it's a two-person set, so I bring his arms up, because he puts his hands on my shoulders, I come up, and then I turn and turn, and then bring one arm under the other, and lock him in. I pull him down, knee him in the groin, and then, single knuckle punch. I'm trying; I'm just learning this, I'm trying to do this, and I just bring my arms up slowly, and my mind freezes, and I'm just standing there, and, since I'm pushing him backwards, he just drifts off into the background, waving goodbye as he goes. I just burst out laughing.

And then, he showed me ten animals frolicking. I could never get that.

RAL: Five Animal Frolics?

Five Animals frolicking, whatever, yeah. Anyway, some of the stuff is just like, it's gone. And then he showed me his crane frolicking. You stand on one leg, one hand outstretched, the other back, body roughly horizontal to the floor, and even he is bobbling while I watched him. He turned around and I said, "Mr. Chan, where did they come up with this stuff?" And he turned to me and said, "I was just asking myself that today," and we both just bust out laughing. Because it's absurd. How are you going to do this stuff? How could you think of it? Maybe you have to be a stork.

RAL: What styles did he teach?

Mr. Chan taught Xing Yi, Bagua, Tai Chi, at least Chen and Yang style. The Yang family style, I think it was. And there is a difference, evidently. It was not Chen Man-Ching's Yang style. He did Ngo Cho, which is a Southern style. They used weights and power sets from what I could see. Mr. Chan was built like a tank. When he blocked you, you knew it. He was gentle with the students, of course. Thank God. And one hand was a different color than the other, from his training.

RAL: And what was the cause of that?

Iron Palm training. He trained it using sand, pebbles, and iron filings. He had traditional training. As I remember, he said when he was six years old, they would put him in horse-stance, and he would stay there until an incense stick burned down. So much horse stance. His legs were like tree trunks and his back was a slab.

He wasn't built like an American bodybuilder, but his back was like a complete slab. One of the things he taught me was when he was turning and I couldn't see what he was doing inside, I would put my hand on his back and then I could feel him turn. When he saw that I could do that, he said, "Ah, direct transmission," and that was great.

When I felt his knees separate when he was doing the Yi Jin Jing, that was really mind-boggling, to feel the knee joint expand with the elbows at the same time. It was just incredible.

And breathing.... Let's see, I'll say this, the throat breathing... Hang on. I don't know if you can see this throat expansion... (demonstrates breathing into the throat)

RAL: Yes, yes, I can.

There is also blood flow control, just watch the blood vessels. (shows his forearm)

RAL: Yeah, yeah, your blood vessels are popping.

Yes. And so that is changing blood flow. I'm working on doing it with alternate hands now. That is taking a little doing, though.

RAL: So, when you're talking about alternate blood flow, what is happening?

Good question. I do it through feeling.

It is the same feeling again you get from feeling what's going on inside in the Yi Jin Jing. But the quieter you can get the body, the more you can feel it. And then you begin to feel what the blood flow feels like inside your body. You must really slow down for this. The way I would describe it is it feels like time flows around you, that is the only way I've found of putting it. Obviously, that's not happening, because I'm not traveling at the speed of light, but that's what it feels like. And once you feel that you can gently feel the feeling shift; you can shift from one side to the other. That's how come the alternate lung breathing is important. It is not just being able to physically do it but feel what is happening and how it's going on, and to slow it down. Once you can slow it down, then you can feel what is happening.

Once you have that, feel what is going on in your legs? Explore your whole body.

Once, I remember I was doing standing exercise with my eyes closed. Then, while I was standing, my left hand started humming, and I thought to myself, "damn, I'm hot today!" I can feel it in different hands. I started smiling, but when I opened my eyes there was Mr. Chan with his left hand pointing into my left hand. He had just come up and I hadn't heard him. That was memorable.

RAL: Yes, yes. Did you ever make it up to the Tai Chi Farm?

No, that I didn't do. That was him. It was another group. I don't know if there was or how much communication there was between groups. That I couldn't tell you.

RAL: Why do you think that was? Did Mr. Chan purposely separate groups by skill or by number of years they had been with him or what they were studying?

Not that I know. He also taught at William Chen's school. William and Sifu Chin were friends, they knew each other. Upstate was another group. There was a also whole bunch of students in the East Village. I knew some of them, like Cooper. But it was simply different schools, and it wasn't that much interchange between the schools, at least not that I was aware of.

RAL: Did Mr. Chan ever talk to you about his background in China, his days in the Philippines? What made him come to the United States? Why he left China? Why had he left the Philippines?

Yes, let me think. He didn't really mention that. He told me a couple of little stories. The only one I remembered was, I forgot the business type, but some guys came in, threatening the business and Mr. Chan. He said, come with me, went outside to a telephone pole and hit the pole, which vibrated and shook. He turned and said, "If you are stronger than that pole, I will fight you." They quietly left, and that was that.

RAL: This was in the Philippines.

Yeah.

RAL: Jeff, I just have one more question to ask you. Well, two. And they're short, I guess. A while back, I asked you, what was it about Mr. Chan that made him unique as a person? So my follow-up question is, what do you think it was about Mr. Chan that made him unique as a teacher of martial arts?

He thoroughly explained everything in detail. And that, I love, that is what I needed. Some people can do it; they will be shown a form, and they can do it. For me, that is hard.

He would go into as much detail as you needed. If you wanted to learn for hours, he was there, at least for me. That was generous. Whatever small thing you wanted to learn, or if you had a question, he would answer. As an example, Mr. Chan would say, "Open the hand." I thought you were supposed to keep your thumb out, and he says, "Watch. See, when you hit, the thumb goes out, then, the thumb comes in, so you don't get it caught. That's how it works."

Oh, yeah. Here's another thing. He said, "Don't believe a word I say."

RAL: Mr. Chan said this to you?

Yes, he said, "Don't believe a word I say, test it yourself and see if it's true." And he said that again and again and again.

RAL: Last question, Jeff. What life lessons did you learn from Mr. Chan?

How to just be. In the way that he showed it. I can't put it into words. There are so many ways of doing that.

But just to be able to be still. That stillness was the most important thing for me.

Then, there is the breathing, how it works, how we need it. You can feel how the back swells, how everything works at once. It's helpful, for me at least, to get to feel what's going on in the body. Intellectual understanding is only part of it.

As an example, if you're going to protect the neck, inflating is only one part. Rotating the collar bone inward while lowering it and closing the gap with the ribcage is another. There are so many small details, but the overall importance of alignment and stillness is key.

RAL: Well, Mr. Chan certainly made a lifetime of that. Yes. His legacy hopefully will live on.

There is one other thing that was fun. Mr. Chan used to do little sculptures of his own, like art trouve, and he would put stuff together, which I thought was great.

RAL: Oh, interesting. What was the subject?

He would just use stones, shells, and whatever he found, to make little figures or landscapes. The other thing was, he had a camera. I was going to give him points on photography and then I looked at each one of his photographs and they were so well-composed already, I just laughed to myself because I figured, of course he's going to do that. That balance is part of who he is. So, I shut up.

One more. I was in the street with Mr. Chan in Union Square and some guy is yelling at somebody across the street, walking toward us - a huge guy. As he walks by, Mr. Chan scratches his head. He's got his elbow next to the guy's throat, but he's just scratching his head. Little Chinese guy scratching his head and the yeller didn't notice, didn't see. So that was fun.

RAL: Those are the kinds of stories and memories that I think are going to make the book memorable.

"He Hung Out With the Boys"
—Dr. Richard Chin

RAL: You learned Chen style Tai Chi from BP Chan.

Yes.

RAL: What was he like as a teacher? Anything stand out?

Let me explain it, then you write it your own way. His style was technical. This is two inches from here, this is two inches from here, that kind of thing. That was his style. Difficult, because it's so difficult that you can hardly move. Literally, the toe should be one inch and this toe should be five inches and the angle should be this and that. So he was being very precise. I think maybe that was my fault because he asked me how to teach Americans. And I think I gave him the wrong answer. He said he wanted a lot of information, so I think he overdid it. That *is* a method, though. That's how he taught. And that's why he was popular, because you ask questions, he'd tell you more than you ever wanted to know. He went the other way. He simplified so much.

My approach is transition. BP's is more posture.

The power is in the transition. From one posture to the other, it's the flow. See, posture is here. How do you get there? That's where the power comes in. Power is movement. Physics is force. Posture is structure. As you transition into your structure, that's how the force is created. If you don't have the structure, the force is weak. Once you have the structure, the force is strong. Yin and Yang.

RAL: So when you're applying a technique, or an application, are you in posture or are you in transition?

Think of golf. It's your posture, it's your posture into your transition. Don't think of either/ or, because it isn't that way. It's both. It has to be. So don't get caught in that.

There's what we call the Six Coordinations. Remember, it's not static. Six Coordinations, the word coordination. Moving into the four forces: swallows, spits, sink, float, it's all meshed together. Just think about physics in life. Static is nothing. It's physics. Force is movement. It's moving one energy to the other is how you create force. So that's why I stress flow and force. Because then you'll get it. Once you understand flow, how do you get that into energy?

Then you start to settle in your stance and start to move.

RAL: And even when you're settling into your stance, your posture, there's some movement there also.

Yes.

RAL: It's subtle movement.

There you go. You're always in motion. You're always in motion, so you're never static. So that's why there's movement. Somewhere there's movement. Does that make sense to you? It could be internal movement. Okay. Now, there's your answer. Movement. If there's nothing moving, nothing's happening.

There's got to be some movement. Somewhere you have to create movement. It's pure physics.

RAL: Interesting turn of the conversation from Mr. Chan's teaching style, which was basically very, very technical, to a discussion about transition.

But that's more advanced. He didn't have many students ever get to that level.

RAL: Standing was his thing.

Okay, so if you can't stand, you can't talk about movement.

RAL: It must have been hard for him. Coming from such a diverse and skilled background in the martial arts, it must have been hard for him to deal with this. It must have been very difficult for him to simplify things so much that......

No, I wouldn't say that. He enjoyed, you know, he enjoyed his...... I'll give you my personal experience. Remember when we were talking about professional amateurs?

I enjoy working with my students. They don't understand what I'm teaching. You go to college, there's a professor, you're a freshman. You're not at a PhD level. It doesn't really disappoint him. There's interaction. So I don't downplay or look down on my students. I'm disappointed they're not as good as they could be.

I want them to be, but that's not even the right word. I wish they were better. It's not disappointing. It's who they are. I'm disappointed that my craft, my student body isn't more highly skilled, but it's not anything personal. So I think BP's like that. I guess what I'm trying to say is we're not teaching professionals. If I was teaching a professional team or BP was teaching a professional team, we'd be aggravated. In other words, let's say we're going to go to war. Now we'd be upset because nobody's good enough. But as a social thing, it's fine. You know what I'm saying? I don't think he was disappointed. He's only disappointed in people that really mess up.

When BP was training those guys in the Philippines, he wasn't the nice...... Okay, here in the USA he was the godfather, father of all his followers. You have no idea what BP was really like. None of his students could have any idea what he's like back in the Philippines, his reputation. Because there, they were professionals. That's a different training.

RAL: What was his reputation like in the Philippines? Do you know?

Very respected. Just respected. One of the main guys.

RAL: But as you said, not one of the premier top-level guys.

No, no, was not. But that's okay. You see, that doesn't take anything away from him.

RAL: You're saying that within the Asian martial arts community, he was good, but he wasn't a grandmaster.

He was not groomed to be the lineage head. Does that answer that?

And again, who are you talking to? None of his students here were professionally trained. They were not professional martial artists. So he did not train them that way. They didn't see him that way. That's where the mythology comes in. See, they don't know the BP who trained in the Philippines. They don't know how tough he is. I'll give you another insight. So here in the US, when you talk to people, like you said, he was godlike.

RAL: He was revered in this country by his students..

In the Philippines, he rode motorcycles. He hung out with the boys. People don't know that. His leather jacket, let's go! They don't know that.

RAL: Who would know that?

Only us that really knew him. And it's not a secret. I know him. People don't know who he is. When you speak about my earliest students, they didn't know me either because I wasn't really close to them because we only had a student-teacher relationship. My students today know me better. Why? Because we're colleagues. I see them as colleagues. I teach them all at the same level. So we're inter-reactive. They're not white belts. They're not beginners. We're the same.

But something happens in martial arts where we look down on the beginners. I don't like a lot of masters because they act like they're gods. Only in martial arts do we have that. That is incorrect. I'll tell you where that comes from. I thought about it, because people ask. Martial arts were introduced in America after the war. World War II, the Korean War. Who introduced it? The GIs. The first teachers in this country were all military. So the martial schools were run in a military fashion. We don't do that in Asia. It isn't what you think in Asia. It isn't like you've seen. We are polite to seniors, we respect the seniors, but we don't look down on the men.

We treat them correctly, but not rank-wise. That's military. And that's also Japanese. It comes from the ranking (belt) system. So in Taiwan, which was occupied by Japan for many years, the Chinese schools are run like that. Shuai Jiao is run with the ranking system. You talk about occupation, Japanese influence. So it's very much like that there. But in China, no. You have your senior, but it's not like that. So that's where a lot of the misunderstanding comes from.

In China, you don't talk back to the teacher. They don't want to hear from you, but that's something else.

RAL: And there's the dan system in China?

Yes, now everybody has a ranking system. Everybody's got something. Yes. Because it's easy. It's a nice gimmick. Now everybody's ranked.

So, you ever see the old movie, Kung Fu, the original TV series Kung Fu?

RAL: Oh yeah, I have all the DVDs.

Okay, in the first movie, the very first one, the kid goes to the monastery. The monk says, he's master of mantis, he's master of tiger, then you have the abbot. Well, BP Chan would have been a master of Tai Chi. He would have been one of the masters of the shaman. Not the abbot. That's the difference. He's a Master. He is, right? He'd be head of his department at a university. He'd be head of the Qigong department. And you wouldn't understand a word he's saying because he's teaching PhD level. What he had to teach was actually PhD level. His students didn't get the bachelor's degree yet. So that's why he's teaching how to do this, how to do that. People didn't appreciate him because he went up to his level. The ones who did, like me, we could talk. And then there's the abbot, who knows all the stuff. My grandmaster was the abbot.

As a man, you have to look at BP as a man. As a man, great achievement, evolving, as full potential. He did everything he could to get the best out of his life and the best he knew about all this stuff.

RAL: Because in the end, that's all you can ask for, right?

In the end, he achieved more than many of us. He actually achieved those aims. Most of them never achieved that. That's him. But walking on water and all that stuff? No. As a great master of martial arts, in the traditional sense, no. Was he a master? Yes. A great master? No. That's different. That's a totally different category.

He should be honored for what he is. There are many sides to him. He was human. I'll tell you why he's a master. He showed me what's at his best mastership. He was working at Paragon. He's a stock clerk. You know, all he wanted to do was work a couple of days a week.

RAL: Paragon Sporting Goods?

Yes. Yeah, so Jeff (Pascal) ran all the stores, Paragon, Hudson, all the sporting goods. Jeff ran a computer system. He created the whole thing for them. So when BP needed a job, I said, don't worry, I'll fix it up. So I called Jeff, BP needs a job. Don't worry, we'll get him a job. BP had stores in the Philippines, remember?

But BP's not into business, doesn't want to learn how to do stores. Business is not his thing. Just Tai Chi was his thing. But he needed a job. So Jeff got him a job. Stock, doing stocks. That's what he wanted. A couple of bucks, leave him alone, stock. Each store he worked at, they loved him.

They want to promote him, the manager, this and that. He said, no, I don't want any of that. The stores never ran so well as when he was with the store. Everything was in place. You know Paragon Sporting Goods, okay? Huge, right? He organized a whole basement. Everything was in place. Everything. So now we weren't having lunch every day because now he's working, but I go visit him. One day this woman comes in. I'm talking about a Westchester type princess, a queen. Oh my god, she comes in: "Where's lkadliksjd%kkkj (mumbling and growling)?" and she comes to me. I don't work there so she can't say anything to me. "Who's in charge here?"

BP goes, "I'm in charge." And I go, oh my God. This woman is going to kill him.

Here's the true master of BP. He gets up, turns to me, looks at me, says, "Soft conquers hard." And he winks at me, walks away. Half hour, comes back, she's eating out of his hands, he has total control of her. She's yelling at me, "Why are you letting this man do that? He has too much work, what are you doing to this poor man?" All I can say is "I'm going, I'm going, I will promote you to Grandmaster!"

That's a fight I never would have won, I would never challenge this woman. He said to me, "Soft conquers hard." These are the really good martial arts stories. That's the martial arts. Forget fighting, breaking bricks. You know what I'm talking about. I thought for sure she was going to chew him up. I said, wow. I can say you're good. That's all I can say.

RAL: He didn't graduate from college, right? He didn't have a college degree or anything. He didn't take any sales training or anything.

All he knew was soft conquers hard. Here's what people ask: How come they weren't educated? Didn't they go to college? Listen, there was a problem during that period. It's called World War II. They were running from the Japanese. That was their college. They were running from the Japanese, hiding in caves. So that's my best story, my best memory of him was that incident in the basement of Paragon.

Okay, you know what I'm talking about. You've been in sales. You know how these people are. They're monsters.

Brief Discussion of Pak Mei and Other Internal Styles....

Pak Mei is very close to the Chen style Tai Chi because we're firing energy. Firing Pak Mei is known for its firing energy and the difference between the Chen style and the Yang style is the firing energy, Fa Jing, the Fa Jing. Yang doesn't do it.

RAL: You also said that there was some Bagua there.

The Bagua form is in the application. They're all intermixed.

Okay, so it goes back to what we call the Red Boats. Have you heard of Red Boats? The legend of Shaolin is all the masters met in the Shaolin. When it was burned down, they all went out to spread the art. And it's called the Red Boat Tradition. The Red Boats were the river boats that went up and down all the rivers in China. They were called Red Boats because gambling, prostitution, everything happened.

Think about the Mississippi. Everybody traveled through the Red Boats. That's where they taught the martial arts. It makes sense, right? Because they traveled up and down the river. So in the boats, on the boats, you had Hung Gar, Chou Li Fut, Tai Chi, Bagua, Xing-Yi, and they all fought each other, and they all taught each other, and they all meshed with each other.

If anybody was any good, he had elements of something. Just think, sports, you have a move I haven't learned. Show me that move. You know? Like that. And that's how they learned. It wasn't systemized back in those days.

It wasn't that you learned the first form, then the second form. Everybody just learned what they could. So most of the martial arts came out in that tradition. We don't talk about it, because it isn't glamorous like the Shaolin and the master learning from the divine. They learned in their Red Boats! A friend of mine is writing a movie about it. And we're opening up now. We're talking about where the systems came from.

RAL: What about loyalty to your current teacher, being respectful, and not engaging other martial arts teachers to train you while you're still training from your current teacher?

What you're saying is not wrong, but you couldn't see the

world. In the old days, they threw you out. But I come from that tradition. Way back, I remember, then in Hawaii, a grandmaster in Hawaii, from a big school in Hawaii, helped me a lot in teaching and how to adjust to the Western world.

He said, "Don't worry about students learning other styles." He said, Today's students know more styles than you'll ever know." In other words, get out of that mindset. They know all the styles. It's America. Because we're in America you can go find other stuff; in China you couldn't. The loyalty was close-knit; as a family, you didn't share. So that's where that comes from. But nowadays it's not like that.

Today, it's not like, I'm not going to share with you, because you're going to talk to him. We're not in that type of world. That will not stop you. That's what he was saying to me. Don't get into that. They know more styles than you ever will know. Just do what you're going to do. You're going to have your own loyalty followers. They're going to follow you because they like you. Forget all the other stuff.

That's trust, you know, so I say to my students, I don't care what you want to do.

RAL: Yeah, that's probably a healthy attitude to have because if they want to, they will.

They will. Every one of my Florida students is a master of another style. In Pak Mei itself, most students of Pak Mei are masters of other styles, because it's an advanced system. And talking about Tai Chi, most masters of any style all end up learning Tai Chi.

When they get later in life, they all begin to study Tai Chi. Most of them do Yang, because they already do the Fa Jing from their style. What they're missing is the meditative part of the Tai Chi.

RAL: I had heard or read that towards the end of his life Bruce Lee was studying Tai Chi.

Bruce Lee always studied Tai Chi.

RAL: I didn't know that.

Bruce Lee studied Hakka; he studied a lot of stuff. Bok Rui, it's Hakka. He studied many of our styles. He gives Wing Chun its name, and that's a mistake he made.

In his first article, this is what happened, the very first article Bruce Lee made when he became famous, he was asked what do you study? He said, well, I study Wing Chun. He named three styles, Wing Chun, Pak Mei, Southern Mantis. These three styles are very similar. My teacher is Ip Man, and everybody went crazy. Ip Man became famous, Wing Chun became famous because he said that, okay? That's where Pak Mei first makes its appearance. And the Southern Mantis, and all those styles became known, because he said it.

So that's the truth behind that. So that's how I met Bruce. I met Bruce in 1966, something like that. At that time, my group was running the All-American Tournament at Madison Square Garden. He was the guest of honor at the demonstration. So I met him, and then we started to be friends, and we worked out ever since. So that whole group is my generation.

24. THE FINAL YEARS AND LEGACY

"Everyone gets the invitation, but we do our exercises so ours comes a little later."
- *BP Chan*

In the 1990's a series of events occurred that must have rattled BP Chan to his core.

In 1992, Mr. Chan's wife, Ester (Esther), passed away. In 1996, Mr. Chan's friend from the Tai Chi Farm, Master Jou, was killed suddenly in an auto accident. In 1998, one of Mr. Chan's daughters passed away. Also, during that decade, William C.C. Chen moved his studio to a new location where there was not enough space for Mr. Chan to keep his weapons on site. Is it coincidental that several of his students from the 1992-2002 decade point out that he was not as attentive to detail in his teaching as he most assuredly was in prior decades? Was he just going through the motions? Did he lose any interest in the things he loved to teach? Maybe not entirely, but enough so that it was noticeable to some of his students.

Eventually, an enlarged heart, and complications from that, put him in the hospital and may have ended his life.

From my conversations with students, it's not clear to me that Mr. Chan took steps to designate or specifically groom a successor. I know he had conversations with some of his students before he died, urging them to teach others. I am not aware of any arrangements that BP Chan put in place for continuity of his teachings with his students in a class setting in the various schools in which he taught. Perhaps this was because he shared space with several teachers and did not want to step in front of them and name a successor. Maybe it's entirely possible that he did have side conversations with some of his students for the purpose of taking over his class offerings. My sense is that he was the keystone in the arch, and that once he was gone his classes eventually faded and students went their separate ways.

Many of his students moved on to teach martial arts and meditation, either privately or in their own schools that they established, or both. Several have written books. Some students have taught medical or healing Qigong to cancer patients. His legacy and teachings live on.

My hope is that Mr. Chan's teachings continue to thrive as 2nd generation students, like me, help to continue his passion by teaching new, young student-learners about his philosophy of life and martial arts. Hopefully those who have never heard of BP Chan or know little about him will seek out one or more of Mr. Chan's 1st generation students in this book to further their personal development.

25. BP CHAN'S FAREWELL LETTER TO HIS STUDENTS

How many martial arts teachers, or for that matter, how many teachers of any stripe, would make a personal call to you to see how you were doing? How many will send you a hand-written holiday card at the end of the year? When it's close to their time to go, how many teachers will write their students a "Farewell" Letter, thanking THEM for THEIR "patience" with their teacher?

Not many, for sure.

BP Chan did all of that.

Mr. Chan passed away in 2002, the year of the Horse.

"Thank you, you're keeping me alive
by coming to class."

-BP Chan, to his students,
often heard in class by Bob Schefsky

年
YEAR

馬
HORSE

DEAR PRACTITIONERS.

I AM VERY honored to have the CHANCE TO PRACTICE together AND to exchange WHAT IS "our SAME LIKEING"

WE ARE ALL brothers AND SISTERS IN the world. "ME COMES FROM WE" WITHOUT "WE" there is no "me."

WE HAVE BEEN brought together by FATE. That is why we can get together — for SHARING, SERVICE AND RESPONSIBILITY — like BrothERs and SISTERS, WITH the help of mother NATURE, to keep this WORLD IN PEACE foREVER,

Thank you ALL for YOUR PATIENCE AND ENDURANCE.

FRIENDLY yours
Chan

MANY THANKS

26. FROM TAI CHI MAGAZINE VOL 26 NO. 2

B. P. Chan Dies

Bun Piac (B. P.) Chan, who taught internal martial arts for more than 25 years in New York City and was a fixture at Jou Tsung Hwa's Tai Chi Farm, died Sunday, March 17 in New York City. He was 81.

Chan was born in Fukien Province in China and started his martial arts studies at the age of 10. He learned many styles of internal arts, as well as Northern Shaolin forms.

He came to the the U.S. from the Philippines in 1976 and was introduced to William C. C. Chen shortly thereafter by his daughter. He and his daughter at that time were living close by William Chen's T'ai Chi school in Manhattan.

Chan subsequently began holding classes at William Chen's school, continuing right up to his death. William Chen assisted him in getting residency in the United States.

In a letter to his family that was read at his funeral, B. P. Chan commended his family for loving one another and thanked his students for their love and support.

He also thanked William Chen for petitioning him, which enabled him to come to the U.S. while he was in his 50s and to bring his family, one by one, from the Philippines.

Chan was a low-keyed teacher and declined publicity, writing books or articles, as well as being videotaped.

His first teacher in China was Chen Jin Ming, a Shaolin master. He learned other Northern Shaolin forms from Lian-Dak Fung in 1933.

Later he went on to study Bagua, Xingyi Tung T'ai Chi Ch'uan, Chen style, T'ai Chi staff, T'ai Chi Knife, push hands and Tam Tuei. He studied Bagua with Lui Hing-Chow and

Please see page 48

B. P. Chan teaching a seminar at Tai Chi Farm.

B. P Chan

Continued from page 13

Xingyi with Chow Chang-Hoon. He also taught T'ai Chi Ruler and qigong meditation, which he learned from Lui Chow-Munk.

William Chen said that when Chan's daughter introduced him 24 years ago, they discussed what martial arts B. P. Chan practiced. "When we talked, he said he was willing to share with anyone.

"The next day, I said I will post at my school what he knows. Many students signed up for his class and then we became like partners. I helped him to apply for residency. Subsequently, Chan was able to bring his entire family, which included eight children, to the U.S."

William Chen said the time with B. P. Chan went very fast. "We worked well together and never had any disagreements. I got a lot of return from the partnership.

"To me he was a very, very nice person and a very high level martial artist. He was very kind and very giving in his classes.

"He was very humble and never criticized anyone. He was very sincere when he taught. Sometimes I felt his class was running late but he didn't want to end the class."

Chan was also a regular at the T'ai Chi Farm in Warwick, NY. He helped create the Bagua garden and would go there Saturdays with students to work on it and frequently taught seminars there.

David Saltman, who studied with Chan for 27 years, said Chan was a very simple person without pretensions. "He said, 'Don't call me master. You are only a master when you are dead because then you know the whole thing.'"

"He would say, 'I am just a guide. You have to take everything I say and you have to test it for yourself and if it doesn't work for you, then throw it out.'"

Saltman said B. P. Chan was very exacting and demanding as a teacher, focusing on precision teaching of the movements. He was very detailed and emphasized accuracy of movement.

"He had an uncanny intuition about

people. He knew stuff without knowing how he knew it."

He said Chan specialized in teaching applications. "He would demonstrate applications for forms and believed that it was important to know applications and uses.

"He believed that T'ai Chi works for health and self-defense because they are the same process. The process and movement and attitude has to be the same for both."

As an example of the precision teaching, Saltman said that in learning the eight palms of Dragon Bagua, he was taught only one palm per year.

"He said it was better to learn one move right than a thousand moves wrong. If you can really do one move right, then you can do a thousand moves right."

Saltman said Chan was a specialist in qigong and meditation and new thousands of methods.

Andy Lee, who met B. P. Chan in 1988 at the Tai Chi Farm, said, "It was raining at the farm and I decided to spend the whole time in the Zhang San Feng building. I figured because it was raining only their best teachers would be indoors.

"And so masters came and went, teaching and sharing information. Finally, I thought it was over even though the schedule showed another teacher by the name of B. P. Chan. There was a circle of people around a small teddy bear of a man. I said, 'Master?' He said, 'No.'"

Andy Diaz, who studied with Chan for many years, said that one day in class he asked Chan what he did on his days off.

"He told me that he sits and looks out of his window and thinks of all the questions that his students might ask so that he would be able to respond without hesitation. 'As a teacher one has to be prepared because we are in the business of teaching others how to be prepared.'"

"I will miss him greatly. I respected him as a man and as a martial artist."

Drake Short a relatively recent Bagua student of eight months, said, "You couldn't meet a more beautiful, more genuine, disciplined man.

"Each week he would stop in between lessons and talk about what you are doing and the reason you are doing it. He would break it down different ways and tried teaching it in different ways. He was gifted that way. I wish I would have known him much longer." •

> As an example of the precision teaching, Saltman said that in learning the eight palms of Dragon Bagua, he was taught only one palm per year. "He said it was better to learn one move right than a thousand moves wrong. If you can really do one move right, then you can do a thousand moves right."

27. TAI CHI MASTER B.P. CHAN DIES AT 80

by Frank Allen

REMEMBERED FOR HIS HUMBLENESS AND KNOWLEDGE

Master B.P. Chan, who taught at the William C.C. Chen School of Tai Chi for the past 27 years, passed away Sunday morning at 9:35AM, March 17, 2002. He was 80 years old and teaching up until 2 weeks before his passing, which was gentle and completely accepted. Master Chan was laid to rest yesterday with a combined Roman Catholic and Buddhist ceremony. Although many of us will carry on his teachings within our own amalgamations, Master Chan's successor who will carry on his teachings in their pure form is Sifu Michael ben Aaman.

Master B.P. Chan was the humblest martial arts teacher that I have ever come into contact with and in fact hated to be called even a teacher, much less a master. He asked all of his students to simply call him Mr. Chan and at least once a class, every class, would say, "Remember that I'm not teaching you. We are just practicing together." He also almost never said anything about who his teachers were or where he learned his arts. On the other hand, he was a walking Chinese Martial Arts Encyclopedia, knowing and at different times teaching Yang and Chen Styles of Tai Chi, Pa Kua Chang, Hsing I Chuan, a number of Chi Kung

Sets, and a number of different Shaolin Styles from his home in Fujian.

He did tell us that he began his martial studies with a friend of his fathers who taught a local style, when Mr. Chan was 10 years old. He also mentioned once that his Pa Kua style was that of Chiang Jung Chiao and that he learned some of his Hsing I in the Chinese army. As his students, we noticed that his Hsing I seemed very similar to that of Sun Lu Tang and that Mr. Chan seemed to have a very deep respect for Wang Hsiang Zai. Chan always taught his students that martial arts were for preserving health and peace of mind and said that he had never been in a fight — but that the Second World War and the time that the two guys tried to mug him in Manila didn't count. He and his family apparently had moved to Manila to escape the Japanese during the Sino-Japanese war of the late 1930's and got there just in time to live under the Japanese occupation of the Second World War.

During his years in Manila, Mr. Chan taught for 3 hours every morning in the park before going to work in his father's used furniture store, a store that he often referred to as, "Not the biggest, not the best, The Only Used Furniture Store in Manila!" After coming to New York in the mid-1970's he taught for The William C.C. Chen Tai Chi School and other various venues around the New York area, right up until a couple of weeks before his death. He was especially noted for how much he loved Master Jou's Tai Chi Farm and the time he spent there teaching and working on the facilities with his students. B.P. Chan was one of the last of that rare breed of simple and humble Kungfu masters, [as much as he hated being called a master], and he will be sorely missed by everyone who he ever came into contact with.

Reprinted with permission of Master Frank Allen
https://www.usadojo.com/b-p-chan-remembered-humbleness-knowledge

This essay originally appeared in Tai Chi Magazine Vol 26 No 3

28. IN MEMORY OF B.P. CHAN (1922-2002)

By Mark Jones

On March 17, 2002, the world lost one of the greatest martial artists of the century. B.P. Chan passed away at the age of 80.

He knew that he was ready to go and prepared the time and place, just as did Chao Kang Tao, the master of the Tai Chi ruler, one of the many systems taught by Mr. Chan. Like Tao, Chan was strong, vital, happy, and quick thinking right to the end.

When names of great martial arts masters throughout history are discussed, rarely if ever does the name of B.P. Chan come up. In fact, most readers of this article will wonder who, in fact, he was. That is precisely the way Chan wanted it. In an age of self-promotion, hype, and a race after the almighty dollar, Chan was the opposite - a humble, reclusive martial artist and teacher who was dedicated purely to the art and to those who wished to learn it. He would call this "fishing in a small pond."

In an age of masters, sifus, grandmasters, and gurus, the biggest insult you could give Chan was to refer to him as a master. He would say, "You can call me anything you want when you put me in the ground." What he meant was, if you are a master, you have nothing left to learn; you have already mastered the art. And art, like life, is continually changing, so you must continually adapt and create. To master is to stagnate. Chan made it incumbent upon himself to learn something new every day.

The only title he would allow himself to be called was that of fellow practitioner. He only claimed to have been doing it a bit longer so he could help guide you, but you had to do the work. Chan was the real deal. The old traditional Zen master, you'd have to somehow seek out and prove your dedication to learning the art. In a materialistic climate of franchises, trophies, certificates, and tournaments, he never even had his own school. He would teach in William C.C. Chen's school, at the Tai Chi Farm, and in parks, libraries, and other public places that his students arranged. He refused to write books, make videos, be interviewed for magazines, or even have his photo taken. Although I feel this was excessive, he believed that doing was the only way to learn. Words were cheap. Learning to feel was the only way to study an art, and that couldn't be gained from books or videos. He would teach the principles, the laws of nature as applied to the human body, and it was up to the student to do the work, to learn how to listen to his body.

For example, when giving a workshop, he never used the term "workshop." He called it a "shopwork." You get many concepts during it, shop around, and find a couple you connect with, then go home and work. Try them out. Practice. The four stages of development were believe, analyze, do, then prove. One needs to have faith in the art. Analyze what one is going to try in order to make sure to be in center at all times and all intersections are exact. Then practice it many times and finally prove it by trying it out on an opponent to see if it actually works.

The only thing Mr. Chan ever wrote to my knowledge was a nine-page document entitled "How to Prepare to Do One Move." In it, he spoke of being in harmony with nature - learning from it, not trying to go against it, of finding motion in stillness, and stillness in motion.

His teachings were living Taoism - doing becoming knowing, not learning in the mind first. Knowing something from only the neck up is not knowing. Chan eschewed all the esoteric Chinese names for things, especially chi. Instead of talking about tendon changing, Ming Men points, or Fa Jing, he would talk about car engines and wheels, corporate structures in the workplace and bridge design - the engineering principles of efficient practical structure.

You would be learning all the Chinese concepts by not knowing you were learning them. He taught that if you didn't have Qi to begin with, you'd be in a pine box. Everyone already has it, the life force, breath. By focusing on it, you will only block it. It is better to concentrate on posture, alignment, and center. When you are able to realign the body and open it up, internal energy will naturally flow by itself. Have no expectations. Just enjoy the process.

Chan was one of the most brilliant men I'd ever met and was a virtual encyclopedia of fascinating ideas, especially when relating to body mechanics and philosophy. He seemed to take special pride in being a simple farm boy with no formal education, giving all this wisdom to over-educated college graduates who were completely out of touch with their bodies. He was able to decipher the true concepts behind the commonly held translation of the classics and what they actually meant (which was far different than what was typically practiced.) He also loved to play with words, double meanings, visual symbols of letters, feelings the body had by speaking certain sounds, opening, constricting, lifting, etc.

How counting from the pointing finger down caused your spine to curve, but counting from the little finger up caused the spine to lift.

Tucking the thumb inside a closed fist
will keep you warm on a cold day.

When carrying a briefcase, you can counterbalance
the weightwith the other hand by extending
down the fingers.

How to lift and throw a heavy object
(by first turning the opposite direction in a
circular motion.)

How to cure various illnesses through Qigong
exercises and diet.

How balance and alignment are affected by the eyes,
which control the central nervous system.

After one hour with him, you felt like your head was going to explode with information, but your life was also changed for the better. Everything he spoke of was designed to make you a better person, to make one more selfless, pure of heart and intention, less stressed out, more inclined to help others. His questions to answers were rarely given directly in a Western sense. They would be poetic parables that made you ponder, until one day you arrived at the answer, if you put in the time and effort to find it. If you did, the answer would mean more and become a part of you rather than if he had just answered it and you shook your head up and down.

His martial abilities were beyond prodigious. They're on a level we've read about the old masters possessing yet probably will never see again. He concealed his deepest abilities for the most part, but several people have witnessed him performing feats of extremely high internal levels, such as tossing huge people around with very little external movement and temporarily paralyzing people with one finger or even at a distance, although he never hurt a student. Not only was his body as strong as steel, but he could move his internal organs at will and hold excruciatingly difficult postures with no effort. He also had an uncanny way of knowing what you were thinking.

Bun-Piac Chan was born in Fujian province in China and began studying in the Shaolin Temple as a child in the 1920s.

His earliest teachers included Lian-Dak Fung and Chen Jin Ming. He also furthered his Qigong training with Lui Chow-Monk. Throughout the century, he delved into long-term deep study of Bagua, Xing-Yi, I Chuan, Tai Chi ruler, staff, knife, Yang and Chen family Tai Chi forms, and applications and other arts. His Bagua lineage came through Yin Fu to Gong Bao Tien, and to him from Lu Yun Chow (Liu Hing Chow.) His Xingyi lineage came through Gao Yu Shen, Li Tsun I, Shang You Chang, Liu Tsu Yen, and to him from Chow Chang Hung (Hoon). Though not clear, it is rumored that he learned his I Chuan directly from Wang Xiang Zhai. His direct Tai Chi instructor was Tung Yin Ch'ieh, who was Yang Cheng-Fu's closed-door student, the one Yang demonstrates applications on in his photographs, and Chan's photograph appears in in Tung's "Red Book" in a group shot titled "January 4, 1953, Ing Yi Tai Chi School." Mr. Chan moved to New York and began teaching in the 1970s and his postures and weight distribution looked unlike anyone else's until books like Douglas Wile's, "Tai Chi Touchstones, Yang Family Secret Transmissions" came out showing the actual photos of Yang Cheng-Fu and Tung Ying Ch'ieh, which looked like Chan's. Chan learned directly from the old masters as a closed-door student, not the popularized Yang style postures that exhibited different weight distributions and intersections.

His Chen postures were also not like the modernized ones, but like those from bygone times that are no longer seen. For Chan, all postures had to make logical sense from a structural and application standpoint. Flowing, pretty movements executed while one was out of center could get a person killed in a fight. And he was able to battle test his art in hand-to-hand fighting during the war, it has been said.

Yet Chan rarely mentioned any of his teachers, especially if asked.

He would snap, "You study with me, not my teachers." What also set him apart was his ability to synthesize his learning from all these great masters, find the common principles in them, and express them in a refreshingly creative manner to his students, giving each individual exactly what he needed, when he needed it. Despite his reclusiveness since arriving in the United States, many students took classes with him, and many used his name as a credential, despite only spending brief tenures with him. Only a few core students remained with him for a long period of time, and in turn practiced and taught in small groups quietly with little fanfare.

They never entered tournaments for sport, wrote books or made videos. Like Chan, they've kept a low profile, working with those who found them. One senior practitioner who studied with him for over 25 years and who Chan trained to teach has been in the New York metropolitan area, teaching in the same low-profile manner.

Although Mr. Chan said he didn't care what he was called after he was in the ground, I suspect he would rather be eternally recognized not as a grandmaster but as a fellow practitioner, as the martial arts and the understanding of life have no ending, just the continual flow of becoming.

This essay originally appeared in Tai Chi Magazine Vol 26 No 3

29. MEMORIES OF MY FIRST QIGONG TEACHER: B.P. CHAN, A TRUE PERSON OF NO RANK

Updated: Feb 20, 2018

This essay originally appeared in the Summer 2002 edition of Qi: The Journal of Traditional Eastern Health and Fitness © Kenneth S. Cohen

On March 17, 2002, B P. Chan, one of the first generation of qigong teachers in North America, passed into spirit. Chan, born on May 30, 1922 in Fujian Province, China, lived for many years in the Philippines, and, finally, moved to New York City, where he lived for the rest of his life.

When Chan arrived in New York City in 1974, he planned to stay for about six months, long enough to teach a basic course in Bagua Zhang, one of the "inner martial arts" (nei jia quan) related to Taiji Quan, at the studio of his friend and colleague, William C. C. Chen. Not wishing to miss the rare opportunity to study with a teacher and person of Chan's caliber, students flocked to his classes. Six months later, he decided to "visit" a bit longer, to teach the next level of Bagua Zhang, as well as an introductory course in Xing Yi Quan and Chen Style Taiji Quan. Within a year, he had decided to remain in the United States.

Chan began studying Chinese healing, contemplative, and martial arts as a young child. He learned Taoist meditation and qigong from monks and masters at the An De Guan (安德觀 Monastery of Peaceful Virtue), not far from his home. At age 11, Chan began training in Northern Shaolin Boxing with Master Lian Dak Fung, and not long thereafter learned Taiji Ruler Qigong 先天氣功太極尺 from Lui Chow-Munk, a direct student of the system's greatest proponent, Zhao Zhongdao. He also studied with the famed Master of Wu Zu Quan (Five Ancestors Boxing 五祖拳) Chen Jingming 陳景銘, from whom he learned Fujian White Crane Boxing, Standing Meditation (Zhan Zhuang), and various qigong techniques. Chan was deeply connected with the tradition of Sun Lutang 孫祿堂 through his training in various arts (most likely Xingyi Quan 形意拳) with Sun's famed disciple Zheng Huaixian (1897-1981) 鄭懷賢. In the Philippines, he continued cultivating the Tao and learning Bagua Zhang and Xingyi Quan with Liang Jici 梁紀慈 (Leung Kay-Chi in Cantonese), with whom he taught for many years. I have also heard from some of Chan's other students that Chan may have learned Xingyi Quan from Chow Chang-Hoon, though I was unable to corroborate this during his lifetime.

Chan probably had other teachers as well, including combat instructors in the military. He knew and taught Yunnan Consecutive Step Boxing 雲南連步拳, which was part of standard training for Nationalist troops during the Second World War. I have pieced these details together over the years, through bits he shared, conversations with colleagues, and research. Chan rarely spoke about his background. He was an incredibly humble and honorable man who did not wish to attract attention or admiration; nor did he seek fame because of his lineage. He taught qigong and martial arts out of love of the arts and in a spirit of service.

Chan was an avid reader and deep thinker. He especially admired the book "A Study of Xingyi Quan" 形意拳學 by Sun Lutang 孫祿堂 and often, during private classes, quoted passages from it. He also loved the inner martial arts writings of Jiang Rongqiao 姜容樵. Chan was constantly refining his practice and teaching style.

A biographical sketch gives little indication of the extraordinary range of B. P. Chan's skills. When I lived in New York City during the 1970s, he was teaching classes in Yang and Chen Style Taiji Quan; Bagua Zhang; Xingyi Quan; Yunnan Boxing; Taoist Meditation; Taiji Ruler Qigong; Lying Down Qigong (Wo Gong); Standing Meditation, and more. Yet, Chan was no dilettante. He had a comprehensive understanding of the systems he taught, and when students were ready, he organized intermediate and advanced level classes. Xing Yi Quan students progressed from the Five Element Exercises to the Twelve Animals, to fluid "linking forms" that combined elements and animals in graceful choreography, and, finally, to two-person martial application sets. Similarly, the Taiji Ruler course included multiple levels of training. At first students learned gentle rocking exercises in which the hands make vertical or horizontal circles, designed to build a strong reservoir of qi in the dan tian. Later they learned the rarely-taught advanced techniques, such as the Taiji Ball. While standing, the student holds a stone or wooden ball between the fingers or palms, several inches in front of the dan tian. This develops qi and strength. Or he or she rolls the ball on a table top to develop tactile sensitivity and "listening" (聽勁) ability– a student who can "listen," that is sense energy, can feel blockages and detect illness in the body and, in the martial arts or other sports, can anticipate an opponent's moves.

I enrolled in Chan's very first class, and also took weekly private classes for several years. He was my first qigong teacher, and if I have been able to reach any heights in qigong, it is only because of the deep foundation Chan gave me. Because I spoke Chinese and had similar interests and values, we developed a special bond of friendship, and I believe that I got to know him well. Chan balanced wu gong 武功, martial ability, with wu de 武德, martial virtue. Unlike so many teachers, who expect their students to take pride in their teacher's name and reputation, Chan preferred to remain anonymous. He was a "no name teacher" (無名師.) When I asked Chan what B.P. stood for or if he would write the Chinese characters for his name, he replied, "Do you want to learn the martial arts or my name?" "Then how can students verify my lineage or find out if I am authorized to teach?" I asked. Chan replied, "Teach when you know. Good qigong follows qigong principles and creates health and happiness; it is not a matter of lineage. You do not become good because of the name of your teacher. Do not mention my name." As you can see from this essay, I am a very poor student, who cannot help mentioning the name of his beloved teacher. Perhaps, since he was also my friend, it is permissible. I was very touched when around 1981 Chan gave me a photograph of himself, on the back of which he wrote, in Chinese, "To my classmate and friend Ken Cohen," signing it with the Chinese characters for his first name, Bun Piac in Fujian dialect, Wen Bai in Mandarin.

Chan was always "Mr. Chan" to his students. He wouldn't allow us to call him "Master," though sometimes I got away with "Chan Laoshi," Teacher Chan, in Chinese. Chan was what ninth century Chinese Buddhist Master Linji called "A True Person Of No Rank" (無位真人): "True" because his inside matched his outside– he walked his talk, lived his spirituality every day; "Of No Rank" because he wouldn't accept titles and he saw each human being as having equal beauty and value.

The following sayings, stories, and anecdotes may give insight into Chan's teachings and character.

THE TEACHINGS OF B. P. CHAN *LINGUIST EXTRAORDINAIRE*

Chan loved language. He spoke several fluently: Fujian and Mandarin Chinese, Tagalog, and English. He told me that the Chinese terms used to describe qigong and Taiji Quan posture have hidden meanings. Sometimes the meaning is tied in to the very sound and energy of the Chinese words. For example, while practicing qigong students should han xiong ba bei, release the chest and extend the back. Chan taught that when you say "han xiong," your chest automatically loosens, becoming yin; when you say "ba bei," it is easy to feel energy rising up the spine and lengthening it. Another example: Xu ling ding jing, "Empty spirited energy is maintained at the crown of the head." When you say, " xu" (empty), the body and mind become light and empty. As you say "ling" qi rises to the crown. With "ding jing," the energy is maintained at the crown. Chan always stressed that we should have the feet firmly rooted in the ground, while the head lightly reaches towards the heavens. "The feeling of a suspended head is the secret of speed in combat," he once commented.

English words also have power. Chan felt that "relax" was an unfortunate translation for the Chinese word song. "The word 'relax' makes people tense," he said. "Better to say loosen and release."

STANDING MEDITATION

At my first private class, Chan revealed a "secret technique" called "Standing Meditation" (Zhan Zhuang.) He said that it was the most important exercise in qigong. I stood with bent knees, straight back, and arms rounded in front of my chest. After ten minutes, my legs began shaking. Chan told me to take a break. We sat together and chatted about martial arts. Then I tried it again, with the same effect. He told me that, in the beginning stages of qigong, shaking was natural. "It means that there's water in the pressure cooker, but the lid is not properly sealed or tight- it is bobbing up and down. In other words, your body is not yet strong or stable enough to hold the qi." He told me to go home and practice every day. At next week's lesson, I could stand for twenty minutes, but then both my hands and legs shook! This went on every week, stand a little, shake a little. I felt like a fool. But until I could stand for a full hour, without moving, he wouldn't teach me anything else. "If you can't stand, how can you walk or move? If you don't have enough energy to stand for an hour, how can you practice martial arts?" He told me that to master qigong, you must master the "Four Virtues" (Si De): lying, sitting, standing, and walking.

SOME PRINCIPLES OF STANDING MEDITATION

"What is the meaning of song kua, yuan dang (release the inguinal area, round the groin)? Be aware of the crease between the thigh and hip–keep this area soft, and imagine that your legs and hips form a rounded arch way. An arch can support more weight than a pillar. Conversely, if you imagine that your legs are pillars, you will tire more easily.

"Practice the Four Empties (四空): Use intent (yi) to make the feet, palms, chest, and mind empty. 'Empty' means open and receptive.

337

"Practice the Three Levels (三平) Keep three areas level: eyes, hips, shoulders. (Level movement is also important in "walking the circle," the basic practice in Bagua Zhang. Sometimes, while Chan was practicing, his teacher held a wooden block with a nail through it just above his crown. If he rose up, he would be skewered!)

"Keep the crown point (bai hui) and perineum point (hui yin) on one line. Gradually qi in the vertical axis will reach the feet, and then the hands.

"Never correct yourself by looking at yourself. Use nei shi, 'inner gazing.' Be like a sentinel on a wall. To see the enemy, look out, not down the wall."

BAGUA ZHANG AND STANDING

Chan exemplified the qigong principle of "a steel bar wrapped in cotton." He was soft and flexible, like water, but he could hit like a tidal wave. Sometimes, during Bagua Zhang practice, I felt that his grip was like a steel vise, and was thankful that he never tightened it beyond my tolerance! Because I had probably watched too many martial arts movies, I was beginning to suspect the "real reason" for Chan's martial arts prowess. He undoubtedly did finger pushups and spent hours each day slapping bricks and thrusting his fingers into heated sand, probably followed by the application of herbal liniments. One day, during a private class, I decided to ask Chan about his personal training. "Why are your fingers so strong?" He immediately dropped into a low squat and struck his fingers full force onto the concrete floor. Then he stood up, rolled and tapped his fingers in the air and said, "You see, no pain, and I can still play piano." "Yes, I can see that," I said, "But how?" He replied, "You won't believe me," whereupon he bent his knees and raised his arms into a rounded shape, as though embracing a tree. "Standing," he said, "is the secret. And the only reason the old masters had such great ability is because they had more patience than people today. They stood!"

KEEP ON LEARNING

One Sunday afternoon, the esteemed Taiji Quan teacher, T. T. Liang, then in his late seventies and directing a school in Boston, dropped in unexpectedly at the end of one of Chan's martial arts classes. He was probably looking for his old friend, William C. C. Chen. Chan shook Liang's hand warmly, introduced his students, and then, to our astonishment, asked Liang, "Could you give me some correction on my Taiji Quan form? Perhaps one or two words of advice?" Our teacher was asking for correction! Liang tried to refuse, but Chan insisted. Chan admonished us, "What's wrong with you? What kind of teacher would I be if I didn't take advantage of this golden opportunity?"

I have always believed that a great teacher is a great student, and the two roles are often interchangeable. Sometimes one is a student, sometimes a teacher. One of Chan's ingenious teaching devices was to ask a student who had just learned a technique to "play teacher" and teach it to the other students. As the student attempted to teach through both demonstration and explanation, Chan would offer gentle correction. It was a great learning experience for everyone.

THE GREATEST SECRET OF ALL

I had just had an exhausting lesson in which Chan corrected every tiny detail of my Bagua Zhang form— aligning the index finger of my left hand exactly with my nose, the thumb of my right exactly with my navel, making sure that my heels were on an imaginary circle, with my feet pointing at a specific angle, and so on, and so on. At the end of the class, Chan asked me, "What is the reason for all this complicated choreography? You know-hold your hand this or that way, step exactly here, not there." It was obvious that Chan wanted to answer his own question, so I hesitated. He continued, "The reason we learn qigong and martial arts is to find out 'is this arm my arm, is this leg my leg?' A person might think that, of course, my leg is my leg. But if this is true, if he is one with his leg, why can't he do this?" at which point Chan slid into a low stance, one knee bent and the other leg stretched out along the floor, his hands grasping an invisible opponent– an exquisite Bagua Zhang move called "sparrow skims the water." Chan then paid me a great compliment. "I can tell you these things because you think for yourself, like me. Other students might believe I am crazy." I assured him that many students would understand. He then summarized his philosophy. "The purpose of qigong is nei wai, shang xia he yi 內外上下合 (inside and outside, upper and lower harmonized in unity.)" He continued, "This is easy to say, difficult to practice."

A GREAT HEART

I asked Chan about the meaning of the ancient philosopher Lao Zi's saying "Do without doing." (wei wu wei 為無為.) He said, "Do and act for the earth, including the environment. Do for heaven by developing yourself spiritually. And do for all living beings."

After teaching a group of students some powerful martial arts grappling and striking techniques, a young woman asked, "Which technique is best? Which should we use in a dangerous situation?" Chan said, "Here's what you do. First, spit in the attacker's eye. This will startle him. Then do a shin kick, turn around, and run away. And always remember that we do martial arts to make friends, not enemies."

I asked Chan if he had any special guidelines for teachers. He said, "You should always remember that teachers are easy to find. But true students are hard to find. And class payment is just a token. Real payment is in character."

"Your brain doesn't control your body. Your heart controls your body. We should use our hearts more." Chan lived from the heart more and more during the last years of his life. His kindness was catching, and our relationship was transformed by it. Sometimes, when he phoned, if no one was at home, he would leave a beautiful message for me and my wife. "This is Chan. I love you." We told him the same. Life is too short, and I am too old, to waste time not saying what I am really thinking and feeling. Love is a greater power than qi.

B.P. Chan is survived by six daughters and two sons. His rich legacy was passed on to thousands of students.

30. A TRIBUTE TO MASTER BP CHAN, A "WARRIOR WITH HEART"

by Paul Gallagher

A rare martial artist and human being, Master BP Chan, passed away in March of this year. Though his martial art abilities were profound, and he was a master of six separate martial arts Systems" (each "System" being equivalent to a PhD in the West), what was perhaps most remarkable about Master Chan was his humility and quality as a heartfelt human being. I hope these few stories of my experience with him convey some of the "wit, wisdom, and heart" of a great man, teacher, and friend.

Master Chan began martial arts studies at the age of 10, when his father brought him to one of South China's "Five Tigers of Shaolin" for instruction. His first year of study consisted of holding the "Standing Post" position until he could do it for one hour - that, and serving the Master. Master Chan related how he would see the other children of his village playing and he wished he could join them. But during his practice time, there was no respite. Sometimes, thinking the old Master was not watching, he would stand up to rest his weary legs. But the wily Shifu would sneak up behind him and with a tap from his two fingers (which Chan described as feeling like a ton) he would "gently" nudge the boy back into position.

One time, Chan observed the Master grinding ink from the stick of compressed ink prior to practicing calligraphy. He noticed that the Master's entire body was coiling around the central axis of his spine and this subtle coiling motion was transferred to the ink stick. That gave young Chan a powerful enlightenment into the martial arts, and their common principle of unified energy emanating from the spine. This insight later became a part of all his martial arts.

What set Master Chan apart from so many martial arts teachers was his absolute authenticity and quality of heart. A consummate Master, Chan always referred to himself as a "guide." When I began studying with him and inquired about his "lineage,"-who his teachers were and where his system had originated—he steadfastly refused to even discuss this. "I am not a Master, only your guide. I have simply gone a little farther on the path than you have. What difference does my teacher's name make?"

This same modesty caused Master Chan to be absolutely disinterested in promoting himself or seeking any sort of publicity. He simply taught his classes (and seminars at T'ai Chi Farm in New York State) and relied on a few flyers and word of mouth to bring him students.

On one occasion I was visiting T'ai Chi Farm during a busy summer seminar weekend. It was always somewhat amusing to see the younger masters "strutting their stuff" and hawking their wares at the entrance to the Farm. Chan, of course, was never there, since he absolutely refused to advertise or publicize himself. As I walked past the stalls and tables with goods for sale, Chan suddenly seemed to appear out of nowhere. "Mr. Paul, come see my gardens. I built something new." He took me by the arm, and we inspected the new bridge he had built across the stream, using only natural wood which he had found on the site. It seemed so fascinating and touching that this highly accomplished master would be totally uninterested in "selling his wares," but quite enthralled about the natural gardens he had built.

Though he was an extremely thorough and demanding teacher, he never kept an artificial distance between himself and his students. He was always friendly and available and ready to help any willing student. Often his "two hour" seminars would stretch for the better part of a day, if he felt the students were truly sincere.

Through the years, long after I had stopped studying formally with him, Master Chan would send me a Christmas card each year always with a poem or some special word of greeting. If we hadn't spoken for a while sometimes my phone would ring (usually late in the evening) and I'd hear the familiar voice, "Mr. Paul, this is Chan. I haven't heard from you in a long time...." My heart would sink a little, because it is always the student's responsibility to "pay respects" to the teacher-not the other way around. But Chan was so humble and natural, he never stood on ceremony. And always gave a few valuable practice pointers during the phone conversation.

One of Master Chan's proudest accomplishments was building beautiful training gardens and a temple at T'ai Chi Farm in New York State. Along the stream which ran through the property, Chan and his students built separate Hsing I, Pa Kua, and T'ai Chí training gardens. Up on the hill he built a "T'ai Chi Temple," all with scrap lumber and natural wood and stones he found on the property. "Always revere Nature, he would say, Nature gives us everything we need."

He was a great synthesizer in the internal martial arts, always basing his teaching on the most fundamental anatomical and functional qualities of the human body and mind. Though his Hsing I, Pa Kua, and Tai Chi Ch'uan were all at an exalted level, he felt that there was something beyond all of them, the wisdom of Nature herself. One of his articles entitled, "How to Prepare to Do One Move," said in essence that the student's entire life is preparation to "do one move," because doing one move correctly involves understanding and becoming one with the entirety of

Nature. An expression Chan's students heard time and again was "The whole Universe is one story." Whatever the activity—martial arts, or even grinding ink, the principles go back to Nature and ultimately to the Universe itself.

Master Chan could be both humorous and compassionate with his students. On one occasion, during a Pa Kua class, I watched one of the students walking the circle with a deep scowl on his face, and very aggressive, jerky movements. When the class was over Chan sat on a small bench near the studio exit and said goodbye to each student.

As this particular student approached Chan he abruptly asked, "Hey Chan, does this stuff work?" Chan had not been in the U.S. for long at that time, and I could see he was having difficulty understanding the question. The student repeated more loudly, "Hey Chan, does this stuff work, is this stuff any good?" I was mortified. Here was a student in effect challenging the master in an extremely rude manner! Chan was still struggling to understand... "Work?... work?" he said, "I don't understand. What do you mean-work?"

The student then said, "Is this stuff any good, does it work on the street?" At last Chan understood. In similar situations I had seen teachers propel students into walls or demonstrate a quick take-down. I awaited the Master's reaction with bated breath.

Chan's face broke into a broad smile. "If you think like that, you'll be in big trouble. We only practice to know that our hand is truly our hand." What an elegant reply! No ego, no need to show off his skills (and I later learned they were profound), simply a moment of deep teaching. The student shrugged and walked out the door.

I last spoke with Master Chan on Chinese New Year's Day of this year. He sounded altogether well and healthy and, as always, gave me some advice on my training. The thing which I will always remember and cherish are his last words to me, something he had said so often throughout the years I knew him. "We are all brothers and sisters-all one family. We must always use our art to help others." It is this thought that I'll always carry with me when I remember Master Chan.

On one visit to T'ai Chi Farm, I brought with me a dear martial arts friend who had very deep and varied experience with numerous combative arts. Though he was always respectful toward the Chinese "internal martial arts," I sensed my friend was secretly a little skeptical as to their effectiveness in combat. We went to one of Chan's teaching sessions and then to various other events at the Farm.

Later, as we drove home, I asked my friend how he had enjoyed our trip and the events at the Farm. He said he had found it all somewhat interesting, but that Master Chan had profoundly impressed him. "He is the real thing," my friend said.

And truly, for his remarkable qualities as exquisite teacher, Mentor and friend, I could truly say of Master Chan, "He was the real thing."

Paul Gallagher and I exchanged emails early in 2023. He wanted to talk to me about his memories of Mr. Chan. Unfortunately, Paul passed away on March 24, 2023, before we were able to talk.

Printed with permission from Becky Herdt.

31. SOME FINAL THOUGHTS

New York City in the 1970's was a deteriorating, corroding stew of social, political, and economic tensions. Amidst all that, BP Chan's classes offered students structure and a place to temporarily escape the chaos outside. He did this by teaching them how to strengthen their bodies and minds…… not by being hard, but by being "calm," even though their city was beset by difficulties.

This was a period of self-examination and exploration, pushing boundaries of the mind and searching for meaning in a country troubled by Vietnam. High School and College students and many young people in their 20's and 30's turned anti-establishment and sought alternatives to the order of things. BP Chan's teachings and demonstrations must have seemed magical, almost mystical to his students. They saw him do things they had not seen nor experienced before, even though some of them had prior martial arts training.

Some students, I'm sure, just wanted the martial arts training. Young men in their 20's and 30's are full of testosterone. Liberated young women in their 20's and 30's wanted the confidence that comes with knowing that they could protect themselves. As Frank Allen said in his 2020 Whirling Circles Podcast titled "Martial Arts in New York City",

"New York City in the 60's, 70's, and much of the 80's was relatively tough, and you had to know how to handle yourself in the streets."

They may have come initially for self-defense, but they stayed for the good stuff - the Qigong and the meditation.

Mr. Chan's personal life philosophy of sharing, kindness, and brotherhood was an integral part of his personal being, and he delivered that to his students through his teachings and through his relationships with them. Mr. Chan's "Farewell Letter" is the ultimate example of the kind of world he sought for his students.

It's no wonder that young people in their 20's and 30's loved the man so much. He was a role model and a father figure to many. Did he walk on water? No. He had faults, like all of us. He had a sense of humor. He was human. He was intentionally understated, not trying to attract attention or impress.

In my opinion, the most important traits that BP Chan possessed was his ability to appreciate people for who they were and to be able to communicate effectively with them.

32. IS BP CHAN RELEVANT TODAY?

If you are a student or teacher of the Chinese Internal Martial Arts ......

Is Sun Lutang relevant today?
Is Yang Chengfu relevant today?
Is Cheng Tinghua relevant today?
Is Wang Xiangzhai relevant today?

Of course.

Is BP Chan relevant today? BP Chan is not a household name in the world of Martial Arts and Qigong in the United States. He is not one of the foundational pillars of the Internal Martial Arts like those names above. How many people can be?

Today, many martial arts teachers and schools offer digital (remote) instruction via Zoom or podcasts in addition to traditional class and/or workshop settings. What precipitated this was Covid, of course, because during Covid, remote learning was the only mechanism that stood between a martial arts school closing its doors and a martial arts school living to exist another day.

Could BP Chan have thrived in today's digital world?

1. The iPhone was released June 27, 2007, five years after Mr. Chan passed away. If the iPhone was introduced

while he was still teaching, would he be one of the first to sign up for the iPhone 1?

2. Would Chan be comfortable using Zoom to teach if it existed back then (Zoom was launched 1/25/2013)?
3. Would Chan have the desire to create a series of podcasts?
4. Would Chan have been interested in using social media (Meta/TikTok/X) if those platforms existed at that time?

I don't think so.

Chan lived simply and loved simple things. Remote teaching is not simple. There are cameras, microphones, and software to be managed.

Chan didn't like to be photographed, recorded, or videoed. Hard to avoid that when teaching remotely.

Chan was big on teaching and showing students how to "feel." That's very difficult to replicate when teaching remotely.

But he can still be very relevant to both students of the martial arts and teachers of the martial arts.

Students today who want to learn Tai Chi would be well advised to seek out a teacher like BP Chan and steer away from initially learning Tai Chi from a screen. Could a beginning student learn the Yang Style form if taught via Zoom? Maybe, but the form would only be an empty shell. How do you teach "listening skill" remotely? For beginners, the whole "internal" experience is difficult - perhaps impossible -to communicate via remote learning, because a teacher must be able to get students to replicate an internal feeling that cannot be seen or felt remotely. Touch and contact with a qualified teacher are what drives skill development in the Internal Martial Arts. You can't get that from a screen. I'm not saying that remote teaching/learning has no benefit. Certainly, remote teaching has provided students today at all skill levels the ability to sample instruction and education from martial arts teachers around the world. We would not have this opportunity if the digital world did not exist.

So, is BP Chan's teaching style, his communication style, relevant today?

BP Chan not only wanted but needed to be in proximity to his students. His ability to communicate with his students was extraordinary, as you have read in this book, clearly described by every 1st generation student. My belief is that his teaching style and approach is more relevant now than ever. The various Qigong systems and martial arts systems (the WHAT he taught) are important, yes, but HOW he taught them, and the WAY he taught them, sets him apart, in my opinion. The relevance of BP Chan to today is in the HOW (of his communication style) and in the WAY (of his communication style) that were the foundations of his teaching.

33. THE STUDENT GUIDES

To supplement and reinforce his class teachings, BP Chan would provide 8 1/2" x 11" "handouts" to his direct students. I believe that the figures were drawn by his students and the Chinese letters were written by Mr. Chan himself. His earliest students apparently may not have received many of these, but it was very common for Mr. Chan to give these out in the 80's and after. Many of Mr. Chan's direct students have kept these for over 40 years!

Were these guides created only for the use of his direct students? Initially, yes. Did he want his direct students to secret them away in a basement filing cabinet, never to see the light of day again, never to be shared or further guide students of his direct students, or other martial arts students who might want to explore Chan's systems and teachings? I don't think so. Mr. Chan was very much into sharing.

If you never studied with BP Chan and want to make these two-dimensional sheets come alive for you, take lessons from one of Mr. Chan's 1st generation students mentioned in this book. You won't regret it.

I do not recommend practicing any of these exercises without the guidance of a direct student of BP Chan. You cannot understand, experience, or feel the full benefit of practicing ANY of these unless you have the knowledge and experience of one of

BP Chan's direct students to guide you. As with all internal systems, a qualified, experienced teacher is necessary to derive the full benefit from these systems.

Believe me, I know.

Contact information for some of Mr. Chan's direct students is provided in Chapter 34.

The handouts that follow represent only a portion of the available content that BP Chan shared with his students....

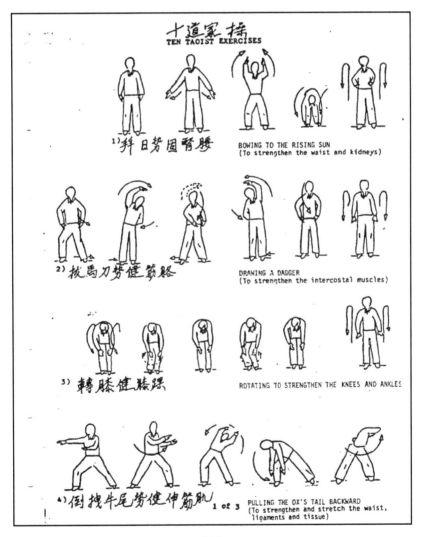

十道家操
TEN TAOIST EXERCISES

1) 拜日势固肾腰

BOWING TO THE RISING SUN
(To strengthen the waist and kidneys)

2) 拔马刀势健筋胳

DRAWING A DAGGER
(To strengthen the intercostal muscles)

3) 转膝健膝踝

ROTATING TO STRENGTHEN THE KNEES AND ANKLES

4) 倒拽牛尾势健伸筋肌

1 of 3   PULLING THE OX'S TAIL BACKWARD
(To strengthen and stretch the waist,
ligaments and tissue)

TEN TAOIST EXERCISES cont.

4) cont.

5) 搖兒勢健伸筋肌

ROCKING THE BABY
(To strengthen and stretch the tendons)

6) 三脚虎拳增氣力

THREE-LEGGED TIGER WITH FIST
(Increasing energy and force)

7) 旋轉双手松筋胘   2 of 3

SWIVELING THE TWO ARMS
(To loosen the ligaments and torso)

TEN TAOIST EXERCISES cont.

8) 三盤落地強健腰腿

THREE PLATES FALLING ON THE GROUND
(Squatting to strengthen the waist and legs)

9) 武松打虎調理周身

WO SONG HITTING THE TIGER
(To regulate the whole body)

9) cont.

10) 擺轉身手按摩腎與神經

SWINGING THE ARMS BACK AND FORTH
(To massage the kidneys and central nervous
system)

355

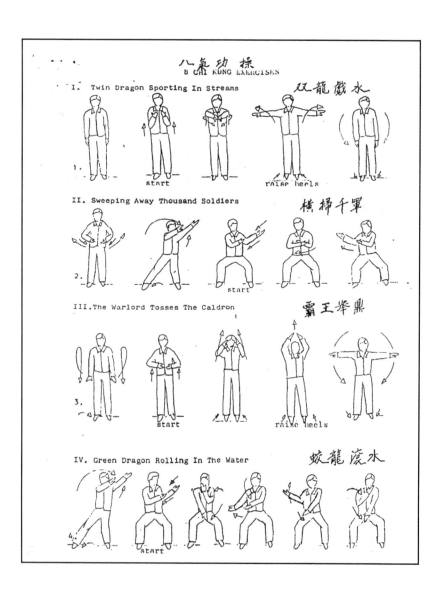

Ron Lambert

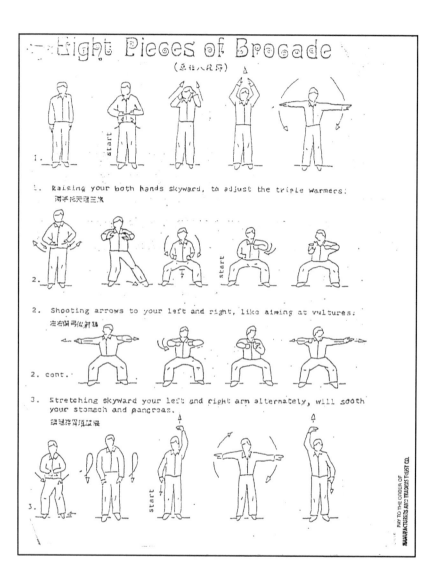

4. Looking toward the back of your body, will mend your five toils and seven injuries. 五勞七傷往後瞧

5. Shaking both your head and tail (like a lion), to get rid of your indigestion. 搖頭擺尾去心火

6. Raising your heels and bending backward seven times, all your diseases will disappear. 背後七顛百病消

7. Clench your fists like in anger, will increase your strength. 攢拳怒目增氣力

3 views as seen from the side—

... ... will strength kidneys.

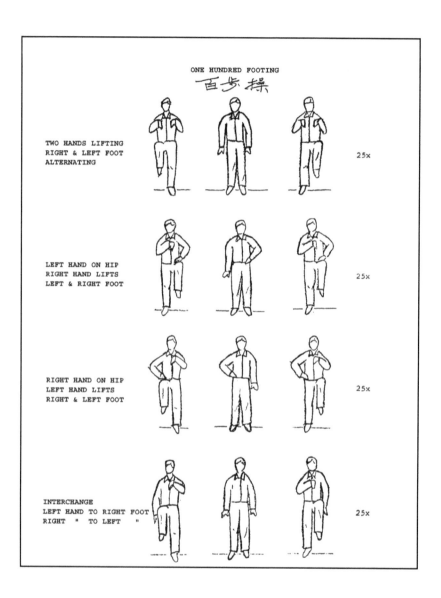

ONE HUNDRED FOOTING
百步操

TWO HANDS LIFTING
RIGHT & LEFT FOOT
ALTERNATING

25x

LEFT HAND ON HIP
RIGHT HAND LIFTS
LEFT & RIGHT FOOT

25x

RIGHT HAND ON HIP
LEFT HAND LIFTS
RIGHT & LEFT FOOT

25x

INTERCHANGE
LEFT HAND TO RIGHT FOOT
RIGHT " TO LEFT "

25x

Commencement of San-Ti

3. Step up punching fist (peng chuan)

Green dragon coming out of water

Black tiger coming out of cave

5. Step back white crane rises its wings

Step up pounding fist (pao chuan)

Step up chopping fist (pi chuan)

Following step crossing fist (heng chuan)

Wild cat washes its face

Left drilling fist (tsuan chuan)

Step up right drilling fist (tsuan chuan)

Wild cat climbs up to the tree

13. Step up right turn standing form

14. Right trun step up wild cat climbs to the tree

15. Step up punching fist (peng chuan)

16. Step back green dragon coming out of water

Step up black tiger coming our of cave

Step back white crane rises its wings

17. Step up pounding fist (pao chuan)

20. Step up chopping fist (pi chuan)

21. Following step crossing fist (heng chuan)

22. Wild cat washes its face

23. Left drilling fist (tsuan chuan)

24. Step up right drilling fist (tsuan chuan)

25. Wild cat climbs up to the tree

26. Step up right turn standing form

27. Right turn step up wild cat climbs to the tree

Step up punching fist (peng chuan)

Step back green dragon coming out of water

Courtesy of Peter Chema

形意　八式拳（内包含五拳三篇）　EIGHT FORMS CHUAN　　HSING-I

1.三体式 — Commencement of San-ti

2.鹞子束身 — The hawk binds its body

3.鹞子入林 — The hawk flew into the woods

4.上步崩拳 — Step up punching fist

5.退步横拳 — Step back crossing fist

6.上步劈拳 — Step up chopping fist

7.上步金鸡独立 — Golden cock stands on its leg

8.上步金鸡食米 — Golden cock eats rice

9.上步鹞子入林 — Hawk flew into the wood

10.退步横拳 — Crossing fist

11.龙虎相交 — Dragon & tiger meet at entersection

12.上步黑虎出洞 — Black tiger coming out of cave

13.缩步掩肘 — Draw back step & cover with elbow

14.缠肘上步穿林 — Winding the elbow & get into the wood

15.退步白鹤亮翅 — White crane rises its wings

16.顺步炮拳 — Following step pounding fist

17.上步右攒拳 — Step up right drilling fist

18.叶底看花 — Looking flowers under the leaves

19.回身燕子抄水 — Turn back swallow skims the water

20.鹞子束身 — The hawk binds its body

21.鹞子入林 — The hawk flew into the wood

22.上步崩拳 — Step up punching fist

23.退步横拳 — Step back crossing fist

24.上步劈拳 — Step up chopping fist

25.上步金鸡独立 — Step up golden cock stands on its leg

26.上步金鸡食米 — Step up golden cock eats rice

27.上步鹞子入林 — Step up the hawk flew into the wood

28.退步横拳 — Crossing fist

29.龙虎相交 — Dragon & tiger meet at entersection

30.黑虎出洞 — Black tiger coming out of cave

31.缩步掩肘 — Draw back step & cover with elbow

32.缠肘上步穿林 — Winding the elbow & get into the wood

33.退步白鹤亮翅 — Step back white crane rises its wings

34.顺步炮拳 — Following step pounding fist

35.上步右攒拳 — Step up right drilling fist

36.叶底看花 — Looking flowers under the leaves

37.回身燕子抄水 — Turn back swallow skims the water

38.鹞子束身 — The hawk binds its body

39.鹞子入林 — The hawk flew into the wood

40.转身肘底穿捶 — Fist thrust under the elbow

41.回身上步右攒拳 — Turn back step up right drilling fist

42.退步横拳 — Step back crossing fist

43.收式 — Conclusion

Courtesy of Peter Chema

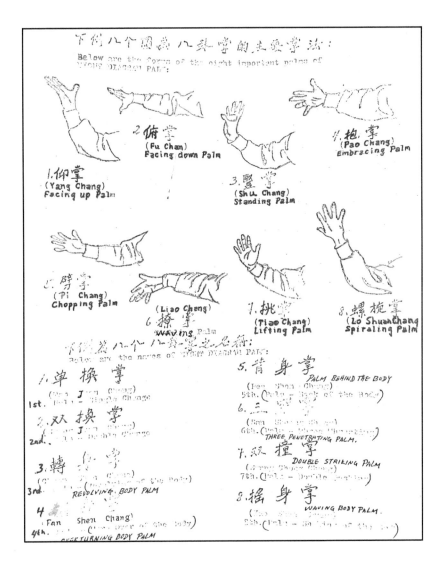

Courtesy of Peter Chema

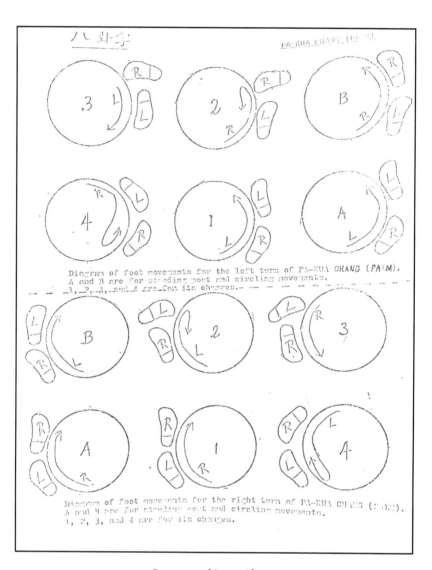

Courtesy of Peter Chema

The exercises of the "Five Animals Play" (五禽之戲) are as follows:- every exercise has five movements.

A. 1. Bear Steps' Posture
     Shion Pu Shih 熊步式
   2. Rocking
     Kan Yun Shih 憨運式
   3. Pressing downward
     An Yun Shih 按運式
   4. To Resist and Shoulder Stroke
     K'ang K'ao Shih 扛靠式
   5. Pushing and Pressing Forward
     T'ui Chi Shih 推擠式

B. 1. Deer Steps' Posture
     Lu Pu Shih 鹿步式
   2. Pushing Out Its Body
     Teng Shen Shih 迸身式
   3. Forward Its Body or To Spy
     T'an Shen Shih 探身式
   4. Looking Backward
     Hui Shou Shih 回首式
   5. Hopping
     Ting T'iao Shih 踏跳式

C. 1. Monkey Steps' Posture
     Hou Pu Shih 猴步式
   2. Peeping
     K'uei Wang Shih 窺望式
   3. To Present the Fruits
     Hsien Kuo Shih 獻果式
   4. To Pluck the Peaches
     Chai Tao Shih 摘桃式
   5. To Flee or Run Away
     T'ao Ts'ang Shih 逃藏式

D. 1. Tiger Steps' Posture
     Hu Pu Shih 虎步式
   2. Roaring (Flaring)
     Fa Wei Shih 發威式
   3. Leaving Its Cave
     Chu Tung Shih 出洞式
   4. Leaping and Pressing or to Flap
     Pu An Shih 撲按式
   5. Fighting, To Grasp
     Po Tou Shih 搏鬥式

E. 1. Crane Steps' Posture
     Hao Pu Shih 鶴步式
   2. Raising Its Wings
     Lien Chi Shih 亮翅式
   3. Stands on One Leg
     Tu Li Shih 獨立式
   4. Landing
     Lo Gan Shih 落雁式
   5. Flying
     Fei Hsiang Shih 飛翔式

SIX SOUND BREATHING EXERCISE
六音呼吸鍛煉
THE NATURE OF FIVE ANIMALS PLAY
五禽之性

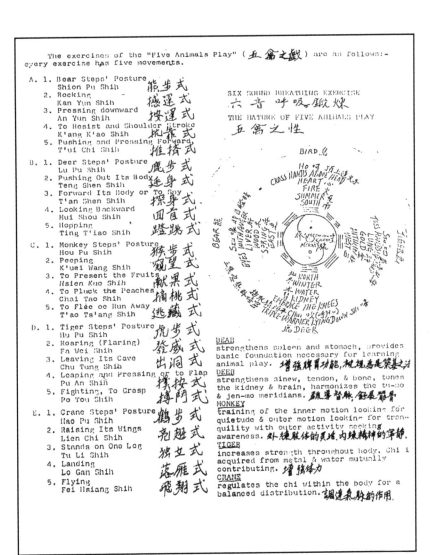

BEAR
strengthens spleen and stomach, provides basic foundation necessary for learning animal play. 增強脾胃功能，視規為是築基之法

DEER
strengthens sinew, tendon, & bone, tones the kidney & brain, harmonizes the tu-mo & jen-mo meridians. 翻導智絡，鈖展筋骨

MONKEY
training of the inner motion looking for quietude & outer motion looking for tranquility with outer activity seeking awareness. 外練肢體的靈培，內練精神的寧靜

TIGER
increases strength throughout body. Chi is acquired from metal & water mutually contributing. 增強體力

CRANE
regulates the chi within the body for a balanced distribution. 調達氣脈的作用

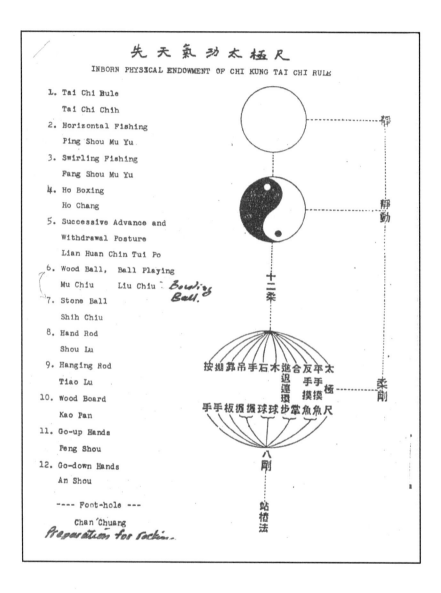

八 輔助功 太極尺 操
EIGHT SUPPLEMENTAL TAI CHI RULER EXERCISES

Perform each exercise eight times using natural breathing. Begin each exercise on the left side, then do the right side.

左右橫向托尺

1. Toss ruler to the sides (figure 8 pattern): In a shoulders-width stance, toss the ruler diagonally to the left side while inhaling; point fingers of the left (outer) hand inward (to help the body turn back to center). Look to the center of the ruler while turning. Turn back to the front while exhaling; bring ruler back to the center below the tan t'ien. Follow the same directions for the right side.

   Two Methods
   (a) To Tonify: Toss ruler to the side moving from bottom (center, facing front) up (diagonally to the left); bring back inward to center (top) and relax (bottom). Follow the same directions for the right side.
   (b) To Get Rid of Toxins: Toss ruler to the left side from top (center, facing front) down (diagonally to the left); bring back to center (bottom) and raise to solar plexus (up). Follow the same directions for the right side.

蹲身捶放尺

2. Squat while exhaling and extend ruler 45 degrees diagonally forward; look to the center of the ruler. Rise while inhaling and raise ruler with circular motion to solar plexus level; bring ruler in toward the center using circular motion, which leads to the next squat.

左右擺抖尺

3. Electric Fan: Following instructions for tossing the ruler given for exercise #1, turn both legs 45 degrees to the same side as the toss. (Front arrow footwork: turn on the way, heels substantial, balls insubstantial.) Return to center, facing front with parallel footwork, as one move. Toss ruler and turn body and legs to the other side, then return to center.

彎腰垂抖尺

4. Bend at the waist while exhaling, extend ruler 45 degrees diagonally forward. Rise slowly while inhaling and raise ruler to shoulder level, then bring in toward the body along the center line. Look to the center of the ruler.

   Do not bring the ruler too close to the body or the next bend will be harder to do.

壯丹田

5. Hold ruler horizontally with center at tan t'ien, right hand over the
   left. With feet pointed straight, turn the body and shift the weight
   in a figure 8 pattern. Complete exhaling as the weight is shifted to
   one side; inhale while shifting. Perform this _slowly_ to adjust the
   figure 8 turns.

站式攝摟

6. From a stance the width of the head, squat while exhaling and roll
   ruler along the center line of the legs until it rests at the top of
   the kneecaps, held with the heels of the palms. Rise while inhaling
   and roll ruler up the center line to crease level, held by the fin-
   gertips. Eyes look 45 degrees diagonally forward during the squat,
   straight ahead while rising.

提舉

7. In a stance the width of the head, raise ruler from tan t'ien to
   above the head, looking up slightly, while lifting one leg (raising
   the toe, foot parallel with the ground). Lower ruler to tan t'ien,
   looking straight ahead, while lowering the leg. Shift weight internally and repeat while lifting and lowering the other leg.

   At first, raise the ruler to eye level, keeping the raised foot parallel. Later, raise ruler overhead and bring the toe up as the foot is
   lifted.

捶料

8. From shoulders-width stance, bend the knees to lower the body and
   "drop" the ruler simultaneously; extend away from the body at a 45
   degree angle. (The extension of the hands makes it possible to return to the original posture.) Rise slowly and raise ruler to solar
   plexus level. The eyes look past the ruler as it "drops" when the
   body is lowered but look straight ahead as the body rises.

   At first, don't try to control the speed or cause the body to rebound.
   Practice until the ruler feels heavier than the hands; then it will
   rebound.

Additional Exercises

1. Use the edge of the ruler to massage between the ribs. Use the center
   ball for the bottoms of the feet or for the spine. Use the end to tap
   (stimulate) the lao kung points on both palms.
2. Twirl the ruler using the middle finger and thumb, then clench the
   hand to stop the motion.

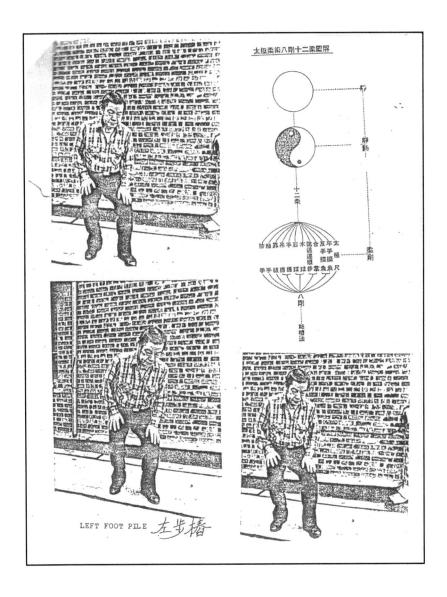

太極柔術八剛十二柔圖解

LEFT FOOT PILE 左步樁

34. TO LEARN MORE

The reader who has not learned the various systems BP Chan taught may be asking, "OK, but where are the pictures of BP Chan's Five Elements and 12 Animals Xing-Yi, his Yang and Chen Style Tai Chi Forms, his Bagua System, his Qigong Sets, his weapons sets.... Are they in this book? No. Neither pictures, nor complete written descriptions, of those systems are in this book. In my opinion, still pictures cannot convey internals and still pictures cannot convey transitions. In addition, written descriptions of movement often cannot convey subtleties that exist within the movement.

These direct students of BP Chan can provide personal instruction and insights into the Qigong and Martial Arts Systems of BP Chan.

RAY HAYWARD

218-341-9894
Email skrayhayward@gmail.com
Patreon https://www.patreon.com/rayhayward?fan_landing=true&view_as=public
YouTube https://www.youtube.com/@rayhaywardtheinspiredteach8246/featured
Tai Ji, Xing Yi, Bagua, Yi Quan, Wu Dang Sword, Chin Na, Qi Gong, Taoist Meditation, Tao of Love

RON GEE
Rongeeart@gmail.com
rongeeart.com

RUDY CURRY
347-407-1261
rudy9086@gmail.com

REV. LINDA MYOKI LEHRHAUPT, PHD
E Mail: LindaLehrhaupt@aol.com
Phone & What's App: +49 (0)175-370-4823
Home: Germany and France Expertise: Tai Chi, Chi Kung, Zen Meditation

MARK JONES
(914) 414-2943
oygevalt@optonline.net
www.marknjones.com
Qigong, Taijiquan (Yang Family, Old-Frame Chen Forms, Tung Ying Chieh styles), Baguazhang, Xing-Yi Chuan, Chi-Na, Applied Combat, Tai Chi Ruler, Meditation, Philosophy

FRANK ALLEN
Wu Tang Physical Culture Association
baguarat2@gmail.com
917-854-8868
www.wutangpca.com
TINA ZHANG
TinaZhangTaiChi@gmail.com
347-558-5674
TaiChiNYC@NYC.net

INTERNET & LIVE CLASSES AND WORKSHOPS
Tai Chi Quan, Bagua Zhang, Xing Yi Quan, Chi Gong, Nei

Gong, Internal Alchemy, Meditation, I Ching, Philosophy,
Classical Northern Wu Style Tai Ji Quan, Earth Qi Gong For
Women
Available on Amazon: The Whirling Circles of Bagua Zhang
(Book)

DOCUMENTARIES:
Tai Chi Club - available on Amazon Prime & Vimeo
Whirling Circles - available on Vimeo
Whirling Circles Podcast
YouTube - Spotify - Wu Tang PCA Website

PETER CHEMA
shuaichiao@gmail.com
Xing Yi, Bagua, Tai Chi and Shuai Jiao

MARSHA NOLAN
Email is yellowjasminetaichi@gmail.com
Phone is 609-661-2981
School is yellowjasminetaichi
Website is yellowjasminetaichi.com
Field of Experience Wu Ji Jing Gong Form and applications, Wu
Ji Jing Gong QiGong, Yang style, Chen Style, Two Person San
Shou.

JAMES FOGARTY
Tai Chi
Cornwall N.Y.

35. MORE FINAL THOUGHTS

I know I miss him much.........Master Chan taught me to walk again after massive surgeries.

-Florence Nielson, Student of BP Chan

B.P. Chan was the ultimate low-profile teacher. He would tell his students, "No videotapes, no photos, no articles." So there was no article in Tai Chi Magazine about him, although we certainly would have been glad to feature him. The best I could do was to take some photos of him at Jou Tsung Hwa's Tai Chi Farm while he was holding workshops. B.P. Chan was very much treasured by his students for his knowledge, skill, and character.

- Marvin Smalheiser, from Editor's Notebook,
Tai Chi Magazine, Volume 26 , #2, April 2002

One thing I remember about Mr. Chan is that you would feel he cared about his students. I remember we had early morning classes at five in the morning in Tompkins Square Park. He never charged us for them. I believe it made him happy to have students devoted enough to get up so early to come to a class.

- Patti Walsh, Student of BP Chan

ABOUT THE AUTHOR

RON LAMBERT has been practicing Martial Arts for 23 years. He studied for 18 years with a direct student of BP Chan in Mohegan Lake, NY, where he learned several of Chan's systems there, including Bagua Outer Palms, Bagua Inner Palms, Bagua Standing Set, Bagua Two-Person Sets, Bagua Push-Hands, Eight Brocades, 10 Daoist, 8 Chi Kung, Hanging Leg Set, Sitting Down Set, Lying Down Set, Standing Set, I Chuan, Eight Immortals Staff, Eight Immortals Sword, Full-Body Massage (An Mo), Deer, Turtle, and Crane Breathing, Tendon & Ligament Stretching, Muscle Stretching, and more.

He studied with Tom Bisio, where he learned a circular Bagua Staff Form taught to Tom by a brother of Gao Ji Wu. Study with Frank Allen enabled Ron to learn several of Liu Jing Ru's weapons forms: a Straight Sword (Jian) Form, and a Bagua Needles Form. He also learned a Bagua Broadsword Form and a Bagua Elbow Knives Form from Frank. In addition, he learned the 64 Hands Form taught to Frank by Liu Jing Ru.

Ron can be contacted at tentaopublishingllc@gmail.com.